Learning Science Outside the Classroom

Informal, non-classroom-based contexts can make an important contribution to learning for pupils studying science. Whether the outcomes are measurable in terms of their contribution to the planned curriculum, or in terms of the development of the individual, their impact is significant and long lasting.

This book shows how a wide range of contexts for learning science can be used with pupils, including:

- Learning at museums, science centres and planetaria
- Learning from newspapers, magazines and through ICT
- Learning at industrial sites and through science trails
- Learning at zoos, farms, botanic gardens and residential centres
- Learning in school grounds and from freshwater habitats

Using case studies and with contributions from practitioners in all fields of science education, *Learning Science Outside the Classroom* offers practical guidance for teachers and others involved in primary and secondary education, enabling them to widen the scientific understanding and experience of pupils.

The book has been checked for safety by CLEAPSS.

Martin Braund is Lecturer in Educational Studies and Curriculum Area Leader for Science in the PGCE Course at the Department of Educational Studies, University of York. **Michael Reiss** is Professor of Science Education and Head of the School of Mathematics, Science and Technology at the Institute of Education, University of London.

Learning Science Outside the Classroom

Edited by
Martin Braund and
Michael Reiss

RoutledgeFalmer
Taylor & Francis Group

LONDON AND NEW YORK

First published 2004 by RoutledgeFalmer
11 New Fetter Lane, London EC4P 4EE

Simultaneously published in the USA and Canada
by RoutledgeFalmer
29 West 35th Street, New York, NY 10001

RoutledgeFalmer is an imprint of the Taylor & Francis Group

Typeset in Melior by
Keystroke, Jacaranda Lodge, Wolverhampton
Printed and bound in Great Britain by
TJ International Ltd, Padstow, Cornwall

British Library Cataloguing in Publication Data
A catalogue record for this book is available from the British
Library

Library of Congress Cataloging in Publication Data
A catalog record for this book has been requested

ISBN 0–415–32117–4 (pbk)
ISBN 0–415–32116–6 (hbk)

To Sally Braund and Anne Scott

Contents

List of figures

List of tables

Anne Bebbington has worked for the Field Studies Council since 1970. As a Senior Teaching Officer she is currently based at the Field Studies Council's Residential Field Centre in Surrey – Juniper Hall. Here, as well as teaching environmental studies at all levels from KS1 to university level, she runs specialist botanical courses for adults, both beginners and those working at a more advanced level on university-accredited courses. She is part of the Field Studies Council's KS2 Staff Advisory Team. Her interest and expertise in illustration plays an important role in her work.

Peter Borrows read natural sciences at the University of Cambridge and then did a PGCE and a PhD in inorganic chemistry at London University. He was a science teacher, including being a head of chemistry and head of science, and senior teacher in London schools for over 20 years before becoming a science adviser. He is now Director of the CLEAPSS School Science Service, based at Brunel University. He developed the idea of a chemistry trail when teaching the 'Change and Decay' option in Nuffield O-level chemistry at Pimlico School. He realised that within 100 metres of the school there were large-scale examples of most of the chemistry in the option and that it could be made much more relevant to the students by showing them what was in their immediate environment. The idea developed from there and for the past ten years Peter has had a regular column on chemistry trails in *Education in Chemistry*.

Martin Braund lectures in Educational Studies at the University of York and was previously Head of Environmental Science at Bretton Hall College of the University of Leeds. He has over 25 years of experience of leading and organising learning outside the classroom both as a teacher in schools and universities and as an adviser, consultant and teacher trainer. He has worked on science education projects at The National Museum of Wales in Cardiff and at several museums in York. He has researched a number of areas in science education and is a regular contributor to journals in the field. His most recent book, *Primary Plants*, has been critically acclaimed.

Joey Britto is currently an adviser working for the Gibraltar Department of Education. Although originally qualifying (St Mary's College, Twickenham) as a teacher of English, he has taught science at Key Stages 2 through to 4 and ICT across the primary and secondary sectors. He is currently responsible for overseeing an ICT 'masterplan' for Gibraltar schools. Joey is currently in the process of researching how children and young people 'teach themselves' ICT skills. This research study is part of his doctoral studies with the University of Sheffield's EdD programme.

Susan Humphries was the headteacher of The Coombes School in Arborfield from the school's opening in 1971 until 2002. The site she inherited was deprived in every sense of the word. She had a vision for children's learning to be set in a 'kindergarten', and work to improve the school's outdoor landscape started immediately. For more than thirty years, Susan sought with her colleagues to improve the school's outdoor landscape and to transform the school grounds into the richest and most diverse learning/teaching resource. Susan is the co-author of several books relating to early years' education. She has contributed to television work focused on early years' education and is a regular contributor to international conferences/workshops across the world. She is a trustee of both the Learning Through Landscapes Trust and the Campaign for Learning.

Ruth Jarman is a lecturer in education in the Graduate School of Education at Queen's University Belfast. She co-ordinates the science course on the PGCE programme, teaches on the Continuing Professional Development programme and supervises PhD students. Her research interests centre around the school science curriculum and out-of-school learning in science. Her current research includes a number of projects which focus on the use of newspapers in the science classroom and she has published widely on this theme.

Sue Johnson was, until recently, the Senior Education Officer for the Royal Horticultural Society at Wisley. Here she developed strategies for teaching and learning science in the wide range of outdoor settings presented. Here too teachers and trainee teachers were offered guidance and inspiration, unavailable elsewhere, on the teaching and learning possibilities latent in school gardens and gardening. She spent 17 years in mainstream education using outdoor contexts as an aid to learning, environmental education and students' personal development. She was chairman of the Botanic Gardens Education Network in 1998/9. Currently, she is developing the teaching and learning potential of the Harris Garden, the University of Reading's botanic garden, and working with the Darwin Trust to introduce Darwin's scientific methods to schools.

Martin Lunn became Curator of Astronomy at the Yorkshire Museum in York in 1989, and was seconded to work with the North Yorkshire Science Team. Here he helped produce the 'Earth and Space' project. This was a series of practical astronomical projects that attracted over 30,000 primary children. He was the author of the BBC Factfinder book *Earth and Space*. He now takes travelling science exhibitions into primary schools in Yorkshire. In 1998 he was created an MBE for services to astronomy and education.

Billy McClune has a background in physics teaching. He now lectures in science education at Queen's University Belfast where he teaches a number of courses on the continuing professional development (CPD) and post-graduate certificate in education (PGCE) programmes. He maintains research interests closely linked to school science and is currently involved in a number of projects related to science literacy and physics education. Recent publications highlight an interest in the role of newspapers in science education.

Joy Parvin graduated in chemical engineering before training as a primary school teacher. She is currently the Primary Projects Manager for the Chemical Industry Education Centre (CIEC) at the University of York. In the 10 years that she has worked for the CIEC, she has been involved in the development of written material that enhances the link between science (predominantly) and industry, and in-service training for primary teachers. She currently manages the Children Challenging Industry project, and is the Director of the Primary Science Enhancement programme. Before working for the CIEC, Joy taught in primary and middle schools in Leeds and Bradford. Joy has an MA in Science Education.

Michael Reiss is Professor of Science Education and Head of the School of Mathematics, Science and Technology at the Institute of Education, University of London. His research, writing, teaching and consultancy expertise is in the fields of science education, health education and bioethics. After a PhD and post-doctoral research in evolutionary biology and animal behaviour, he trained as a school teacher and taught in schools before returning to higher education in 1988. He is the author and editor of a number of science education books, the latest one of which is *Understanding Science Lessons: Five Years of Science Teaching*. He is the Director of the Salters-Nuffield Advanced Biology project and Chief Executive of Science Learning Centre London.

Susan Rowe has been headteacher at The Coombes School since January 2003. Prior to that she was the deputy headteacher at the school. Her key interests lie in the fields of teaching science and mathematics to the very young. She is the co-author of several books relating to early years' education and has also contributed to television work focusing on this area. She is keenly interested in educational issues in West Africa. She is a tutor for the Open University's Specialist Teaching Assistant Course (STAC).

Miranda Stephenson after ten years of teaching chemistry is now manager of the Chemical Industry Education Centre – a joint initiative of the Chemical Industries Association and the University of York. Her interests are in curriculum development in science and technology; context-led science curricula, industry–education partnerships, and chemical and allied industry data and practice as a resource for teaching. She has been co-author or editor of over 60 teaching and learning publications including *The Essential Chemical Industry* (4th edn 1999), *Understanding Food Additives* (1st edn 1998), *Green Chlorine* (1st edn 1996), *Educational Site Visits for Schools* (1st edn 1999). Her overseas work includes the European Chemical Industry Council, Education–Industry Partnership Working Party, consultant to Department of Chemistry, University of Saõ Paulo, Brazil, and contributions to conferences in many countries.

Elizabeth Swinbank after a PhD in radio astronomy trained as a teacher and taught physics in schools for nine years before moving to the University of York where she is Fellow in Science Education. She has worked on a number of science curriculum and teacher-education projects, both at the University of York and as associate lecturer and consultant with the Open University. Currently, she directs the *Salters Horners Advanced Physics* project and the *Teaching Resources Unit for Modern Physics* (TRUMP), teaches undergraduate physics and edits *Physics Review* magazine. The Institute of Physics has awarded her the Bragg medal for her innovative contributions to the school physics curriculum.

Sue Dale Tunnicliffe graduated with special honours in zoology from Westfield College, University of London and then took her post-graduate teaching qualification in science education at the London University Institute of Education. She taught pupils in grammar schools between the ages of 11 and 19, in adult education and then primary schools, spending five years in a multi-cultural school in Slough. She left the classroom to set up and run the advisory team of teachers for primary science and technology for the London borough of Richmond-upon-Thames, a post she left after five years to become Head of Education at the Zoological Society of London. She worked part-time in a historical museum and then as an education consultant at the BBC and studied for her PhD in science education at King's College, London. A former Ofsted inspector she is a Senior Associate member at Homerton College, Cambridge and project co-director of the project 'Children's understanding of the natural world' at the Institute of Education, University of London. She is a member of the Zoos Forum, the government's advisory body on zoos.

Jerry Wellington began his teaching career in Tower Hamlets, London before moving to Sheffield where he is now a professor in the School of Education at the University of Sheffield. He has published widely on science education and has also written a number of science textbooks for the 8 to 16 age range.

Chapter 1

The nature of learning science outside the classroom

Martin Braund and Michael Reiss

Overview

The chapter acts as a prelude to the rest of this book. Personal and historical perspectives on the value of using out-of-classroom contexts for learning science are given. These are discussed in relation to the debate about the purposes of school science. The nature of learning that occurs in out-of-classroom contexts is considered in terms of its definition, its characteristics and a model that helps us understand how it is different to more formal learning in classrooms. A brief summary of each chapter is provided.

Introduction

One of us (MB) recently attended a reunion of students to whom he had taught biology in the sixth form of a large comprehensive school. Most of the original group had come to the reunion and a pleasing number had continued with biology in some form or other. There were teachers, biochemists, a doctor and even the warden of a large nature reserve in Canada. We got talking about old times and one topic kept resurfacing – 'that wonderful week's fieldwork on the Hebridean Island of Mingulay'. It seems the experience was remembered and treasured by all, irrespective of their future careers, and was quoted as being a key influence by those who had continued with biology. The other of us (MR) similarly has a selection of evaluation forms from students whom he has taken on week-long field trips to Slapton Ley Field Studies Centre. As one student put it 'I enjoyed everything. I can't believe I feel so good about this experience; I've done more work in this week than in the whole year. Every night I went to bed exhausted and satisfied. It's good to be EXCITED about learning'. When he left his last job, he too recalls students fondly remembering their residential field trip – and even offering to come and help with future ones.

Many teachers tell similar stories of the positive influences that contexts for learning which occur outside the normal classroom have had, both on their pupils and on themselves. The gains for teachers' own professional development in terms of their developing knowledge about learning and pupils' emotional and intellectual growth can be significant. At York, teachers at the end of their first year in teaching are invited to talk to current student teachers about their experiences. These practising teachers reflect on the key moments in their professional lives and offer advice to the novices. We are struck by a common and recurring theme. As one teacher put it:

> My best advice to you is to get involved with anything you can outside school. You know, it could be a school trip, fieldwork, outdoor pursuits, a school holiday; anything where you see pupils and how they learn in a different light. You learn so much more about them, what motivates and drives them. You share their fears and aspirations and they share yours. It's the most rewarding thing I have done this year.
>
> (Comment made by a teacher to PGCE student teachers at the University of York, June 2003)

This book is about the ways in which we can educate school-aged pupils and students in science using a variety of what we call 'outside-the-classroom' contexts. This is not to say that the methods discussed in this book necessarily require special visits or organised excursions. Each chapter includes examples of activities that can be 'brought in' to the classroom context to make science learning more relevant and accessible to pupils. There has been much debate about the current school curriculum for science in the UK and its usefulness and relevance for young people in the twenty-first century (Millar and Osborne, 1998). Questions have been raised about the central purpose of science education, challenging its traditionally narrow focus on preparation for further study. The argument is made for a curriculum more in tune with the needs of a population increasingly faced with lifestyle decisions relying on some understanding and appreciation of science so that people can have better access to the debates and arguments that underpin personal choice. Amongst the recommendations is one stating that:

> School science should aim to provide a populace who are comfortable, competent and confident with scientific and technical matters and artefacts. The science curriculum should provide sufficient knowledge and under-standing to enable students to read simple newspaper articles about science and follow TV programmes on new advances in science with interest.
>
> (Millar and Osborne, 1998 p. 29)

The contexts described in the chapters of this book are well placed to meet these aspirations for science education. The learning that results from them, however, may not only be derived from the hours spent in formal schooling. We should remember that school-aged children spend only about a third of their waking lives in school. The impact that home-based learning can have on school-based outcomes should not be underestimated. One of us found evidence of this when researching pupils' understanding of animal classification (Braund, 1991). Pupils' performance in formal tests of reasoning ability were compared with their performance on classification tasks and a number of cases were found where pupils performed on the classification tasks well above the predicted level. When pupil responses to questions about hobbies and interests were examined, it transpired that in every case these were pupils who had some out-of-school interest that involved learning about animals, their names and so on. Fishing, bird-watching, trips to zoos with parents and watching wildlife programmes on TV all featured. The extent of such influences is suggested in work one of us has carried out with Sue Dale Tunnicliffe (Tunnicliffe and Reiss, 1999, 2000). Pupils aged from 4 to 14 years were shown a range of preserved animals and living plants and asked a series of questions about them. For both girls and boys, the home and direct observation were more important as sources of knowledge than were school or books.

So far we have set out some personal perspectives on learning science outside the classroom and how we see this in the wider context of the purposes of science education. Our views are not unique. Many educators, particularly in the past, have sought to justify and promote a variety of situations outside the classroom in which school-aged children might learn.

A historical perspective

The curriculum of UK schools today can seem rather crowded and constrained, dominated by government legislation and an objectives-focused framework. Curriculum documents prescribe a curriculum yet often without clear philosophical justifications for and argument about what teachers might do and learners should learn. Contemporary educationalists often overemphasise, frequently implicitly and apparently unwittingly, the importance of formal school-based education without recognising the contribution that home-based learning and informal contexts can make. This has not always been the case. A number of thinkers in the past promoted a pedagogy and a curriculum based on wider agendas.

Johann Comenius (1592–1670), for example, believed that education should be universal, focusing on family and social life as well as schooling. Comenius' ideas of an 'authentic curriculum' contain many references to learning outside the classroom and continue to influence teachers today as can be seen from reading Susan Rowe and Susan Humphries' chapter on 'The outdoor classroom'.

A century later the French philosopher Jean-Jacques Rousseau, in his classic novel *Emile* (1762), wrote about the value of an experiential approach to teaching and learning and its importance for the development of the individual. Much of Rousseau's advice on teaching drew heavily on examples based in nature and outside contexts.

The important contribution that an outdoor space can make to the learning environment of young children fundamentally influenced British primary education and school design in the early part of the twentieth century. Maria Montessori and later the MacMillan sisters in London both promoted the inclusion of experiences in outdoor spaces such as gardening, eating and even sleeping out-of-doors as an essential component of schooling for the young (Anning, 1991). Their influences can still be seen in the design of some primary schools built in England in the 1930s. After the Second World War, a tradition of fieldwork including the use of residential centres developed and blossomed as part of national trends in conservation and environmental education. The history of this movement and its impact on science education are discussed by Anne Bebbington in Chapter 5.

In Victorian times, learning about the latest scientific and technological discoveries was popular in the UK and *de rigeur* for people from all social classes. A great tradition of mass, public interest in science and its applications developed. This included visiting the newly constructed national and regional museums, attending public lectures and debates, and viewing zoos, botanical gardens and the great fairs and exhibitions that were established to celebrate and promote the latest achievements. Out of this grew a vigorous and well-established education service based in museums and other places that provided for pupils both within the confines of the centre or building and as an outreach service. Although this service declined following the First World War its resurgence, started in the 1960s, continues today. A new emphasis on education is being called for by the UK government and museums and galleries are once again at the forefront as important providers of learning for schools and the wider public and as part of a contribution to what is often called 'lifelong learning' (Anderson, 1997).

Defining the learning that takes place

Trying to define learning is an almost impossible task. So much depends on the context and the perspective and intentions of the author. Definitions are often framed in the psychological theories and models that attempt to explain how people learn, or are focused only on measurable outcomes. We have, however, found a definition that takes a wider view more suited to the nature of learning described in this book:

> Learning is a process of active engagement with experience. It is what people do when they want to make sense of the world. It may involve the development or deepening of skills, knowledge, understanding, awareness, values, ideas and feelings or an increase in the capacity to reflect. Effective learning leads to change, development and the desire to learn more.
>
> (Based on a definition first used by The Campaign for Learning, 2003)

The last sentence of this quote seems to hold the key to understanding what goes on in the contexts described in this book and the value placed on experiences by pupils and their teachers. We believe that science is a fundamentally interesting subject to learn about, yet so many young people seem to reject it as they grow older claiming, for example, that it is boring, impenetrable and irrelevant to their needs (Bennett, 2003). Science is indeed hard to learn as much of the research into children's learning has shown. Yet, when pupils visit or are taught in places that explain science in new and exciting ways, they frequently seem to be more enthused. There is, we believe, something about these contexts and places that brings about change through increasing the desire in people to find out and understand more.

Teachers might look for evidence that knowledge and understanding of science have improved as a result of using informal, out-of-school contexts but we believe that this may be missing the main point. Whilst there may be some small changes in scientific knowledge and understanding resulting from these contexts (and there is evidence for this as some of the authors in this book cite), is this likely to be significantly more than a conventional school science lesson can achieve? Perhaps the main changes come about in terms of pupils' attitudes to science or in terms of the values that they place on the processes and modes of learning that they encounter in contexts beyond school. The next two sections of this chapter develop this idea.

Domains of learning

Authors writing about informal learning contexts often talk about the contribution made within three types or 'domains' of learning. These are:

- the cognitive domain
- the affective domain

■ the psychomotor domain.

This terminology can be traced back to the work of Bloom (Bloom *et al.*, 1956). Bloom went on to describe a hierarchy of educational objectives under the first two headings that is still commonly referred to, although the third domain was never fully explored in terms of its implications for schooling. Table 1.1 summarises the key characteristics of each domain as we see them and shows some examples in each domain of science learning activities that might take place outside the classroom.

Specific details of how activities suggested in this book relate to each of these domains and the learning outcomes that ensue can be found in the other chapters of this book. The reader must make up his/her own mind on what specific gains in learning might result from using them. To understand more about how informal, out-of-school contexts affect learning in science it is useful to think in terms of a contextual model.

Table 1.1 The three domains of learning and examples of activities in learning science outside the classroom

Domain of learning	Examples of science learning activities
The cognitive domain The development of knowledge and intellectual skills including: recall of knowledge, comprehension of meaning, application of knowledge, analysis of data, synthesis of new meaning and the evaluation of process, artefacts or solutions.	Recalling safety rules before setting out on a seashore study. Observing and raising questions about a fossil specimen in a museum gallery. Applying knowledge of chemistry to interpret observations, e.g. of the carbonation of limestone seen on a chemistry trail.
The affective domain The manner in which we respond to and show appreciation of and enthusiasm for phenomena and events. The ways in which we develop attitudes and values and how these relate to those of other people.	Pupils discussing a visit to a cave and expressing their feelings and fears. Pupils talking in groups about conservation of the great apes after visiting a zoo.
The psychomotor domain How sensory inputs are filtered and lead to actions. Learners' actions become more skilful, co-ordinated and adapted as experience and expertise develop.	Using senses of touch and smell to identify household artefacts at a hands-on science museum. Co-ordinating with others in a group to measure the rate of flow and depth of a stream.

A contextual model of learning in informal contexts

Falk and Dierking (2000) have devised a model that helps us understand learning in situations that are relatively 'informal' when compared with normal schooling. By 'informal', Falk and Dierking mean that pupils have some element of choice in what they do, the directions of learning they follow or the amount of time and effort spent. We recognise that the degree of control over the agenda for learning that teachers may wish to impose will vary (for very good reasons, e.g. health and safety, links with previous and future learning in school, the needs of examination specifications and so on), but the model is still very useful in helping us understand what learners experience and how experiences can be enhanced to get the most from these contexts.

Falk and Dierking's contextual model is discussed in some detail, as it relates to learning in science museums and galleries, in Chapter 8. The basic elements of the model are shown as Figure 1.1.

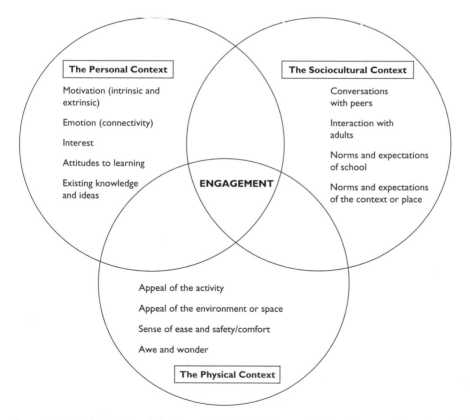

Figure 1.1 A contextual model of learning in informal, out-of-school contexts (based on Falk and Dierking, 2000).

The model is based on three overlapping contexts, each affecting the engagement of the learner and ultimately the quality and quantity of what the learner gains from their experiences.

In the personal context pupils' learning flows from a set of emotional and motivational cues. In this way pupils operate in the affective domain discussed above and this often sets up the desire to want to find out new things or go deeper into learning about something already encountered. The impact can be surprisingly long-lasting and even life-enhancing as we illustrated in the introduction to this chapter.

The physical context has a lot to do with providing these emotional and motivational cues. The examples described in this book have a vital ingredient in common – instant appeal. For many pupils science comes alive when they experience phenomena, specimens and artefacts in natural settings. Susan Rowe and Susan Humphries have much to say about the value of these types of experiences in Chapter 3. At times, though, such learning environments can spark initially negative reactions. For example, pupils' initial views of factories and manufacturing sites are often stereotypically of dark and threatening places pouring out pollution. Teaching science using industrial contexts and visits, however, is capable of changing these perceptions as Joy Parvin and Miranda Stephenson explain in Chapter 9.

What we learn in any situation is often mediated through our gestures and by conversation with others. The ways in which we act in and react to different learning situations is a product of our culture. Our culture and society and the ways in which we have been brought up impose a set of social norms which set expectations and give rise to rules about how we behave in different situations. These are key aspects of what Falk and Dierking call the sociocultural context. School groups working outside the classroom act as a 'community of learners'. Each community of learners has its own characteristic behaviours and the actions of its members depend on previously established cultural and educational norms. In school, teachers know what these norms are and with experience can predict pupils' likely reactions and behaviour. In out-of-school and informal contexts the norms of school begin to break down and may even conflict with the approaches to learning and expectations that the informal situation provides. Teachers can see this as a problem or as an opportunity. It only becomes a problem if we do not realise that new norms and sociocultural expectations apply in these circumstances and when we fail to make allowances for them. For example, it seems an anathema to us to force pupils to go around a hands-on science centre clutching worksheets to fill in by the end of the visit or not to take time to wonder at the beauty of a sunset or the calls of seabirds on a field trip.

New opportunities for learning science abound. Working in such contexts allows pupils to express themselves in ways that school does not. The richness of pupils' conversations can often be improved by the well-judged intervention of adults, though teachers must be careful not to slip into their own more formal school-based norms when doing this. In Chapter 7 Sue Dale Tunnicliffe uses her experiences of analysing conversations at zoos and farms to show us just how important this 'scaffolding' of dialogue can be. There are many other examples in this book of how teachers and other adults can effectively stimulate pupils' interactions and discussions and develop co-operative learning.

Organisation of the book

In Chapter 2 we look at the specifics of what is needed to organise and undertake science work outside the classroom. We pay particular attention to safety issues and practicalities.

In Chapter 3 Susan Rowe and Susan Humphries describe how they have developed (over a period of more than 30 years!) the outdoor landscape at their primary school to support a wide range of learning experiences in the school grounds. Their school now has everything from suitable habitats for fungi, plants and other living organisms to a labyrinth based on the one at Chartres Cathedral. The grounds are used throughout the year. For example, in spring the bounds are beaten using sticks from the school's own trees and in November the children study fire and the effects of heat.

In Chapter 4 Martin Braund examines the particular contribution that freshwater habitats can make to pupils' learning. Suggestions are included for how both still and running freshwater can be used, and findings from a survey of school ponds show how ponds can better be used to support learning in science. Ways in which pupils can study rivers or streams and generate data for analysis and to measure pollution are discussed.

In Chapter 5 Anne Bebbington looks at learning at residential field centres. Advice is given on how to plan a visit to a field centre taking account of health and safety issues, cost implications and the need to decide in advance on the course content. Detailed examples suitable for a range of ages are described to illustrate how curriculum needs and teaching objectives can be addressed. The social and personal development benefits of residential field work are discussed.

In Chapter 6 Sue Johnson looks at how botanic gardens can be used for learning science and developing environmental literacy. The potential for holistic teaching and learning is presented and the way in which hands-on learning permits a diversity of learning styles is discussed. The importance of plants to human existence is brought home by work in a botanic gardens and the experience also allows home- and school-constructed knowledge to be connected.

In Chapter 7 Sue Dale Tunnicliffe argues for the educational benefits of visits to zoos and farms. Such visits provide one of the few opportunities children have to encounter animals other than pets and everyday species. Particular attention is paid to how teachers can use pupil conversations to maximise learning. Differences between zoo and farm visits are examined and the need to consider religious, cultural and dietary beliefs of pupils is stressed.

In Chapter 8 Martin Braund reviews the ways in which museums and hands-on centres and galleries can be used by teachers to promote pupil learning in science. The model of Falk and Dierking introduced above, is developed to help understand the nature of learning in such places. The particular opportunity that handling objects provides for science education is described and a range of actions are suggested for teachers to optimise pupil experiences at such sites.

In Chapter 9 Joy Parvin and Miranda Stephenson begin by looking at reasons why industrial companies may host school visits and go on to provide suggestions for teachers to help them gain such access. They then look in depth at a primary school case study before moving on to look at taking older students into industry for science activities.

In Chapter 10 Peter Borrows looks at chemistry trails. Pupils generally fail to see the relevance of chemistry. A chemistry trail can help identify instances of chemistry 'happening' in the immediate surroundings of the school. Advice is given on undertaking a chemistry trail and examples are given, for a range of pupil ages, that are to do with building materials, metals, air pollution and other topics.

In Chapter 11 Elizabeth Swinbank and Martin Lunn look at how visits can be used to enhance learning in physics and astronomy. Planetaria, star-domes and star parties can bring to life what can otherwise be a somewhat remote area of the curriculum while star parties are also a good way of involving parents in pupils' learning. Visits to telescopes, the National Space Centre and research organisations can help pupils learn about 'Big Science' while visits to observe physics in the workplace can help teach physics in context.

In Chapter 12 Ruth Jarman and Billy McClune look at how newspapers can be used within the classroom to enable learning about science. Almost by definition newspapers are up-to-date, dealing with current developments and contemporary issues in society. This allows them to be used for 'science and society'- and 'science and citizenship'-type activities. In addition, they can be used to illustrate ideas about science, to stimulate thinking about science and to help pupils write well themselves.

In Chapter 13 Jerry Wellington and Joey Britto argue that science teachers and educators should take serious note of how, what, when and why children learn science via ICTs at home. In particular, comparisons of the school science environment with home learning and learning using ICT reveals the extent to which schools may need to change many of their assumptions about meaningful learning or else risk stifling learning using these new technologies.

Finally, in Chapter 14 we review how learning can be managed outside the classroom. We look at reasons why there is now the beginnings of a renewed interest in out-of-the classroom learning and close with some crystal-ball gazing in relation to educational policy, scientific literacy and lifelong learning and the contribution that the contexts considered in the book might make in these areas.

Conclusions

One of our post-graduate students, training to be a teacher, recently carried out a survey of pupils' views on what they would like to see as improvements to their science curriculum. A number of choices were offered: more practical work (and consequently, in pupils' minds, less writing), more work on topical issues, more visits and fieldwork, fewer tests and examinations. Surprisingly, perhaps, in view of the alternatives that were on offer, trips and fieldwork were pupils' number one priority for better school science. Similarly, the Science Year Student Review of the Science Curriculum found that students rated 'Going on a science trip or excursion' the most enjoyable way of learning science of the 11 alternatives provided (Cerini *et al.*, 2003). These findings reinforce our belief that out-of-school contexts matter and that they should be a key component of any school curriculum for science.

In this chapter we have shown how contexts outside the classroom contribute to learning in science and the particular importance they have in providing a springboard for further learning through improved motivation. We have already mentioned that pupils' attitudes to school science are not as positive as we might hope for and that this has led some to challenge the very nature of the science curriculum on offer. Our experience and that of many of the authors in this book is that the contexts and opportunities suggested here are rich and rewarding for the teacher and the pupil learning science and will go someway to enhancing what is taught in schools. We urge the reader to delve into the richness of the ideas in this book and see how to maximise the potential for learning good quality science in interesting yet challenging ways. We hope that readers will come to value these contexts and ways of working as much as we have.

References

Anderson, J., 1997, *A Common Wealth: Museums and Learning in the United Kingdom*, London: Department of National Heritage.

Anning, A., 1991, *The First Years at School*, Milton Keynes: Open University Press.

Bennett, J., 2003, 'Pupils' attitudes to science and school science', *Teaching and Learning Science: A Guide to Recent Research and its Applications*, London: Continuum.

Bloom, B., Engelhart, M., Hill, W., Furst, E. and Krathwohl, D., 1956, *Taxonomy of Educational Objectives. The Classification of Educational Goals* (two volumes), New York: David McKay.

Braund, M., 1991, 'Children's ideas in classifying animals', *Journal of Biological Education*, 25, 103–10.

Campaign for Learning, 2003, http://www.campaign-for-learning.org.uk

Cerini, B., Murray, I. and Reiss, M. J. (eds), 2003, *Student Review of the Science Curriculum – Major Findings*, London: Planet Science.

Falk, J. H. and Dierking, L. D., 2000, *Learning from Museums*, Walnut Creek, CA: AltaMira Press.

Millar, R. and Osborne, J. (eds), 1998, *Beyond 2000: Science Education for the Future*, London: School of Education, King's College.

Rousseau, J., 1762, *Emile*, trans. Barbara Foxley, 1993, London: Everyman.

Tunnicliffe, S. D. and Reiss, M. J., 1999, 'Building a model of the environment: How do children see animals?' *Journal of Biological Education*, 33, 142–8.

Tunnicliffe, S. D. and Reiss, M. J., 2000, 'Building a model of the environment: how do children see plants?' *Journal of Biological Education*, 34, 172–7.

Chapter 2

Practicalities and safety issues

Michael Reiss and Martin Braund

Overview

In this short chapter we consider the specifics of what is needed to organise and undertake science work outside the classroom. We pay particular attention to issues of safety.

Introduction

In recent years there has been a number of high profile incidents involving pupils from UK schools engaged in school visits. Some have tragically resulted in pupil deaths. The ensuing publicity, and in some cases litigation against the teachers involved, has produced strong reactions. Some teacher associations have gone as far as to suggest that teachers should no longer be involved in out-of-school visits. Whilst we understand these reactions, we are concerned that they go too far and in the long run threaten the evolution of a more balanced education for children of the twenty-first century. Children today are often criticised for being lazy, overweight, unfit and cosseted. It is our impression, and that of many of the authors of chapters in this book, that children today know less about their environment than they used to. In many cases schools provide the few opportunities where children get the chance to get out into the environment and undertake activities by themselves and co-operatively with their peers.

The amount of fieldwork and outdoor education taking place in the UK has been in decline for some time. To reduce this further in reaction to fears about safety at a time when society demands more of young people in terms of developing their physical and mental well-being, their independence and their ability to make decisions, is at least counter-productive and at worst irresponsible.

Of course there are risks involved in working outside the confines of a classroom. However, one result of the recent spate of high profile incidents is that there is now better guidance and support for teachers than there has ever been (see the resources box at the end of this chapter). The benefits of working with pupils outside the classroom can often outweigh the constraints. We discuss these benefits in Chapter 14; here, we shall review some of the practicalities, including safety issues.

Organising and undertaking science work outside the classroom

If you or someone else in your school has conducted science work outside the classroom, you will be able to get much of the help and information you need from your own notes and/or your colleagues. Your school may have an Educational Visits Co-ordinator (following DfES guidance). If you have not or wish to explore new options for teaching, there are a number of things you need to think about. Clearly, the amount of forward planning depends on whether you envisage a 45-minute trip to a local churchyard within walking distance of your school (to study lichens on graves, for example) or a longer period away from school, e.g. on a residential visit some distance from the school.

In all cases of work outside the classroom (as indeed in it) you should carry out a risk assessment. The school's policy on health and safety will be the starting point to help you in this. The level of risk will depend on the nature of the activity. A short walk to the local cemetery without crossing busy roads carries less risk than one involving transport. Identify hazards; evaluate the level of risk; provide procedures for reducing all risks to an acceptable level. Complete the necessary forms and make sure that they are checked by the relevant persons responsible for safety in the school (and in the Local Education Authority if required). The DfES publications listed at the end of this chapter provide examples of risk assessment and other forms that can be used. Residential trips and work near open bodies of water, in coastal environments or in upland areas present higher levels of risk and may need to be notified to the governing body of the school, and to the Local Education Authority, before they can go ahead.

Well before the visit (15 months in the case of residential fieldwork; 2 to 3 months in the case of a day trip) you need to:

- Consider the function of the work in relation to your planned objectives.
- Check existing school and LEA policies for health and safety. It is also advisable to consult the excellent series of health and safety guidance booklets provided by the Department for Education and Skills (see resources box).
- Identify possible sites or places to go to.

- Identify suitable staff and adult helpers, bearing in mind an acceptable adult: pupil ratio (which depends on the age of the pupils involved), a range of expertise and whether both male and female adults are needed.
- Decide whether pupils will be charged and how you will cope with pupils unable to pay without discriminating against them.

Once a decision has been made to go ahead with the visit you need to:

- Make a visit yourself to where you are intending to go, not only to reconnoitre but also to ensure that adults and/or educators, if any, at the place you are visiting are fully briefed, so that you and they are perfectly clear about the aims of the visit and who is responsible for doing what (see Chapters 4, 5 and 6 for exemplars). If you are visiting a provider of outdoor education in the UK and you intend pupils to engage in certain outdoor activities (e.g. walking above 600 m, canoeing) you should check that the provider has the appropriate training.
- Determine costing and travel arrangements.
- Check your school's insurance policy.
- Compose a suitable letter to parents/guardians which should be checked and signed by the head teacher as well as yourself.
- Brief pupils, staff and any helpers about the purpose of the visit (see Chapter 6 for exemplars).
- Check that everyone has everything they need (e.g. suitable clothing including a change of clothing, lunch boxes, water bottles, appropriate amounts of money, emergency telephone numbers/other contact details) and that a suitable number of the adults have first-aid training (preferably HSE-approved) and access to first-aid boxes whose contents have been checked before the visit.
- Check that any staff driving pupils have the necessary qualifications – a certificate of competence may be required from a designated examiner.
- Ensure you know about any special medical conditions (e.g. diabetes, epilepsy, allergies) and dietary requirements. Collect information on whether or not pupils have had a recent injection against tetanus.
- Ensure that a clear behaviour policy (e.g. with regard to smoking, consumption of alcohol, lights out, movement between bedrooms/dormitories) is communicated to all pupils and their parents/guardians.
- Obtain volunteers from among pupils to take photographs, make drawings, shoot a video and write an account for the school web-site/magazine.

On the visit itself, keep in mind the relevant safety points discussed above. In addition:

- Ensure that the first-aid kits are taken on all excursions.
- Certain environments such as uplands, aquatic habitats and coastal waters carry particular and additional risks. For work in some environments such as high mountain or moorland areas (above 600 m) it is advisable that one member of staff is qualified to lead activities in such places (e.g. by holding the British Mountaineering Council's Mountain Leader Award).
- Have in place methods of communication in the event of an accident or other unwanted incident.
- Obtain good, detailed, local weather forecasts prior to each day's work, e.g. from local mountain rescue services or from coastguard stations.
- Ensure each person has suitable clothing (including footwear and head-dress) and field equipment. Depending on where you are working this might include: extra clothing, an exposure/survival bag, safety goggles (when chipping rocks), knowledge of the times of high and low tides, drinking water, emergency high-energy food, a map, a compass, a watch, a whistle, sunscreen, a torch and a mobile phone.
- Disposable gloves are not necessary when working in aquatic habitats. Pupils should be told about the risk of Weil's disease and of the danger of cyanobacteria (which used to be called blue-green algae) build-ups on lakes. These risks can be minimised by ensuring that hands are washed thoroughly after contact with water.
- The group leader might also carry a lightweight circular survival shelter. Trying this out with pupils, even when it is not needed, is a useful education in safety.

Resources

General issues
Reiss, M.J., 1993, 'Organizing and running a residential fieldtrip', School Science Review, 74(268), 132–5.

Safety
The following website contains key information on safety: http://www.teachernet.gov.uk/visits
The laws governing licenses for driving minibuses are quite complicated. See www.dvla.gov.uk

The documents that should be consulted are:
CLEAPSS Chapter 17.1 'Fieldwork', Laboratory Handbook.
Department for Education and Skills, 1998, Health and Safety of Pupils on Educational Visits, London: Department for Education and Skills.
Department for Education and Skills, 2002, Three-part Supplement to Health and Safety of Pupils on Educational Visits, London: Department for Education and Skills.
Department for Education and Skills and Central Council of Physical Recreation, 2003, Group Safety at Water Margins, London: Department for Education and Skills and Central Council of Physical Recreation.

National Association of Field Studies Officers, 1998, *Field Studies Centres: A Code of Practice – Quality, Safety and Sustainability*, Stibbington, Peterborough: National Association of Field Studies Officers.

Nichols, D. (ed.), 1999, *Safety in Biological Fieldwork: Guidance Notes for Codes of Practice*, London: Institute of Biology.

Chapter 3

The outdoor classroom

Susan Rowe and Susan Humphries

Overview

In this chapter, we describe how we have developed our outdoor landscape to support a comprehensive range of learning experiences in the school's grounds. The teaching of the science curriculum is particularly enriched by the series of planned developments outside, but there are curricular gains in all of the core and foundation subjects at Foundation Stage, Key Stage 1, Key Stage 2, Key Stage 3 and beyond, from this programme of environmental improvement. We believe that the science curriculum lies at the heart of all pupils' learning, along with language arts and mathematical understanding. Knowledge and understanding of the world is a factor underpinning every aspect of our lives.

Our rationale for developing the school site

The Czech educationist and philosopher Johann Comenius (1592–1670) believed that education should be universal, optimistic, practical and innovative, and that it should focus not only on school and family life but also on social life in general. He proposed that 'a school garden should be connected with every school where children can have the opportunity for leisurely gazing upon trees, flowers and herbs, and are taught to appreciate them' (Comenius, 1660). For him, a garden was a perfect place in which concrete learning could be acquired. His beliefs have influenced educational thought for almost four centuries, and our own regard for Comenius's advocacy of an 'authentic' curriculum led us to develop the outdoor setting as our largest classroom.

Although the work we describe here relates to our experiences in the early years setting, the principles underpinning the work can be transferred to teaching and learning at all levels. Secondary schools are usually blessed with more generous amounts of land than schools in the primary sector and thus have more potential for outdoor development. The grounds can be developed and used to support a spiral curriculum up to and including tertiary levels of education. Our own grounds are regularly used by secondary- and university-level students for field work and for practical studies. We imagine, that if older students moved into our premises, most of their study needs would be provided for at a very deep level by the school's environment. It is our belief that all schools and educational institutions can and should develop an ecologically valuable outdoor landscape which will be a multi-purpose resource for study, recreation and aesthetics.

Our school grounds are the teaching guide for us all. We investigate as we move about and we become more aware of our surroundings and the value of sharing information with each other. When the Coombes School opened in 1971 our initial concerns were about the low aesthetic level of our surroundings. We wanted the children to behave responsibly in the outdoor environment, and we wanted to set our building in an hospitable as well as a challenging setting. We inherited the detritus of building work, an ecologically damaged landscape and a featureless square of tarmac playground surrounded by heavy clay soil. Our vision was to set the school out as a 'kindergarten with overtones of care and love'. We had some understanding of the potential of a rich and diverse outdoor school setting (Cornell, 1979), and this set us on our way to energetic improvement. We saw the process as a long one that needed to involve all children, staff and parents. The programme had to be participatory, drawing on the talents and dreams of all those involved in it. Thirty-two years later, our school is set in a young wood. The site is criss-crossed with pathways and there is a range of microhabitats which have been purposefully created to support our teaching and pupils' learning and to add diversity to the landscape.

The school community learns both formally and, in a more relaxed way, by experiencing life in the playground and garden. We organise the playground so that there are designs in it which support logical and lateral thinking. Chess, a hundred square, large concentric circles, alphabet and number ladders and games from other cultures feature as designs on the playground surface. The children are creative in their thinking and in their play situations. They transform the markings into: 'magic roads', certain colours become 'no-go areas' or they are used to divide the playground into tactical zones for informal games. The capacity for learning and teaching out-of-doors is strengthened in a variety of ways to make the outside come alive for children. Children and adults are exposed to growing things and there is tremendous scope for imaginative play and emotional development. The psychology of building a full-bodied environment which appeals to all the senses sets the scene for action-packed learning that is richly motivating.

Trees make a world of difference to the children (Van Matre, 1972). Our progress towards putting the '*arbor*' back into Arborfield (the name of our local village) was slow, but step by step we set out to turn the land surrounding our school into a wooded area including: roosts for birds, shade in the summer and a protective shelter-belt for all seasons. Wild flowers have been introduced and small garden areas created for crops. Shallow ponds were shaped and the soil taken out was used for creating mounds and making new landscape features. Paths of different materials (concrete, mown grass, wood chippings, sawdust and decking) wind through the habitats and bring surprises for children at every turn. Large rocks represent one of the Earth's oldest features and speak of prehistory. Butterflies and dragonflies, rabbits and amphibians live in the gardens with us, as well as three sheep that are rotated through the grounds in a mobile paddock. Good design for children means caves and tunnels so that they can experience: different light values and ringing sound tones, spaces for bonfires, heights for long range views, lots of informal seating areas and dens for hiding. Our small maze and a labyrinth, based on the one at Chartres Cathedral, create different walking experiences and the ground plans are reproduced on paper so that the children may trace them with their fingers. Leaves from the trees and bark chippings on the pathways decompose slowly and the fungal elements in the soil help the process. A good collection of mushrooms and toadstools may be collected from the gardens during the autumn months and children learn to classify them according to colour, shape and whether they have gills or tubes under their caps. We also classify the fungi according to the plants growing in the area of collection and whether the specimens were found on wood, moss, amongst heathers or in grassland. The fungi are fascinating for the children and we explain to them that scientists had to establish a special category for these extraordinary organisms. The fungal sub-kingdom is now known to be vital to forestry and farming, and the decline of mycorrhizal species has preceded the wholesale death of forests in Eastern Europe. When the children gather the fungi, they take care not to pick every plant, but to collect selectively. They display their finds inside the classroom, and collect spore prints by leaving the fungi upturned on white card overnight. The fungi are then put back into the appropriate habitat to decompose. Beware of possible poisonous species of fungi, and take an opportunity to educate the children of the dangers of consuming anything unidentified. Ensure good hygiene by making sure the children wash their hands after handling fungi, leaf litter, etc.

Trees

Trees are the single most dominant architectural feature in the landscape. They are associated with myth and legend, with their products (wood, bark, leaves, blossom, fruit, etc.) and with the eco-communities which they support. In our opinion, the planting and growth of trees has been the single most important element in our design for the outdoor classroom.

Our development in the playground began with painted designs on the surface and the planting of trees along the perimeter. We chose apple, pear and plum for their edible seedcases and their romantic and fragrant blossoms. In late April and May, these trees are snowy with flowers and the children play under the blossoms. Insects pollinate the flowers and demonstrate their part in the fruiting cycle. Teachers draw explicitly on this direct evidence in the programmes of work. The children see the development in a take-it-for granted way as they play outside. Much later, the fruit is gathered during special harvesting days. Flavours are compared, pip counts are taken and each class cooks dishes using the fruits. Menus are organised to show the versatility of the fruit and its changes of state in becoming chutney, jam, sauce, fritters, pies and crumbles. Just as importantly, the children's taste buds are honed upon the produce which they have seen forming on the trees surrounding them. Much of the out-of-doors attraction comes from the lushness and the promise held by well-chosen trees.

Some of the trees around the playground edges are forest types and meet the children's needs to: gather acorns, count and weigh fir cones, make primitive ink with oak galls, examine beech mast and sweet chestnuts, and to crack open walnuts and hazelnuts. Part of the work is to imagine the possibility of feeding from these seeds in a simple hut in a time long, long ago. The children conjecture for themselves the value of autumn stores. In the past, these were vital to support life through the long winter periods. When the children and adults identify and collect these plant products, they have a chance to handle a part of the great cycle of life. Some of the seeds get planted so that the connections are literally deepened, but all seeds and leaves are enjoyed as objects for display, as ephemeral art objects or in categorised exhibitions. Typically, these exhibitions link geography (where the objects were found), nutritional values (in relation to humans and to wildlife), and tree and bush identification from fruits and leaves. This type of approach encourages scientific thinking for all of us, in a meaningful and concrete way.

Picking and eating some fruit straight from the tree is an uncomplicated way of expressing the fact that our food has to be grown, and that we all depend on plants. Blossoms and fruit demonstrate seasonal change and a process of growth and reproduction which is repeated year on year. Plants give us a part of a way to appreciate the concept of time and its passage. The turning of the year brings new learning adventures through its seasonal changes. September is when we harvest and eat the fruit we have grown. November is tree-planting time. The children are asked about the trees which have special merit for them and their comments guide our choice when we buy in the stock. We sometimes start off new trees from seed and we plant whips and propagate from cuttings. Larger specimens are often donated or bought in to mark a special occasion. The different ways of establishing tree cover encourages all of us to think about their origin and to 'read' the landscape for clues about how plants could have started.

Our children are very partial to willow because its young shoots are prized for their suitability for weaving and as sheep fodder. The children weave garlands for Christmas and Midsummer's day, and they take these home. Some is cut to provide rods and sticks for craft work and mathematical resources. The willow has an aesthetic quality beyond that of pressed plastic resources. Each classroom has bundles of ten sticks as well as single sticks to be used in teaching place value. Some of the supple willow is shaped and woven *in situ* as living basketwork and to make dens, bowers and tunnels. The light wood has a high resistance to splintering when subjected to impaction stress. The Montgolfier brothers took advantage of this quality when they became airborne in a willow basket. Modern balloonists have never found a better material to take the stress and strain. The ancient craft of willow weaving is demonstrated to the children by visitors from the local craft guilds and, with help, the children make simple baskets or willow hurdles. There is an implicit connection between what the children are doing in school and what their ancestors would have been doing in the past when using this material. There is also an underlying implication about sustainability; the regenerative properties of willow are well known and understood. Willows are also hosts to a huge number of insects, many of which will feed on other trees as well, but a large number of them use willow exclusively. No other tree except the oak supports more life, and in this country virtually all moth larvae depend on willow. We place white sheeting underneath a willow tree and shake the branches. The children are then able to examine the range of living things supported by it. A main aim in our school programme is to foster respect for all forms of life and to raise the children in an environment where there is planned species diversity. The sheet used for inspection is left overnight, by which time most animals have returned safely to the habitat. Animals brought indoors for further study are returned to their environment at the end of a teaching session, and the children understand the importance of this liberation. The teachers may then draw from this enriched environment in the daily teaching and learning programme.

Tree planting is an important part of our annual programme of environmental improvement. During their time at the school, the children will have had several opportunities to be a tree planter and they get great satisfaction from seeing their trees flourish. Because our school grounds now support a large variety of wildlife including a big rabbit population, it is necessary to protect the young trees from rabbit damage in their early years. We also involve the children in our annual coppicing and pollarding programme. Coppiced branches are trimmed and used as tall claves for rhythm work, or are set in the gardens in piles as wood stacks providing food and shelter. The children learn about sustainability and renewal of resources in a first-hand, experiential way.

We make log piles with dead wood around the gardens, and as the wood rots it becomes ideal for fungi and a huge range of living things. Since we want the children to be able to embark on 'mini-beast' hunts in the grounds, we purposefully set stones, logs, bits of hessian-backed carpet or corrugated iron into the grounds to be heat and humidity traps as well as light excluders. These can then be lifted to reveal a host of animals for study *in situ*, or for bringing indoors for a short time. After we examine each site, we replace the covers carefully and teach about animal sanctuaries and limiting our examination to formal moments when we lift the covers together.

Ecogardens are better places in which to learn about responsible stewardship of the earth, and offer opportunities which a closely mown turf or managed, formal flower-beds do not. Our gardens provide us with a huge range of species for study, and we are now able to set up a series of 1-day natural history museums in the school hall. The children collect their own exhibits, label these and add them to the collection, and we invite specialists to help us to learn more about the species. A recent spider museum will be followed by a beetle museum and a gastropod exhibition. We believe it is vital for children to make living statements about their neighbourhood throughout the year, in order that they can begin to understand more global and geographically distant concerns.

Crops

Our planting design includes food crops for eating. In our experience, children often assume that food originates in supermarkets, that chips grow in packets, that mashed potato starts in powder form, that eggs come from boxes and so on. By growing a few food crops in soil at school, we can deal with some of these misconceptions.

Pumpkins offer spectacular results, and every year the children are given a design and technology task to bring the heavy crops safely and undamaged into school. They work without direct adult help, although a range of resources is made available for them (ropes and string, broom handles, masking tape, blankets, wheelbarrows, sack trolleys, cardboard boxes and the like). As well as pumpkins, we grow potatoes every year. These are a good example of a main food crop and most families eat them every day in some form. The crop needs to be earthed up during the growing stages otherwise the tubers go green in response to light, but it is always possible to use large pots if garden space is not available. Every child will get to plant a seed potato, or part of one, and there is enormous excitement when we go out together to harvest the results of our work. The potatoes are dug out with small trowels that can be managed by the children. The crop is sorted, weighed and measured and then cooked in a variety of ways. The smallest potatoes are washed and simply boiled, and we sit in 'family circles' with a potato in one hand and a little seasalt in the other. There is great satisfaction in eating the results of the planting, and every gardener is aware of the keenness of this pleasure.

We made raised gardens with recycled timber and these are used for potatoes, peas and beans. The advantage of these raised beds is that the seedlings can be examined and the crops taken out without treading the garden. Our youngest children in the nursery unit grow tomatoes in gro-bags. Cherry tomatoes are easiest to share and give relatively carefree gardening without the accompanying chores of weeding or staking.

Later in the autumn term, every child plants at least two daffodil bulbs. Planting bulbs is a clearly different botanical experience from planting seeds, and the differences are pointed out. You need to beware of allergic skin reactions/dermatitis when handling bulbs, cornis, etc. – especially hyacinth bulbs. The daffodils flower around Mother's Day, and the steady year-on-year planting has increased daffodil numbers in the grounds so that all the children can pick about six blooms. Together with some pussy willow, ornamental currant or 'sticky buds', they make a small bouquet to take home. Restoring children's rights to pick flowers can be the basis of a deep regard for growing things, and it ties in well with our school's philosophy of giving 'picker's rights' to those who plant. The children learn to check which flowers may be picked without endangering future year's flowers, and we discourage them from collecting all but the most common wild flowers (buttercups, daisies, dandelions). However, we do believe that it is as important for children to experience the delights of picking flowers and enjoying their fragrance and beauty out of the ground as it is for them to appreciate flowers growing undisturbed *in situ*.

Sunflowers

With its huge bloom and bright yellow colour, the fully grown sunflower towers over the children and makes a kind of tropical jungle when planted *en masse*. Sunflowers in bloom entice many insects and, as they turn to seed heads, they attract birds. A sunflower garden is one of the most popular elements in the school grounds from the time the seeds germinate to the time the blooms are picked. They are significant for their contribution to our awareness of the seed-to-seed cycle and to our sense of awe and wonder. A seed which can be laid across a thumbnail at the beginning of its life, and which becomes a 2-metre giant with a head as big as a dinner plate, is a remarkable thing. One successful seed reproduces hundreds more set in an intriguing and complex pattern. We have been investigating sunflowers for many years and they are always fascinating and rewarding. The development of the plant takes approximately 12 weeks from seed to crowning flower. The beauty of a miniature sunflower field in full flower is impressive, and grown in this dense fashion makes it easier to see the sunflowers as a useful crop. The children and teachers make displays of sunflower related items (from shampoo, cosmetics and perfume to cakes, cookies and bread), and the children are introduced to the work of artists who have been inspired by sunflowers such as Van Gogh, Monet, O'Keefe and Hockney. (The large posters available from museum and gallery shops are ideal. Some poster shops stock a few reproductions of major artists' work, although quality varies.)

In June, the children have two handfuls of sunflower seeds, bought in bulk from the pet shop. They broadcast these in prepared plots, of about 5 metres square, and the plots are carefully netted to protect against feeding birds. The nets are removed when the seedlings are about 25 cm tall, and planting is organised to produce the bulk of flowers in September. Some commercially produced seed is also sown to encourage taller specimens and different varieties, and these may be sown early in pots before being transplanted. We tend to sow three or four times in succession every fortnight in the plots, so that there is a good range of plants (from buds to setting seedheads) when we return to school for the autumn term. The flowers cut for study in the classrooms are taken from the garden in such a way that a winding pathway is opened up through the plot. This path is then used by the children and teachers to get amongst and under the plants for a sense of scale and density. Seeds are re-examined and compared with the plant. Most plants are cut on our annual 'Sunflower Day'. This is a themed day when we celebrate the beauty of the plants and blooms, draw and paint them, eat sunflower bread, sunflower margarine and sunflower honey, and invite parents and carers to produce art work on a large scale outside the school, alongside the children's art work. The children use their own plants as life studies and recreate them in chalk on the playground or carpark surface. Often, the adults work in emulsion paint or spray paints to give a longer-lasting result. The resulting display is both vivid and personalised, until the first rains wash the pictures away.

Ponds, pools and wet areas

Pond watching is one of the most fascinating pastimes for all of us. We follow the progress of the frog, toad and newt from spawn to fully grown amphibian. We often net the pond dwellers and put them in plastic containers or transparent tanks for close-up inspection. This 'hunting' behaviour is a great favourite with the children and the finds are described and shared until it is time to return the pond dwellers gently to their environment. In the early years of our pond schemes, we considered the populations of plants and animals which we hoped to encourage. We felt that we had to go slightly further in our planning than building a single pond, so we dug two large ponds and dredged out the grassland for two smaller ponds to encourage insects, birdlife and plants which need wet habitats. (Learning Through Landscapes has published a variety of useful publications and leaflets about ponds and wet areas. See Resources.) Two ditches act as damp beds and these are a great benefit to wildlife during very hot or dry spells. One of the large ponds has a boardwalk running around two edges, so that the children can look directly into the deeper parts of the pond. The other large pond has a wooden lip about 40 cm across which the children lean on, and on which they rest their tanks, specimen pots and reference books.

Naming the specimens, describing their diet or metamorphosis is all part of the scientific operation, but much more important is the flying start which such practical methods produce. It is about awareness of small organisms, the pleasure of discovery and the 'grown-up-ness' of being warders of wildlife sanctuaries. Hours of contentment are passed detecting grass snakes hunting in the water; searching for the papery sheaves, cast in the dragonfly nymph's final moult; or watching the ballets of damsel flies and whirligig beetles. It instils a keen interest for life.

Water-based experiments in the playground include making artificial rainstorms with a power hose. The outdoor space is the only area where the children can move about under the hose and test their umbrellas and waterproofs (Figure 3.1). In the right conditions, we can make rainbows and look at the colour spectrum. Bubble blowing in a slight breeze can make bubbles soar over the roof of the school and the breeze makes the bubbles wobble, demonstrating their elasticity. We also flood natural depressions in the playground with the power hose so that the children can experience changes in the surface, get reflections and splosh through the puddles to enjoy breaking the surface and listening to the sounds.

In the spring term, we act out the story of the infant Moses floating in a basket on the Nile. Each child models a tiny baby with playdough, clothes it in scraps

Figure 3.1 Artificial rain – testing our umbrellas and waterproofs.

of fabric and sets the baby on a dish which will float. This is partly a Design Technology task, partly a scientific experiment, and partly a way of making our RE programme REAL. The activity is very popular and the children carry their baby Moses in their containers to test out their designs on the ponds and in the puddles. At the end of the day, the model babies are taken home to test in the bath tub.

Fire

In November, all the children study fire and the effects of heat. It is an integrated theme where dance, drama and music help to support the core curriculum through a number of fire-related experiences. The first of these gives clear expectations about combustibility and the techniques for safely investigating fire. We read and then dramatise the cautionary tale of Hilaire Belloc – 'Matilda, who told such dreadful lies' (Simmonds, 1991). The teachers and children make a model of Matilda's house, using a large cardboard box (at least a metre or so tall for best effect) and, using the Posy Simmonds' illustrations, plan the exterior. The poem is then read indoors and out-of-doors, and the house is set alight. The children observe the rapid effects of fire on the cardboard model. The Matilda experience sets the stage for other fire adventures, such as a re-enactment of the legend of the Phoenix, and gives the children and teachers the opportunity to talk about safety issues and the destructive dangers of fire, as well as its benefits to humankind.

The children then move on to a more scientific exploration of fire. They are asked to bring paired (but no longer needed) objects to school (such as two shoes, two umbrellas, two spoons, two pieces of chalk, two pencils, etc.). One of these objects stays inside the classroom as a control, and the counterpart is placed in a wire basket to put into a bonfire. As the children and adults help to build the bonfire, the wire baskets are tucked into the combustible material, as well as lidded biscuit tins, containing foil-wrapped and scrubbed potatoes. These simple ovens are raked out to the edge of the fire as soon as the heat becomes too intense, but the wire baskets remain in place, until they are collected from the cold ashes of the fire on the following day. The lighting of the fire is controlled, and the children stand at a safe distance, having already checked wind direction. The children eat their baked potatoes out-of-doors with a little butter and salt and are encouraged to describe the changes that have taken place in the potatoes. The contents of the wire basket are carefully sifted and any recoverable bits are closely examined and compared with the control objects in the classroom. A glass bottle may be a melted lump, the metal lasts of shoes are puzzled over, the metal ribs of an umbrella remain in working order, plastic may have fused together in the heat of the fire. Most objects, of course, are burned beyond recognition or trace and the impact of this deepens the children's respect for the power of heat and fire. The children are spellbound by this experience, and the occasions result in long-term learning.

A week-long study about the Great Fire of London in 1666, is concluded with a large scale model of the old city being set alight outdoors. Every child makes a model of a medieval or Tudor building at home, with parent help, and a huge floor map of the old city of London is outlined in the school hall. We use a base of reversed old carpets, or of layers of paper glued together, until a strong base is created. The streets are painted onto the map and the children help to name them accurately. The children place their home-made models onto the floor map. The combination of work done at home and at school helps to make this a community project and most parents and carers attend school on the day of the actual fire itself. The map is used indoors over the course of a week to support literacy, mathematics, history, geography, art, music and PE, but at the end of the week is relocated outside on a field area. The children carry out their models and replace them on the base map. A bakery on Pudding Lane is then set alight, and the children see, hear, feel and smell what happens as the 'City of London' starts to burn. The fire is dramatic, and usually every model building is reduced to ashes in a short space of time. The topic is vividly remembered, and provides a crucial part of our safety education.

Later in the term, we light large wooden posts (coated at the top with candlewax and sheep fleece) to serve as huge Diwali candles, and we also float candles on our ponds to mark this Hindu/Sikh celebration.

It is essential that children are given the opportunity to study and investigate heat and fire throughout their years at school and the school grounds are well suited for these investigations. Health and safety issues are carefully discussed and the dangers of playing with fire are seen, felt and heard. Having the chance to be a close first-hand witness to the destructive nature of fire and heat adds to the children's sense of awe at the power of this natural force. Occasionally, our local Fire Service comes to school to provide demonstrations of fire-fighting, extinguishers and smoke alarms, and to give advice to us all about safety.

Geology

There are many ways in which to transform the school grounds into inspiring places where children experience strange and wonderful shapes. One way is to put children in touch with large rocks. In our area, clay underlies a thin topsoil layer and we wanted to introduce specimens of rocks from other parts of the UK in order to make the study of geology accessible. Of course, the huge specimens we have introduced to the school grounds also provide powerful aesthetic additions. Culture and history are expressed through the use of local stone and this led us to want some of the rocks to be arranged in a way which would enhance the sense of pre-history and legend for the children. We started a geology project to do this. Memorable landmarks have been made from blocks of Yorkshire limestone set in a ring where two of the blocks carry a stone cross-beam similar to those seen at Stonehenge. The children now call this landmark, 'Coombeshenge'. Sandstone from Derbyshire was given by a quarry where there was an adjacent dolmen (burial chamber), and this monument stirred us to build a similar dolmen with the four blocks of stone received. The children go inside the chamber and experience the sound quality, the gloom and the unique atmosphere. Stones from a quarry in the Isle of Purbeck in Dorset were put together as a throne on a small mound of earth, and the children call this 'King Arthur's Seat'. We set a staircase constructed from railway sleepers, pebbles and bark chippings into the side of the mound leading up to the 'throne'. Red sandstone blocks from Penrith in Cumbria are grouped together, and one of these was carved into a gigantic head by a sculptor-in-residence; the others stand as sentinels. A large piece of Hornton Blue stone from Oxfordshire has been set into a 'font'-like situation and serves as a birdbath. The stone was carved for us by a stonemason with part of a line from a Robert Frost poem – 'all the difference' (Frost).

A group of Sarcen stones make a notable feature in the front of the school, and there are further large rocks from the Mendip hills of Somerset, from Cornwall, Bangor and Faringdon. Our school landscape gets a part of its attraction from these 11 sets of rock. The boulders typify the earth's surface at an earlier time before glacial action, mosses, lichens and the weather had rendered it into smaller stones and soil particles. History, geography and geology are taught from the rock locations and the rocks improve the relationship between the school building and the school site.

Bryology and compost

Some of the first forms of life on earth were the mosses and lichens, and these helped to shape our planet. Our school site today is full of examples of these primitive plants, and we encourage the children to locate and examine them *in situ*. Moss grows in cushions so that the individual soft, water-filled cells of the plant are supported. We study these tactile plants by collecting them from around the school grounds and arranging them in bryophyte gardens in the classroom. The children take turns to mist them with a fine spray of pond water, and observe the effects of this under hand lenses. After a few days, we return the plants and press them back into their original locations. This ordinary, common plant becomes extremely extraordinary under close examination and the children are fascinated by it.

Leaves and bark chippings set in heaps in the gardens produce heat and steam dramatically when they are cracked open on a frosty day. The children have managed to cook a foil-wrapped raw egg, placed into the middle of a large heap of bark chippings over a 3-day period. The leaves are spread in depth over our garden areas, and quickly decompose to give us a humus-enriched soil for our planting programmes. Over the years, we have fed our clay soil by the addition of tonnes of leaf litter. The bark chippings act as weed inhibitors in some of our garden beds, but are mainly used to cover pathways which criss-cross the school gardens. The bark chippings mean that the children can use these pathways throughout the year in any weather conditions without getting muddy feet; they also add a 'springy' feel as the children walk on them, and emit a powerful fragrance for several weeks.

Maps and beating the bounds

Guided walks around the landscape are regular ventures. An important walk for the whole school is when we re-enact the annual ceremony of 'beating the bounds' early in the spring term. The sticks we use for beating the boundaries are cut mainly from the school's hazel bushes (although we do also cut other stems as well). When we beat the bounds, we visit our school's boundaries, the borders of our woodland and we check for early flowers and seasonal reminders. The children carry maps and are encouraged to 'read' the symbols as they walk around our school site. At every stop, they tap the ground, boundary fence or hedge, and sing. This experience of geography is better than any textbook explanation. It is walk and talk connected with the historical tradition of beating the bounds. Midway through the walk, the groups of children stop for warm drinks and biscuits. They need this on a walk through a winter landscape (we usually do it in February) and it serves as yet another reminder about a sense of place.

We want to help the children to enjoy maps and to be able to interpret aerial photographs. A cartographer friend of the school helped us to draw maps of the school site which are to scale and are of a professional standard. These are reduced and reproduced for the children, who carry them around the site on their journeys and mark them to record their findings. It may be that the children are investigating where bluebells are to be found in the grounds, or where the sheep are grazing in their mobile paddock, or where the daffodils are being planted. As landscape features are added to the school site, the maps are updated. We also make full use of any aerial photographs on which we can lay our hands. Young children understand the direct images (even though taken from a bird's-eye viewpoint) and they are then encouraged to make the connections between bird's-eye views and abstract maps. By the time they reach Year 2, most of the children are able to plot and trace a route on a school map to depict a journey or a specific location. Colour slide images and photographs are also used to keep records of our school site development, to remind us of areas of beauty or interest, or to recall an experience or special event.

Supporting annual celebrations

When we analyse our curricular needs in our teaching and learning programme throughout the year, we are careful to reflect on how the school's outdoor environment might be developed and used to support our indoor work (Braund, 2001). We can then plan for these experiences in advance. For instance, in spring we beat the bounds and use sticks harvested from our own trees; for Epiphany, we journey along all-weather pathways set into the landscape; for Mother's Day, we plant daffodils in the autumn ready for picking in the spring. As Steiner says, 'the festivals are nodal points of the year which unite us with the spirit of the universe' (Steiner, 1909).

Every school has its own way of celebrating Christmas. We accentuate our interest in the natural world by cutting down an evergreen tree grown on site, and decorating our school hall with it. The non-native Leyland Cypress is ideal because of the flat spread of its branches. In the depths of winter, this evergreen is evidence of the life which always continues. It is more resinous than a fir or pine tree and consequently is more heavily scented. We plant a few of these non-native trees each year in order to provide evergreens for Christmas use in the future. The other reminder of continuing life in winter comes from the ivy, holly, santolina, juniper and laurel which we also plant and grow in our gardens. Using branches from these plants, we create a huge Victorian swag or garland to hang from the centre of our school hall. In this way, we aim to make old Christmas customs and traditions a genuine and living expression resourced from our own gardens. Bringing nature into the school as a focal point for a festival is an ancient custom. It is our best and most natural means to enliven the turning point of the year.

Conclusion

Our development of the school landscape over the last three decades has given us a remarkable resource which we use to support the formal curriculum. We believe that the setting for learning is as important as the curriculum content which we are trying to convey to the children. The school's most recent Ofsted Report (Ofsted, 2002) notes that the quality and range of the curriculum are 'outstanding'. Ofsted added, 'in addition to the statutory requirements of the National Curriculum and Religious Education, pupils have a wonderful range of memorable experiences which extend their learning. The use of the school grounds as a learning resource is "exceptional".'

The added benefit is that our school family lives and works in a wonderfully diverse, endlessly fascinating and beautiful setting which changes throughout the year. It is uplifting for all of our senses.

References

Braund, M. R., 2001, *Primary Plants: A Handbook for Teaching Plant Science in the Primary School*, Birmingham: Questions Publishing Co.

Comenius, J. A., *The School of Infancy* (edited with an introduction by E. M. Eller 1998), Chapel Hill: University of North Carolina Press.

Cornell, J., 1979, *Sharing Nature With Children*, Nevada City, CA: Awanda Publications.

Dannenmaier, M., 1998, *A Child's Garden*, New York: Simon & Schuster.

Fowles, J. and Horvat, F., 1979, *The Tree*, London: Aurum Press.

Frost, R., *The Road Not Taken*, available in many anthologies and collections.

Inspection Report 30 September–3 October 2002: Inspection Number 246947. Crown copyright 2002.

Simmonds, P. (illustrator), 1991, *Matilda, Who Told Lies*, London: Jonathan Cape. Based on the poem by Hilaire Belloc.

Steiner, R., 1909, *Festivals and Seasons*, London: Rudolph Steiner Press.

Van Matre, S., 1972, *Acclimatizing*, Martinsville, IN: American Camping Association.

Further reading

Humphries, S. and Rowe, S., 1996, *Working Together*, London: Forbes Publications.

Humphries, S. and Rowe, S., 1993, *The Big Science Book: Materials and Forces*, London: Forbes Publications.

Humphries, S. and Rowe, S., 1993, *The Big Science Book: All About Living*, London: Forbes Publications.

Jeffrey, R. and Woods, P., 2003, *The Creative School*, London: RoutledgeFalmer.

Olsson, T. (ed.), 2002, *Skolgarden som Klassrum: Aret Runt pa Coombes School*, Sweden: Runa Forlag.

Rowe, S. and Humphries, S., 1994, in Blatchford, P. and Sharp, S. (eds) *Understanding and Changing Playground Behaviour*, London: Routledge.

Rowe, S. and Humphries, S., 2001, 'Creating a climate for learning', in Craft, A., Jeffrey, R. and Leibling, M. (eds) *Creativity in Education*, London: Continuum.

Woods, P., 1999, 'Talking about coombes: features of a learning community', in Retallick, J., Cocklin, B. and Coombe, K. (eds) *Learning Communities in Education*, London: Routledge.

Resources

Common Ground, Gold Hill House, 21 High Street, Shaftesbury, Dorset SP7 8JE. Website: www.commonground.org.uk

Coombes Infant and Nursery School, School Road, Arborfield, Reading, Berkshire RG2 9NX, Tel.: 0118 9760751. email: head.coombes@wokingham.gov.uk. Website: www.thecoombes.com and www.thecoombes.com/intranet (please telephone the school for a visitor user name and password to access our intranet, which records all aspects of our work at the school).

Grounds for Learning, Airthrey Cottage, University of Stirling, FK9 4LA. Tel. 01786 445922. Website: gflscotland@stirling.ac.uk

Groundwork UK, 85–87 Cornwall Street, Birmingham B3 3BY. Tel.: 0121 2368565. Website: www.groundwork.org.uk

Learning Through Landscapes, Third Floor, Southside Offices, The Law Courts, Winchester SO23 9DL. Tel. 01962 846258. Website: www.ltl.org.uk

The Conservation Foundation, 1 Kensington Gore, London. Tel.: 0207 5913111. Website: www.conservationfoundation.co.uk

The Tree Council, 51 Catherine Place, London SW1E 6DY. Tel. 0207 8289928. Website: www.treecouncil.org.uk

Chapter 4

Using freshwater habitats

Martin Braund

Overview

The special contribution that freshwater habitats can make to pupils' learning is examined. A progression in learning of key concepts is provided before looking at opportunities for studies in still and running freshwater. Findings from a survey of school ponds show how this valuable resource might be better used to support learning. Ways in which pupils can study rivers or streams and generate data for analysis and to measure pollution are discussed.

Introduction

Places with water hold a special attraction for us. Lakes, waterfalls, rivers and streams are attractions and beauty spots in our landscape that we like to visit. The current trend for water features in gardens is an example of the therapeutic and aesthetic appeal of water. According to research, freshwater habitats are among the most popular sites for study chosen by teachers (Kinchin, 1993) and are the first choice for pupils when thinking about ways of improving the environment of their schools (Manchester Polytechnic, 1977).

There are many sound practical and educational reasons for teaching using freshwater habitats.

Practical reasons for using freshwater habitats

- They are locally accessible and offer a cheap alternative to field trips to distant localities.
- Visits can be re-scheduled if needed and do not rely on pre-booked courses that often result in timetable inflexibility.
- Ponds, troughs and sinks can be established in most school grounds without using large amounts of space and at reasonable cost.
- Relatively large numbers of pupils can carry out fieldwork at any one time.

Educational (ecological) reasons for using freshwater habitats

- Sites provide opportunities for other curriculum studies, e.g. in art, mathematics and geography (this is particularly important for primary schools).
- They have a relatively high biodiversity. Sixty-five per cent of Britain's wetland flora and 55 per cent of its wetland fauna can be found in ponds.
- Taxonomic groups have easily recognisable and distinct features (at the family/order levels). A number of good keys are available and are relatively easy to use.
- Macrofauna are easily collected using straightforward techniques over defined and limited areas. Sampling is not time consuming.
- A range of microhabitats are available for study and comparison, e.g. rapids and pools in streams and margins, substrata and vegetated areas of ponds.
- Physical factors such as temperature, oxygen and pH show interesting variation and correlation with factors such as position, substratum, organic detritus, etc. Parameters can be measured, monitored and analysed *in situ* and over varying timescales. This provides a good use for information and communication technology (ICT) in the curriculum.
- A range of interrelationships is present and allows for studies at a number of conceptual levels progressing from simple feeding relationships exemplified by food chains to more complex food webs, predator–prey relationships and discussions of energy flow.
- An interesting variety of life cycles and reproductive strategies are available for study.
- There is a number of interesting plant–animal associations that can be investigated.
- Seasonal variations and long-term community and population dynamics can be studied.

This chapter explores the ways in which teachers can maximise the learning potential of these places. Habitats will be divided into two main types: still freshwater – including canals, ditches, ponds and lakes – and running freshwater – e.g. streams and small rivers. It should be noted that there are a number of safety issues that teachers must consider before carrying out any fieldwork especially in aquatic habitats like these. These are referred to in Chapter 2 of this book. Specific references to safety literature involving ponds and other freshwater habitats can be found in the resources box at the end of this chapter.

Before looking at the potential for learning in still and running freshwater sites, it is necessary to consider issues of progression so that what pupils can achieve is set in the context of the school curriculum for science.

Progression in learning

There has been some criticism of the lack of progression evident for ecological concepts in the science national curriculum for England and Wales particularly in Key Stages 3 and 4. A major concern is that the study of ecology moves too rapidly from concrete examples of organisms and their interrelationships to abstract ideas (such as energy flow and population dynamics) without being matched by progression in understanding of the whole organism or in the application of observational and descriptive skill (Barker and Slingsby, 1998). Work in primary schools is often praised whereas a fast pace of teaching, without the necessary coherence in conceptual development, seems to characterise much of the work done in secondary schools.

The recently introduced Key Stage 3 framework for learning science is an attempt to clarify progression in the early years of secondary science (DfES, 2002). This framework identifies yearly teaching objectives for what are called 'key scientific ideas', one of which is 'interdependence' dealing with ecological principles. The Qualifications and Curriculum Authority (QCA) has also produced schemes of work for Key Stages 1, 2 and 3 and these contain five units dealing with ecological principles (QCA, 1998, 2000). The units are designed to build on previous work thereby reducing the chance of repetition, although secondary teachers are still often unaware of the content delivered by their primary colleagues.

Table 4.1 shows progression in three key concept areas vital to an understanding of ecology, and in particular freshwater ecosystems and how they function. These concept areas are prominent in the science National Curriculum and in QCA schemes of work and are ones that lend themselves to studies in these habitats. This is not to say that there are not other important ideas in ecology that could be learned. Progression in these areas is shown across Key Stages 1–3 along with some suggestions for studies in freshwater sites. For a fuller treatment on progression in teaching ecology in secondary schools and suggested studies for Key Stage 4 see Barker and Slingsby (1999).

Still freshwater habitats

Still freshwater sites offer a range of possibilities for studying the principles and concepts outlined in Table 4.1. These habitats range in type from the truly aquatic, through marsh, fen and wet flashes to mostly terrestrial, e.g. seasonally flooded woodland. They are transient sites; an unmanaged pond will soon silt up and become overrun by plants until it succeeds to marsh and eventually to woodland. Still waters contain a fascinating range of microhabitats for study.

Table 4.1 Progression in teaching key ecological concepts in freshwater habitats in Key Stages 1–3 (the numbers and letters in brackets refer to relevant units in the QCA schemes of work)

Key Stage	Key concepts and examples of studies		
	Diversity	*Adaptation*	*Interdependence*
KS 1	Different types of plants and animals live in a habitat (2B)		
Studies	*Sample different places in a pond or stream and list or draw what is found.*		
KS 2	Different animals are found in different habitats (4B)	Animals are suited to the environment in which they are found (4B)	Animals depend on different sources of food (4B)
	Keys can identify types of animals (4B)	Different plants grow in different conditions (6A)	Food chains describe feeding relationships. They often start with green plants (4B)
			Interference with a habitat affects organisms that live there (4B)
			Animals depend on plants in a number of ways (6A)
Studies	*Compare types of animals found in ponds with those found in streams. Compare types found amongst vegetation with those found in mud or under stones.*	*Ask pupils to say why animals living in flowing water often live in tubes or have flattened bodies.*	*Use secondary sources such as books, video and ICT to identify food sources – add to a poster or 3-D model of a pond or stream.*
	Encourage pupils to group animals according to observable features and using simple published keys (see Resources box).	*Compare plants growing at the margins, rooted in mud and floating in water.*	*Use drawings of organisms on cards and get pupils to construct food chains.*
			Ask pupils to think what might happen to animals if something killed all the plants in a pond.
KS 3	Organisms are classified according to a recognised system (7D)	Animals are adapted to seasonal change (7C)	Feeding relationships can be described using food webs (7C)
		Animals show adaptations as predators or to avoid predation (7C)	A pyramid of numbers is a quantitative description of feeding relationships (8D)
			Different communities are found in different habitats within a locality (8D)
			Physical factors often determine the distribution of organisms and the structure of communities (8D)

| Studies | Record detailed features of organisms found in streams and ponds and classify using books and databases.

Study the detailed morphology of different organisms and relate to adaptations. | Sample a pond or stream in different seasons. Chart numbers of species found.

Relate studies of morphology of organisms to specific adaptations, e.g. mouthparts, breathing mechanisms, attachment, shape, etc. | Construct food-web mobiles for a pond or stream or place cut out pictures onto a model or poster.

Sample and compare populations in different microhabitats in ponds and streams, e.g. rapids/pools, bottom/surface. Use results to construct food pyramids.

Measure factors such as light, O_2 concentration, pH, water flow-rate and relate to distribution and population of organisms found in different microhabitats. |

These are characterised in two ways: by the position of the habitat as defined by depth and by the nature of plant life that exists. Plant-defined habitats offer the chance to study succession from the land plants rooted in the bank to those that float at the centre. Each zone is characterised by a community of plants showing a range of interesting adaptations worthy of study, e.g. the large surface area of leaves and air sacs in stems of the common water lily. Still water sites are often within close reach of schools, but how much better it is if one is just a few steps away, in the school grounds.

In the last 20 years curriculum changes requiring more ecological work coupled with a desire to develop the aesthetic and environmental appeal of school grounds have stimulated schools to build ponds. Development of school grounds and, in particular, the construction of ponds has been aided by grants from Local Education Authorities (LEAs) and environmental bodies such as English Nature and The Groundwork Trust. The growth in school ponds coincides with that in private gardens, particularly in areas of new housing, and comes at a time of continuing loss of natural ponds. The actual contribution that school ponds make in enhancing wetland landscapes is not known but may be increasingly significant as many are in urban areas where pond loss has been greatest.

A survey of the use of school ponds

Despite the trend for pond construction and the large amounts of money that have been spent, little research has been carried out to evaluate the use of ponds or to explore factors that prevent schools from developing or using them. During 1997 a study was carried out in ten LEAs across the Yorkshire region to establish how school ponds were constructed, maintained and studied so as to focus future advice across the educational sector in the UK (Braund, 1998).

A questionnaire was sent to a random selection of 112 schools. Approximately equal numbers of primary and secondary schools were included. Fifty schools responded and of these, 65 per cent had ponds. This figure cannot be extrapolated to all schools as a larger number of secondary schools with ponds replied and this is probably because they wanted to celebrate the success of recent developments or wanted advice on maintenance and further educational use.

Most ponds were less than 5 years old but a few were built as ornamental features or 'quadrangle' ponds. Most of the newer ponds were planned as part of a wider development of grounds for study and aesthetic/environmental improvement. Over half the schools involved parents and children in planning and construction but less than a quarter involved their local LEA to any great extent.

School ponds were on the small side, 70 per cent being less than 20 m². Larger ponds (up to 150 m²) were almost exclusively found in secondary schools where space was not at such a premium. Most school ponds were rarely over 1 m in depth, the shallowest being around 30 cm. Although two-thirds of schools with ponds reported resident amphibian populations (mainly the common frog or the smooth newt) few teachers could report on populations of invertebrates. It seems that schools do not keep on-going records and that identification and taxonomic knowledge are problematic especially for primary teachers.

School ponds are most likely to be maintained by clearing plants once a year, in response to 'crises'. This was often done by an enthusiastic parent, teacher or caretaker. Children and 'local environmental action' groups rarely seem to be involved. Almost all schools without ponds wanted them but cost, worries about vandalism and lack of knowledge and expertise were the major constraining factors. Interestingly, vandalism was more of a concern for secondary schools than cost.

As far as educational use is concerned, primary schools seemed to use their ponds with different age groups but this was rare in secondary schools. Studies were concentrated in the summer term (May–July) and in some cases several classes studied a pond ('pond dipping') over 2 weeks. Some primary schools used their ponds for year-round study (20 per cent) but this was very rare in secondary schools (6 per cent).

The next section considers some solutions to problems perceived by schools and makes suggestions for improving educational use.

Improving the use of school ponds: some possible solutions

Key ecological principles that pupils should learn about and that can be readily accessed in freshwater habitats were discussed earlier and shown in Table 4.1. Ponds are key places that can be used with a range of ages thereby ensuring a set of coherent and progressive experiences, all too often lacking in schools. The survey by Braund (1998) showed that there were three main areas limiting effective educational use:

- concerns about vandalism;
- pond management;
- limited pupil involvement and multi-seasonal use.

Each of these is discussed below with the intention of offering advice so that teachers and others can maximise the potential for learning and make better use of pupils, adults and the community.

The problem of vandalism

Deliberate damage to schools' ponds is most likely to occur soon after construction. This often involves the butyl liner, which is deliberately attacked or punctured by objects thrown into the pond. The use of bentonite for pond base lining is an alternative but is expensive. Some designers solve the problem by using a liner protected by concrete but this is also expensive. Some success has been reported through the use of 'geotextile' matting, which is laid over the butyl liner (Braund and Kersey, 1998). This material has the advantage of being relatively cheap; it cannot be cut or punctured and looks natural within a short time after construction.

Schools often site ponds in wildlife areas tucked away in the corners of their grounds, some distance from the main buildings. Whilst this may be aesthetically pleasing it often makes it easier for the vandal to gain access without being seen. Some schools in urban areas are now building ponds closer to main buildings or in enclosed yards/quadrangles. Advantages include closer access to classrooms for studies of collected organisms and the fact that rainwater run-off from roofs can prevent pond water levels falling dramatically in the summer months (see Figure 4.1).

One final suggestion for schools that want a more temporary but still worthwhile alternative is to use a cattle trough or rubber tyre pond. The use of

Figure 4.1 Pond sited at the front of an urban school.

troughs for freshwater investigations has been described by Lock and Collins (1996) and suggestions for tyre ponds are given by Braund and Kersey (1998). A tyre pond is shown as Figure 4.2.

Pond management

Schools can easily forget that ponds are transient habitats undergoing succession. Whilst the ecological value in maintaining late successional, highly vegetated ponds is now realised (Williams *et al.*, 1997), such a situation is not practical or attractive for schools. Emergent plants are important aesthetically and as sites for insects to complete their life cycles but many (such as reedmace and yellow flag) are highly invasive and cause problems for small ponds. One solution is to plant these invasive species in containers such as plastic buckets and pots with holes in them at the edges of smaller ponds and maintain these in permanently waterlogged conditions. One of the problems with school ponds is that the traditional conical profile means that they dry out from the margins during the busy sampling periods of summer and children have to stand at muddy margins overreaching to sample in unproductive water. Designs by Kersey (see Braund and Kersey, 1998) avoid this problem by ensuring that a relatively deep area close to hard standing or a dipping platform is always available. Some ponds now include a wooden bridge from which children can

Figure 4.2 A tyre pond.

dip safely into two contrasting areas. Figure 4.3 below shows two plans for the design of pond margins.

Limited pupil involvement and multi-seasonal use

Some educators believe that ecological understanding requires a study of ecosystems at all seasons (Tansley, 1987). However, multi-seasonal studies at school ponds are rare, particularly in secondary schools, yet, arguably, this is

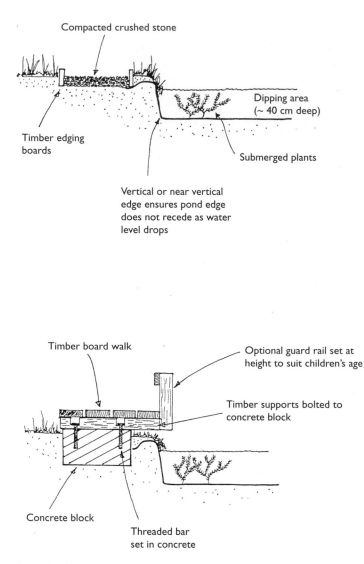

Compacted crushed stone

Dipping area
(~ 40 cm deep)

Timber edging
boards

Submerged plants

Vertical or near vertical
edge ensures pond edge
does not recede as water
level drops

Timber board walk

Optional guard rail set at
height to suit children's age

Timber supports bolted to
concrete block

Concrete block

Threaded bar
set in concrete

Figure 4.3 Designs for pond margins.

where the sophistication of knowledge and understanding required is greatest. As we have seen, good progression in ecological understanding requires a steady build-up in ecological knowledge and its applications. Pond communities are continually in a state of dynamic flux and the patterns of change seen in them can be as much to do with chance as to predictable ecological factors. Coupled with the fact that insect and amphibian life cycles result in large-scale seasonal variations in pond populations, studying the pond only once in the school year means that pupils are missing out on interesting and stimulating learning experiences. The value of longer-term studies in freshwater ecology where data are collated and analysed over several months or years has been well illustrated by Boreham (1994). The subtleties of changes in populations at different trophic levels and in different seasons are shown very well in the studies he described.

Ponds are rarely used for investigative work, for example, to study associations between animal populations and submerged pond architecture. A worthwhile study is to lower wire mesh cages containing strips or larger pieces of plastic (e.g. from a bin liner) into the pond at various sites and at varying depths and to study the macro-invertebrates found after a number of weeks. Such studies allow pupils to simulate and study the influence of pond vegetation on animal community structure with minimum disturbance to the pond. They also provide a chance for pupils to broaden their experience of scientific investigation from the usual laboratory situations where controlled tests of the effect of one single variable dominate to cases where this is not appropriate or possible.

The concentration of pond studies in summer months leads to intensive dipping by classes over a short period of time and this may have consequences for the recovery of invertebrate populations, particularly in small ponds. Kersey (in Braund and Kersey, 1997) recommends that an area equivalent to at least one-third of the pond is left undipped to allow for recovery and recolonisation from undisturbed areas.

Environmental education represents a much broader curriculum area than the study of ecology alone. Three aspects can be recognised:

- education *about* the environment;
- education *through* the environment;
- education *for* the environment.

The first two can be provided for through the kinds of studies already mentioned but the last aspect could involve pupils in enhancing and sustaining the quality of their own environment. It is perhaps surprising, therefore, that the survey by Braund (1998) showed that few schools involve pupils directly or actively in the continued development and maintenance of their outside resources. Educating 'through the environment' might also include using the pond for non-science work such as in art, mathematics and geography. In this way ponds make an essential contribution to the concept of school grounds as 'outdoor classrooms' referred to by Humphries and Rowe in the previous chapter.

Running freshwater habitats

As with still water sites, it is sometimes difficult to distinguish between one type of running freshwater habitat and another. Streams are often just a stage in the development of a river or part of a network of watercourses. It is more usual for schools to study streams since they have a greater diversity of life, show a range of sub-habitats and are more likely to show variation in the influence of physical factors. The key factors that determine the character and hence the communities and ecosystems of streams are the rate of flow and quality of the water. These are themselves the product of other factors such as gradient, available water flow from overground and underground sources and surrounding geology.

Water flow rate determines the nature of the substratum; a place where many animals live. Oxygen content is usually high in fast flowing and shallow streams but may decrease where water collects in pools or where microbial decay of organic matter occurs. The chemical content of water varies with the landscape of the local catchment area, e.g. peat streams in moorland and chalk streams in areas with calcareous rocks. The chemistry of the water can be affected by runoff from agriculture or disused mines. These factors provide interesting variations that can be studied by taking simple measurements, e.g. of the pH or conductivity of the water (as a measure of the quantity of dissolved salts). At advanced levels, more subtle measurements of individual nutrients in water can be made with commercially produced kits or by using colorimetry.

Linear studies

A very effective and enjoyable way of studying a stream or river is to follow a section of it visiting a number of 'stations' along the way, taking samples of the physical and biotic environment at each stop. The stations could be decided according to accessibility for the size of group but should also take account of any likely changes in the ecology such as: amount of shade from overhanging trees; entry of water from tributaries; possible pollution from sewage; runoff from agricultural land or disused mines. Most streams will have rapids and pools at stations in the upper reaches and it is worth comparing the fauna found in these. It is important to involve all members of the class in the collection of data. This can be done by allocating groups specific tasks to carry out at each station. Tasks can be rotated so that each group gets a chance to sample both abiotic (physical) and biotic (living) components of the ecosystem. Table 4.2 gives some examples of suitable activities.

Sampling the biotic environment is most effective if methods are systematic and thorough. For example, an agreed number of small rocks and stones should be

Table 4.2 Examples of tasks for groups sampling streams

Abiotic sampling	Biotic sampling
Measure flow rate, e.g. timing a float over a fixed distance.	Collect samples using nets. Kick or sweep sampling can be used. Different groups could be responsible for different sites, e.g. from rapids and pools, under banks/and tree roots, amongst vegetation, from kick samples, from sweeps, in mud/substratum, etc.
Sketch the site including prominent trees, overhangs and sites of rapids and pools.	Turn over rocks and stones and look for and record numbers of specific types of organisms, e.g. cased caddis fly larvae and black fly larvae. Pupils could record the types of cases of caddis larvae: sand, stone, leaf, stem.
Measure water temperature using thermistors, probes or long-stemmed glass thermometers.	Some groups could be in charge of identification, thus making best use of limited guides and keys. It is useful to rotate this task so that all pupils are involved.
Measure pH using a probe or short-range indicator paper.	
Collect water samples for later analysis or use probes/indicator papers to measure conductivity or specific nutrients such as nitrate/phosphate.	
Measure depth using plastic metre rulers.	
Record the nature of the substratum, e.g. sand, mud, gravel, rock.	

overturned in defined areas of rapids; netting of water should include sites such as under tree roots and overhanging vegetation as well in the main flow of water itself. 'Kick sampling' is a method where the net is held downstream of the feet and the substratum is disturbed so that detritus and animals are washed into the net. All sampling should take place walking upstream to avoid contamination by animals washed into nets downstream of sampling points. It is best to sit on the bank and wash samples from nets into large white painted or enamelled trays so that the animals stand out and can be identified either on the spot or removed into plastic sealed and labelled containers for identification in the laboratory. Do not make the mistake of putting small fish into containers with other animals – unless you want pupils to gain evidence of predation!

Data collected from linear studies allow a number of questions to be answered, for example:

■ How similar are communities found in pools and rapids?
■ How do populations of specific organisms vary along a stretch of stream? Distribution of key species can be displayed by drawing 'kite diagrams'. The

technique is described by Barker and Slingsby (1999, pp. 229–30). Data can be analysed using an ICT package.

- Is the distribution of organisms along the stream related to change in physical factors (e.g. flow rate, pH, O_2 concentration)?
- Is change in one variable related to change in another? Pupils might explore how oxygen concentration varies with depth and/or temperature.

Answering these questions involves a degree of numerical and statistical manipulation and there are a number of sources available to help students (and teachers!). One such guide is shown in the resources box at the end of this chapter.

A simple way for KS4 and 'A'-level students to compare the degree of similarity (or dissimilarity) between two microhabitats such as pools and rapids, is to calculate a coefficient of similarity using the simple formula:

$$\frac{C}{(A + B) - C} \times \frac{100}{1} = ?\%$$

where A is the total number of species in habitat 1, B is the total number of species in habitat 2 and C is the number of species common to both habitats.

Using a 'biotic index' to assess pollution

Studying ecology and carrying out fieldwork are often most effective when the learning has a purpose linked with an issue of environmental concern. Pupils feel that they are engaged in something worthwhile and potentially helpful to others.

Linear studies of rivers and streams lend themselves to a type of analysis that measures the relative amounts of pollution by comparing the presence or absence of key species. The reasoning is that certain freshwater organisms are more tolerant of pollution (especially the lack of available oxygen) than others. These species therefore act as indicators for pollution, hence the name 'biotic index'. Species are allocated a number depending on their tolerance to pollution and then the number of species types, and sometimes their abundance, are used to calculate a value indicating the degree of pollution. Biotic indices used by professional ecologists are most reliable but require a degree of classification often beyond school-aged pupils. The 'Trent Biotic Index' is the one most commonly used by schools but its reliability and validity have been questioned (Dale, 1980). I have found the index used by Atkin and Birch (date of publication unknown) to be easy to use and reliable in a number of types of streams and rivers. This index does not require complex identification and is quick to use. A worked example is shown in Table 4.3. Drawings of some of the organisms used in the index are provided as Figure 4.4.

The ranges of values of the index show the degree of pollution as follows:

0–4: very poor water quality
5–10: poor water quality
11–18: moderate to poor water quality
19–24: moderate water quality
25–29: moderate to good water quality
30–35: good water quality
36+: very good water quality.

Table 4.3 An example of a score sheet for a stream

Animal group (see Figure 4.4)	A Score (based on tolerance)	B Number of different species types found in this group	A × B
Water shrimp (Gammarus)	4	(Only 1 allowed) 1	4
Water louse (Asellus)	3	(Only 1 allowed) 1	3
Baetis (A species of mayfly)	4	(Only 1 allowed) 0	0
Beetle and other insect larvae or nymphs	5	0	0
Leech Snails and bivalve molluscs	3 3	(Only 2 allowed) 1 3	3 9
Water mites Adult beetles	5 5	(Only 1 allowed) 0 1	0 5
Midge larvae (Chirionomid larvae)	2	(Only 1 allowed) 1	2
Tubifex (worms) Cased caddis fly larvae	1 8	(Only 1 allowed) 1 0	1 0
Uncased caddis larvae	5	1	5
		Total score =	32

Source: Based on the index developed by Birch and Atkin.

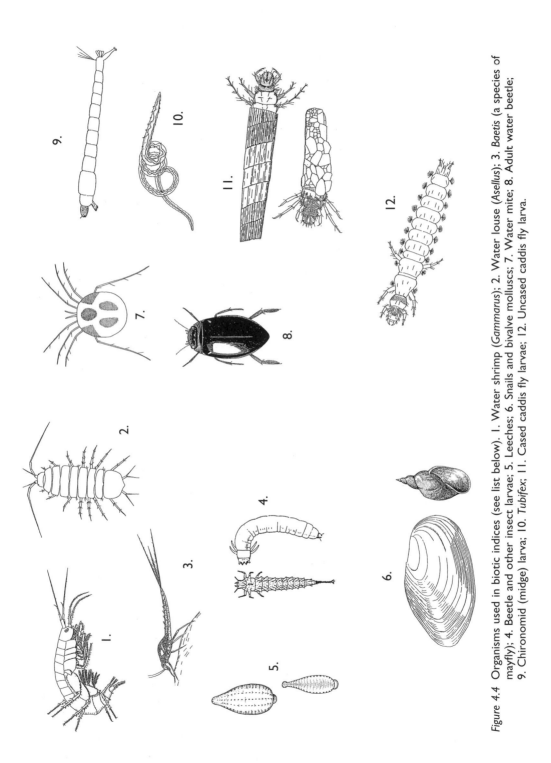

Figure 4.4 Organisms used in biotic indices (see list below). 1. Water shrimp (*Gammarus*); 2. Water louse (*Asellus*); 3. *Baetis* (a species of mayfly); 4. Beetle and other insect larvae; 5. Leeches; 6. Snails and bivalve molluscs; 7. Water mite; 8. Adult water beetle; 9. Chironomid (midge) larva; 10. *Tubifex*; 11. Cased caddis fly larvae; 12. Uncased caddis fly larva.

Conclusion

Research has shown that pupils struggle to understand many ecological concepts (see for instance Leach *et al.*, 1996). Young pupils, for example, often use anthropomorphic reasoning; they might say that a caddis fly larva lives under a stone because it 'likes to live there'. Another common misconception concerns interrelationships between organisms. Pupils might say, for example, that there are greater numbers of small organisms such as insect larvae than there are fish so that fish 'have enough food to eat'. Leach and others call this teleological reasoning. Whilst there is no direct evidence that studying freshwater habitats is more or less successful at dispelling such misconceptions, this chapter has provided a number of reasons for making use of this resource.

As so many of the chapters in this book show, learning science in the field is not only about the amount of conceptual change that takes place. If motivation and personal involvement in learning are taken into account then these places are surely a rich source of stimulation. Freshwater sites provide places where a range of skills in the use of equipment and techniques can be developed and used. Fieldwork has sometimes been criticised for lacking academic rigour because it has concentrated on description and analysis based on qualitative data. On the contrary, this chapter has shown that there is ample opportunity to measure and collect data that help pupils understand key relationships between the two fundamental aspects of an ecosystem, the abiotic and the biotic. Studies in these habitats offer the opportunity for pupils to think about ecological data in relation to real problems such as pollution and to work in their own school grounds as a demonstration of personal environmental action. There is ample scope in both still and freshwater contexts for good quality work with most ages of pupils. The environments in which these habitats exist provide good educational experiences and a chance for pupils to appreciate the contribution that wetlands make to the richness of our world.

References

Atkin, D. and Birch, P. (date unknown) *River Assessment*, North East London Polytechnic: Environment and Industry Research Unit.

Barker, S. and Slingsby, D., 1998, 'From nature table to niche: curriculum progression in ecological concepts', *International Journal of Science Education*, 20(4), 479–86.

Barker, S. and Slingsby, D., 1999, 'Ecology', in Reiss, M. (ed.) *Teaching Secondary Biology*, London: Murray, pp. 214–43.

Boreham, S., 1994, 'A study of freshwater invertebrate distribution and abundance from fieldwork by secondary school students in an Epping Forest pond', *Journal of Biological Education*, 28(1), 32–8.

Braund M., 1998, 'Ponds and education in the UK: current use and future potential', in Boothby, J. (ed.) *'Ponds and Pond Landscapes of Europe'. Proceedings of the*

International Conference of the Pond Life Project, Liverpool: Pond Life Project, pp. 31–8.

Braund, M. and Kersey, R., 1998, 'Are you getting the most from your school pond?', *Primary Science Review*, 54, 8–11.

Dale, C. R., 1980, 'The biotic indexing of water quality and its application to field work in schools and colleges', *Journal of Biological Education*, 14(3), 205–12.

DfES, 2002, *Key Stage 3 National Strategy. Framework for Teaching Science: Years 7, 8 and 9*, London: Department for Education and Skills.

Kinchin, I. M., 1993, 'Teaching ecology in England and Wales: a survey of current practice', *Journal of Biological Education*, 27(1), 29–33.

Leach, J., Driver, R., Scott, P. and Wood-Robinson, C., 1996, 'Children's ideas about ecology 3: ideas found in children aged 5–16 about the interdependency of organisms', *International Journal of Science Education*, 18(2), 129–41.

Lock, R. and Collins, N., 1996, 'Freshwater studies using cattle drinking troughs', *Journal of Biological Education*, 30(3), 166–8.

Manchester Polytechnic, 1977, *Ask the Kids – Planning the School Site*, Manchester: Manchester Polytechnic.

QCA, 1998, *Science: A Scheme of Work for Key Stages 1 and 2*, London: Department for Education and Employment.

QCA, 2000, *Science: A Scheme of Work for Key Stage 3*, London: Department for Education and Employment.

Tansley, A., 1987, 'What is ecology?', *Biological Journal of the Linnean Society*, 32, 17–29.

Williams, P., Biggs, J., Corfield, C., Fox, G., Walker, D. and Whitfield, M., 1997, 'Designing new ponds for wildlife', *British Wildlife*, 8, 137–50.

Resources

Leadley-Brown, L., 1971, *Ecology of fresh water*, London: Heinemann.
   This is still one of the best background texts on freshwater biology and very readable.
Chalmers, N. and Parker, P., 1989, *The OU Project Guide: Fieldwork and Statistics for Ecological Projects*.
   Comprehensive and compact introduction to fieldwork methods and statistics.

Field guides and keys
Fitter, R., and Manuel, R., 1995, *Collins Photo Guide: Lakes, Rivers, Streams and Ponds of Britain and North-West Europe*, London: Harper-Collins.
   Worthwhile having at least one copy to hand.
Orton, R., Bebbington, A. and Bebbington, J., 1995, *The Freshwater Name Trail: A Key to the Invertebrates of Ponds and Streams*, Preston Montford: Field Studies Council.
   Part of a series of fold-out, plastic-coated keys. Worth having multiple copies.

Practical and safety information
Bunyan, P, 1988, 'Safety and the school pond', *Primary Science Review*, 7, 21–2.
   Advice on pond construction safety and security.
DfES, 1998, *Health and Safety of Pupils on Educational Visits: A Good Practice Guide*, London: Department for Education and Skills.
   General advice relating to all out-of-school visits.
DfES, 2002, *A Handbook for Group Leaders*, London: Department for Education and Skills.
   A supplement to the publication above providing additional guidance.

Langton, L., 1997, 'Pond heaven: How to create your own wildlife pond', Bristol: BBC Wildlife Magazine.
A very good short guide to pond ecology and construction.

Useful websites
www.fba.org.uk
Freshwater Biology Association. Updates on research and access to some useful keys for more advanced work.
www.environment-agency.gov.uk
The section entitled 'my backyard' gives detailed environmental data for streams and rivers for any postcode in the UK. The site is useful for exploring a range of data for environmental monitoring.

Chapter 5

Learning at residential field centres

Anne Bebbington

Overview

The special role of field centres in out-of-classroom education today is considered together with the development of the field studies movement. Advice is given on planning a visit to a field centre, taking account of: academic content, cost implications, organisational, and health and safety issues. Three case studies are described looking at the academic role of field work at different age levels. Finally, the social and personal development benefits of a residential field trip are discussed.

The special role of field centres

The core business of field centres is teaching through, from and about the environment, primarily in the context of the geography and science curriculum. Some also offer adventure activities, but these are not considered here. A school with good school grounds or even a pond can, as we have seen in the previous two chapters, carry out a considerable amount of excellent in-house fieldwork. So what are the particular advantages of visiting a field centre?

A field centre provides a new and exciting setting and a contrasting locality. This makes fieldwork particularly memorable, enhancing both affective and effective learning. Specialist staff are available skilled in making links between fieldwork and the curriculum. They are also experienced in planning and structuring fieldwork and have a working knowledge of fieldwork techniques. They also have training in the management of groups out-of-doors and leadership and first-aid training. Field centres negotiate access to a wide variety of sites suitable for different activities. Specialist fieldwork equipment is available, together with teaching handouts and publications designed for particular activities. Many centres also have a library and long-term data sets, e.g. local weather records. Residential facilities are offered by many field centres, providing a particularly valuable opportunity for the development of pupils' social skills.

The development of the field centre movement

Fieldwork has long been an integral part of the life and earth sciences. The work of many of our most distinguished biologists, e.g. Charles Darwin, was based on careful and detailed work in the field. However, for many, fieldwork in the early part of the twentieth century was seen as an interesting, but unimportant, minority activity.

Streeter (1993) describes how, in the early post-war years of the 1940s, three strands emerged in the countryside agenda: the formation of National Parks, the creation of nature reserves and the promotion of conservation and environmental education. Out of the third strand arose a new and novel idea, the vision of a remarkable man, Francis Butler. His notion was to provide residential field study centres in areas of outstanding interest where students from schools and colleges, as well as individuals, could carry out field investigations and receive tuition about natural history and the countryside. By 1948, the Council for the Promotion of Field Studies (now the Field Studies Council – FSC) had opened its first four centres (Figure 5.1).

Figure 5.1 'A new field centre' – Juniper Hall in 1946.

This major innovation heralded an upsurge in environmental education. Curriculum changes, and thinking within schools and university education departments, led to a rapid rise in the development of field study centres. A review of environmental education by the Department of Education and Science (1981) found that by 1979 there were over 600 centres. Local Education Authorities ran 300 of these, nearly 300 were run by independent organisations such as youth hostels with special facilities and ten were run by the Field Studies Council. Day centres, operated mainly by the Local Education Authorities, were numerous. Even with this large number of centres, demand soon outstripped provision. Many schools established their own centres or used hotels and guest houses from which to run their own field courses.

By the 1980s development appeared to have reached a plateau. Over the next 20 years, questions were being raised about the academic value of fieldwork, in particular distant fieldwork. There were also concerns about pressure on habitats, particularly famous and classic sites. Safety and a need for competent and efficient leadership of field study parties were also questioned. In addition, there were increasing financial constraints as Local Authorities put their money into mainstream education in response to government policy aimed at improving the performance of schools and the achievement of pupils. Field studies were increasingly being seen as peripheral to education or an expensive addition.

At the National Association of Field Studies Officers (NAFSO) Conference in 1999, it became apparent that many centres had already closed and others were under pressure to provide evidence of the academic value of fieldwork. Subjective evidence from fieldwork enthusiasts had to be supplemented by real evidence: from inspection bodies, improved examination results and research. This led Nundy (2001) to produce a document providing research evidence, indicating that well-planned fieldwork can improve affective learning which in turn can enhance effective learning across the curriculum.

The position of field studies today

The number of field centres has clearly declined since the 1970s. Recent directories, produced by the National Association of Field Study Officers and the School Government Publishing Company, list 138 centres run by Local Education Authorities and 105 run by independent organisations. These include both day and residential centres. In addition, a few large commercial operators have been established in recent years, e.g. the Kingswood Educational Activity Centres. Kingswood's main focus is on adventure activities but they do provide field study courses for a significant number of students across the curriculum. Today the Field Studies Council owns or manages 17 field centres and is a major provider of field studies in the UK. It is also well-established as an organisation for environmental education in Europe; indeed, many of its ideas and publications are being used worldwide. It also retains its role as a pioneering educational charity and is actively looking at ways in which the case for fieldwork can be made.

In considering the role of fieldwork today at different age levels, three important points emerge:

1   At primary school level, the value of fieldwork in teaching, not only of science, but in helping pupils to make links across the curriculum, is clearly recognised. The demand for courses in this sector may be rising.
2   There is concern amongst educationalists that, on transfer to secondary school, pupils lose their interest in science. Field centres have a particularly important role to play here, not least in maintaining enjoyment and enthusiasm in pupils in the 11–16 age group. The Key Stage 3 Strategy Document for science (DfES, 2002) focuses on five key ideas one of which is 'interdependence'. Fieldwork should be a valuable learning tool in helping pupils to understand this key idea.
3   A particular problem has been highlighted in the 16–19 age group where traditionally fieldwork has been seen as very important in the teaching of biology. Lock and Tilling (2002) report that, in spite of the Government view that fieldwork plays a vital part in science education, there has been a decline in the number of biology students doing fieldwork. Students are nearly always enthusiastic about fieldwork and opportunities do exist, but these are not being taken up.

The three case studies described later in this chapter provide an opportunity for more detailed discussion of these points.

Planning a visit to a field centre

In common with all out-of-classroom activities, detailed planning is essential. There are, however, certain areas that need particular attention.

The course programme

Many field centres have developed packages, addressing different topics within the science curriculum, that can be completed in half-day or full-day visits. The teacher ensures that pupils are offered a series of topics that are linked to each other as well as to what is going on in school. Pre-course discussions with centre staff are, therefore, very important. Field Studies Council centres

Figure 5.2 Cartoon: child in waterproofs with pond net.

encourage teachers, wherever possible, to make a pre-course visit, not only to check domestic facilities and safety issues, but to meet the course tutor. Where the centre is some distance from the school, pre-course taster weekends can be arranged for teachers. During the pre-course visit the teacher should work with the tutor to tailor the course to the particular needs of pupils, ensuring that links between activities are made during the course and to what pupils are doing in school. Pre-course preparation and suitable follow-up work that students might undertake should be discussed. The teacher should find out how fieldwork may be affected by weather conditions. A good field centre will offer advice about what clothes students should bring with them and may also be able to offer suitable protective clothing for adverse weather conditions. Don't forget that hot, sunny weather can provide as many difficulties as cold, wet weather (Figure 5.2).

Health and safety

This is of paramount importance, particularly on a visit to a field centre where the children are working away from the 'perceived' safe environment of school and are taking part in activities which are likely to be out-of-doors that include physical challenges. All relevant school and Local Education Authority procedures for ensuring the safe running of the course must be met. Throughout the visit the teacher remains *in loco parentis*. This responsibility cannot be delegated. Check that the centre tutor understands that if the teacher in charge feels that an activity cannot be carried out safely, for example, due to changing weather conditions, he or she has the right to veto or curtail the activity. Specific health and safety issues are discussed in more detail in chapter 2.

Costs

Once the teacher is happy that the curriculum and health and safety requirements will be met, the financial cost of the course must be calculated. Don't forget to check for possible hidden charges during the course, e.g. transport. Arrangements must be made to manage finances both before and during the course. Don't forget arrangements for children's pocket money.

Communicating with and involving parents

It is essential to ensure that parents are willing to support the course. This is particularly true of primary school residential trips, where costs will be significantly higher than for day trips that the pupils may have attended. It may also be the first time that a child has been away from home. Plenty of forward notice should be given so that parents can make financial plans.

For older students, e.g. those studying for A-level courses, discussion with the students and a carefully worded letter to parents will probably be sufficient. For younger pupils, particularly those at primary level, arranging a special evening for parents and pupils likely to be involved is a very good idea. The academic and social value of the course should be stressed at the meetings. Slides or a video of a previous field trip can be shown and parents and pupils who have been involved in the trip in a previous year could be invited to talk about their experiences. If practical, the centre tutor could be invited to answer parents' and children's questions directly. Pupils' questions may seem very trivial, e.g. 'can I bring my teddy?', 'what happens if I don't like the food?' These issues are, however, very important to children. Make sure that parents have a chance to talk privately and informally about certain issues, e.g. homesickness, the need for a night-light, bed-wetting. Field centre staff are usually well aware of such problems and practised at dealing with them in a friendly way which will not embarrass the child.

Case studies

The three case studies described here have been chosen to show how teaching objectives are met and, in particular, to address the role of fieldwork at different age levels. The description of each case study is accompanied by a short discussion on the issues that emerge.

Case study 1

General environmental studies: A four day residential course for 8–9 year olds (Key Stage 2) illustrating the point that, at primary level, fieldwork is valuable not only in the teaching of science but also in helping pupils to make links across the curriculum.

Teaching objectives

The course was set up primarily to complement the National Curriculum science work that the children had done in school on growth and nutrition of green plants, classification and identification, adaptation, feeding relationships and the importance of microorganisms. The school teacher, however, also wanted the pupils to make links across the curriculum and to help pupils understand the value of all their subjects. The pupils had an opportunity to use their writing and communication skills both in scientific and creative contexts, using a variety of media including ICT. They were also able to use their numeracy skills to deal with real data.

Course plan

A theme of 'colour in the environment' was chosen. A landscape painting exercise was used to focus pupils' attention on their surroundings and to stimulate them to ask questions. These questions formed the introduction to the fieldwork exercises. This course plan was based on the work described in Bebbington and Bebbington (2001). This publication includes background information about colour and describes some of the teaching activities in more detail. A fold-out chart linked to this publication provides a fact file on colour for pupils.

Course programme

The pupils were taken to a local viewpoint, completed a field sketch and collected words describing the colours and their thoughts about the view. On return to the classroom, ideas were explored as to how these words might be expressed. Music, dance, prose, poetry and art were all considered (providing some good opportunities for follow-up back at school). The class was then shown some simple impressionist painting techniques and had a go at producing their own painting, using this as a medium for expressing their feelings and for recording the colours they had seen. All the paintings were displayed and formed the focus of the rest of the week's activities. Throughout the week, the pupils were encouraged to use their background knowledge from across the curriculum to ask creative questions about the paintings. These questions formed part of the introduction of the fieldwork activities, e.g.

- Questions tackling the woodland food cycle and soil formation: Why are the plants green? Why is the soil grey?
- Questions tackling camouflage and woodland invertebrate studies: How might animals use colour?

The pupils were encouraged to make predictions and help design investigations. The need for care and accuracy in collecting data and in making observations was demonstrated and the pupils were given an opportunity to use their numeracy and ICT skills to handle data. In drawing information from the data and interpreting it, there was an opportunity to practise communication skills, both verbally and in writing as well as producing graphs, diagrams and close observational drawings. Pupils were made aware of issues relating to the care of the environment and their own health and safety.

Discussion: making links across the curriculum

The approach in this case study clearly brings art and science together. The pupils learn that skills and knowledge from a wide variety of subjects will help them to answer questions, solve problems and communicate what they have seen and discovered. The topic web shown in Figure 5.3 demonstrates in more detail how a landscape painting can form the introduction to a very wide range of other topics targeting many parts of the science National Curriculum.

Case study 2

> *Feeding relationships in woodland invertebrates*: A day course (09.30–16.00) for 12–13 year olds (Key Stage 3) This case study addresses the concern that, on transfer to secondary school pupils may lose their interest in science. Field work is shown to be a valuable tool in teaching the key science idea of 'interdependence'.

Teaching objectives

These were to provide some practical work, to address the key scientific idea of interdependence. More specifically the following National Curriculum concepts were targeted:

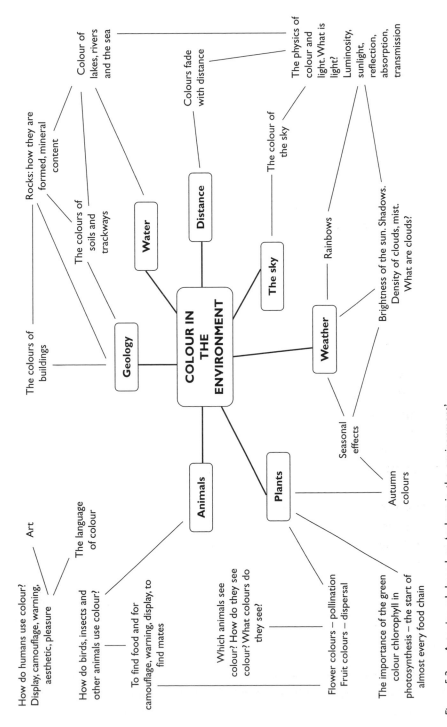

Figure 5.3   A topic web based on 'colour in the environment'.

1   variation due to environmental conditions;
2   the importance of adaptation to daily and seasonal changes in
    environmental conditions;
3   food webs;
4   pyramids of numbers;
5   predation and competition.

The pupils were to widen and improve their investigative skills, understand the importance of what they have learned and have an enjoyable day in the field.

Course plan

The course was designed to investigate the feeding relationships of soil and litter invertebrates in two contrasting areas of woodland. Bebbington *et al.* (1994) and Bebbington and Bebbington (2003) provide identification keys and background information for pupils and class teachers. All fieldwork and data collation were to be completed during the day. Preliminary discussions considered how the data could be interpreted and what had been found. Class teachers were given suggestions and notes to assist with further follow-up work to be carried out back at school.

Course programme

In an introductory session, the pupils considered two areas of woodland, one coppiced and one uncoppiced. They were encouraged to think how environmental conditions varied in the two areas and how the plant and invertebrate populations on the woodland floor might differ. They made predictions and helped to design a fieldwork investigation to test their predictions. Using a random sampling strategy and frame quadrats, the abundance of different plant species in the two areas was estimated. Measurements of: soil pH, relative humidity, temperature, canopy cover and light intensity were made. Soil and litter samples were taken to estimate the abundance of invertebrates. Back in the classroom hand-sorting was used to extract invertebrates. Animals were observed and named with the aid of identification keys, low-power binocular microscopes and a flexicam video camera. Data were collated with the aid of computer spreadsheets and the pupils used diagrams, graphs, tables and charts to describe patterns and relationships in these data. Predictions were revisited, and the evidence examined, to see if their predictions could be supported. In preliminary discussions pupils used their scientific knowledge to explain and interpret what they had found. They considered anomalies in the data and discussed the limitations of their work, making suggestions for improvements and further investigations.

Discussion: maintaining an enthusiasm for science and helping
students to understand the key science idea of interdependence

This important point is vital if pupils are going to maintain their interest in science. Skills and knowledge gained at one level are valued and built on at the next stage. For example, in this case study the programme was designed to recognise the learning from Key Stage 2 that had already taken place, including:

- that living organisms can be assigned to groups;
- to use and construct identification keys;
- that living organisms show adaptations to the place where they live;
- that feeding relationships can be shown as food chains;
- that microorganisms have an important role to play;
- that the environment needs protection.

This course was carefully designed so that pupils' knowledge and skills could be developed and progressed in a number of ways. Pupils used low-power microscopes and their knowledge of classification and their skills in using keys to identify organisms. They found that organisms were not just adapted to the place where they live, but to survive, must also be adapted to daily and seasonal change. They learned that food chains are part of more complex food webs and that pyramids of numbers can be constructed if the number of living organisms at each feeding level is known. They were introduced to the terms predation and competition and were able to see examples of the interdependence of living organisms, not only in relation to one another, but also to interrelated abiotic environmental factors, e.g. light, temperature and soil conditions.

Pupils' investigative skills were further developed. They became aware that the simple laboratory experimental model is often difficult to apply in the field. Particular thought had to be given to variables that could not be controlled and to the way in which samples and measurements were taken. There was also an opportunity to use equipment which was not available in school, e.g. soil test kits, light meters and environmental probes. They were taught to take care of the environment in which they were working, e.g. by causing a minimum trampling effect, keeping collection of specimens to a minimum and returning to the site any animals taken back to the classroom for closer examination.

Working in the field was undoubtedly enjoyable for most pupils. They gained a practical understanding of the implications of interdependence in living organisms and were able to appreciate the importance of what they had learned in practical land management, thus giving a sense of purpose to their studies.

Case study 3

> *Ecological coursework*: This was a 4-day residential course in late June for students following an advanced level course in biology. The problem of the decline in number of students doing fieldwork in the 16–19 age group is considered.

Teaching objectives

To give students who have opted to do course work instead of a written examination the knowledge and skills to carry out an individual investigation.

Course plan

In the first half of the course, students were taught a wide variety of techniques, had an opportunity to practise data handling skills, were stimulated to think ecologically and shown the field centre's resources. On the last two days of the course, they carried out their own individual investigations.

Course programme

In an introductory walk, students were introduced to the variety of habitats around the field centre. Two contrasting investigations were then chosen for the first two days:

1   The effect of human trampling on a grassland habitat.
2   The effect of varying environmental conditions on invertebrate species diversity in a freshwater stream.

These investigations were carried out as a class group, providing students with a model for carrying out an ecological investigation. They were introduced to sampling techniques for plants and animals and shown how to measure a wide variety of abiotic parameters. They were able to use computer spreadsheets to collate data and draw up graphs and charts to illustrate possible trends. Data were analysed using appropriate statistical tests. They were encouraged to use all the field centre's resources: specialist scientific equipment, the library, collections of geological maps, aerial photographs, long-term records, and under supervision, were given access to the Internet. At the end of each exercise students were encouraged to think and ask questions about what they had seen and learned, generating ideas for further investigations in the same or other available habitats.

The second half of the course was devoted to individual coursework. In discussion with the tutor and class teacher, students chose a suitable investigation. Lack of identification skills meant that most were limited to investigations dealing with one, or a few species or taxa of organisms. Difficulties in following the laboratory model of an investigation which was emphasised by their examination boards also placed further limitations on the choice of investigation.

Students were given 2–3 hours to carry out a pilot study. This gave them a chance to formulate a hypothesis, and to design their investigations trying out various sampling techniques and strategies. They took a small sample of data to make sure that they knew which statistical tests they would be using. They made sure that they could identify the organism or organisms that they would be working with and considered safety issues and protection of the habitat. Investigations were refined and modified in the light of this pilot study and further discussion with the tutor and class teacher.

As required by the examination board, each student wrote a plan for the investigation, which was marked and assessed by the school teacher with help and advice from the tutor at the centre. The amount of help students received and any further modifications that needed to be made were taken into account in this assessment. The students then carried out their investigations. The tutor and teacher were at hand to ensure that projects were carried out safely. They were also available for advice, but students were aware that the amount of help given would be taken into account in the final assessment of their work.

Discussion: the declining number of students doing fieldwork in the 16–19 age group

Lock and Tilling (2002) suggest a number of reasons for this. Their suggestions are considered here in more detail in the light of the case study above.

Lock and Tilling made the point out that there is a need for more real evidence of the academic value of fieldwork. There would be a real impact on students' chance to experience fieldwork if this were made a core part of the 16–19 curriculum. For many advanced level students the main opportunity for fieldwork occurs if they opt to do ecological coursework instead of a written examination, as described in the case study here. Nevertheless, such coursework often produces very good results, so why are more students not choosing this option?

Fieldwork undoubtedly places a considerable extra work load and responsibility on teachers, not just in the organisation of the field course itself, but also in the assessment of the work. Lock and Tilling suggest that teachers would be more likely to be enthusiastic about fieldwork if they were more confident in their own knowledge. There is thus a need for training in fieldwork skills for teachers at all levels, both for those in service, and for those in training. It is encouraging that the new 'Professional Standards for Qualified Teacher Status' (TTA, 2002) specifically require that trainee teachers demonstrate that they are able to plan opportunities for pupils to learn in out-of classroom contexts such as fieldwork. Training courses are offered by many field centres but due to the pressure of work at school, lack of encouragement from management and lack of funds these courses are often under- subscribed. A new joint venture by the Field Studies Council and the British Ecological Society may help to address this problem (see Resources box for details).

For those teachers and students who do ecological coursework, there are also some problems encountered in trying to fulfil examination board specifications. Most examination boards award highest marks to those students who are able to show an ability to draw on selected and relevant biological knowledge, principles and concepts. Lock and Tilling suggest that the peak time for fieldwork is in June/July; with a second peak in the autumn. Many students, therefore, like those in the case study described here, have to carry out their coursework before their advanced biology course has started or at the beginning of it. Students would be better able to carry out a mature, synoptic analysis of their fieldwork data if coursework was carried out towards the end of their course.

The laboratory approach to an investigation emphasised by many examination boards is not always suited to the study of whole organisms in an ecological context, and may therefore limit the choice of investigation. Examples of specific difficulties encountered are as follows:

- the complex interrelationships between living organisms and abiotic environmental factors make it difficult to identify or control variables and attribute change to any one factor;
- the high degree of variability encountered in data dealing with living organisms may lead to problems in sampling analysis;
- the slow response time of living organisms, especially plants, to changing conditions has to be taken into account.

Coursework requirements should be revised to allow a less formal approach to ecological investigations.

The perceived unimportance of identification skills means that little time is allocated for teaching them and the choice of investigation may be limited. Results of a preliminary investigation by the author, suggest that 80 per cent of advanced level biology students were only able to identify one or two very common wild flowers. This problem is also becoming apparent at university level and will need to be addressed.

Beyond the academic curriculum

There is little doubt that most pupils benefit academically from fieldwork. This benefit is almost certainly linked to pupils' enhanced motivation to learn, their social development and increased confidence in their own abilities. Fieldwork can therefore also be seen as a vehicle to assist the development of the capacity to learn (Nundy, 2001). This is particularly true of fieldwork carried out in residential settings, as is described below.

Intellectual opportunities

Pupils learn to appreciate that science is not entirely a factual subject, but requires creative thinking and the ability to ask questions. In addition, they learn the importance of planning and teamwork in dealing with complex situations.

The extended time available on a residential course gives pupils time to think and allows them to concentrate on one problem at a time. Different subjects are no longer separated into lesson blocks and students can use their intellectual skills to bring knowledge together from across the curriculum to solve problems. Learning is not confined to school hours. For younger pupils, a short safe walk from dusk until dark is often the highlight of their stay. They are able to experience the way in which their own ability to see changes as darkness falls. For some, there is the challenge of overcoming a fear of the dark. They learn that, for many animals, darkness is the greatest period of activity. They hear and, if they are lucky, see nocturnal animals and learn the value of being quiet. They consider what is happening to plants. There are opportunities to think about the moon, stars and planets and climatic changes. Field centres often have equipment for sampling and observing animals at dusk and during the night, e.g. 'Longworth' small mammal traps, moth traps, bat detectors and drift nets. Older students may be involved in more formal studies of periodicity where they look at varying animal activity over a 24-hour period.

Personal and social development

This aspect of a residential course is especially important for the younger pupil, for whom it may be the first time away from home. Teachers using Juniper Hall Field Centre in Surrey gave the following reasons for choosing a residential course: 'all the children have the freedom to run and play together in a novel but safe and controlled environment and there is plenty of opportunity for healthy physical exercise'. Children have to face new challenges, e.g. being away from home (see 'Jackie's first trip'). They learn self-reliance, e.g. looking after their belongings, being in the right place at the right time, thinking about their own safety. They develop awareness of others: helping each other, learning to share and work with others, coping with relationships and being tolerant. They learn specific social skills such as eating a meal together, setting a table, making a bed, making sandwiches and handling money. They have to cope with adverse weather and know how to dress appropriately for different weather conditions.

Jackie's first trip

Comments from a teacher accompanying a group of 9–10 year olds

'I have always noticed how the children bond and become a much closer-knit group as a result of their residential field trip. Jackie had never been away overnight and both she and her Mum were very worried about this. We approached it a day at a time and I gave her the option that if she was really unhappy she could go home. Even though I was woken up in the early hours of the morning a couple of times during the week and she had to be comforted and reassured, she made it to the end of the week. Jackie was so pleased that she had managed a whole week away and her Mum was delighted by this milestone. Interestingly the rest of the class was really proud of Jackie and made a big fuss of her.'

Figure 5.4 Cartoon: child eating a sandwich.

A residential course also provides an opportunity for students and teachers to see each other in a different light. For some students, with a history of trouble at school, the field trip may present the opportunity for a fresh start and to see teachers as normal human beings! For the group as a whole, the experience usually provides an excellent bonding experience. For older students, meeting, socialising and working with students from other schools is often a valuable experience.

Teachers also feel that there are important benefits for themselves. They comment, for example, that there is:

- time and space to think, uninterrupted by the school routine;
- a chance to observe someone else teaching – always valuable;
- a chance to share and swap ideas;
- a chance to learn new skills and techniques;
- a chance to find out how much pupils have learned from the classroom-based teaching. This may influence the way in which teachers approach their classroom teaching.

It is sad that increasingly, because of a shortage of time in school, teachers are having to spend a proportion of their time at the field centre marking and dealing with administrative work and so are not able to take maximum advantage of these benefits.

Memorable and defining moments

A residential field centre offers students an opportunity to live and learn in contrasting setting to their school or home, creating new events and images. These may apparently have nothing to do with the curriculum or exams but as Nundy (2001) states can, 'significantly enhance long-term memory recall, knowledge and understanding'.

From time to time students (and teachers) will have an experience which, for them, is special and which they will remember for the rest of their lives. It may even define the direction of their future career.

These experiences are things that cannot be planned but a wise teacher will do his or her best to include and make the most of whatever opportunities arise. It is not only the student who will appreciate these moments. For many teachers and centre staff, it is what makes all the hard work and additional responsibility of a residential field trip worthwhile.

Some special moments from the author's own experience

A group of lively 9 year olds sat on the edge of a badger sett at dusk. A female badger brought her cubs out to play about 5 metres away. The children remained frozen with delight for about 30 minutes.

A group of sixth-form students from an inner city school revealed that they had no experience of seeing the tidal movements of the sea. Low tide was at 4 a.m. We rose early and watched as the water crept up the shore with the added bonus of a fabulous sunrise.

Walking past a neighbouring farm on the way to a local woodland, a farmer invited the children to watch a lamb being born. They were fascinated and questions flowed thick and fast. The woodland study had to be curtailed but it was worth it.

Conclusions

Fieldwork, particularly in a residential setting, results in enhanced cognitive learning as well as gains in personal and social development. For many, there will have been special experiences which they will remember for the rest of their lives.

At primary level, the value of fieldwork across the curriculum is clearly recognised. Fieldwork also has an important role to play in maintaining pupils' interest in science at secondary level, particularly in the pre-16 age group. With the introduction of interdependence as one of the 5 key ideas in the science strand of the Key Stage 3 strategy (DfES, 2002) there are opportunities for studying whole organisms and ecosystems. This will help to redress the balance of recent years where the study of whole organisms has taken a back seat.

Post-16 biology students should be aware of recent expansion in the areas of biochemistry, biophysics and genetics. Careers in these new areas of biology bring with them good financial rewards and these are often powerful messages extolling their importance. At post-16 level, the amount of fieldwork experienced by biology students has clearly declined (Lock and Tilling, 2002) and is very often centred around one piece of coursework. In these times of real concern about the global environment, however, many organisations are deeply concerned that there is a critical shortage of biologists with skills to support work in conservation and sustainable development. There is therefore a strong case for more fieldwork in post-16 education.

Great efforts have been made by those providing field studies today to address the problems of health and safety and leadership issues and to ensure that courses are well-planned and clearly address curriculum issues. The continued existence of field centres with their special role in teaching about and for the environment is vital as we move through the twenty-first century.

References

Bebbington, A. and Bebbington, J., 2001, *Colour in the Environment: Teacher's Guide. Occasional Publication 63*, Shrewsbury: Field Studies Council.

Bebbington, A. and Bebbington, J., 2001, 'Colour in the environment: fold-out-chart', Shrewsbury: Field Studies Council.

Bebbington, A. and Bebbington, J., 2003, 'Bugs on bushes: fold-out-chart', Shrewsbury: Field Studies Council.

Bebbington, A., Bebbington, J. and Tilling, S., 1994, 'The woodland name trail: fold-out-chart', Shrewsbury: Field Studies Council.

Department of Education and Science, 1981, *Environmental Education: A Review*, London: HMSO.

Lock, R. and Tilling, S., 2002, 'Ecology fieldwork in 16–19 biology', *School Science Review* 84(307), 79–87.

Nundy, S., 2001, 'Raising achievement through the environment: a case for fieldwork and field centres', Peterborough: National Association of Field Studies Officers.

Streeter, D., 1993, 'An address given at the 50th anniversary celebration of the Field Studies Council', *Field Studies* 8, 193–6.

Resources

The Field Studies Council – a key provider of Field Studies in United Kingdom: Head Office, Preston Montford, Montford Bridge, Shrewsbury, Shropshire SY4 1HW. Tel.: 01743 852100. Email: enquiries@field-studies-council.org Website: www.field-studies-council.org

Kingswood Educational Activity Centres – provide adventure activities and field studies. The Kingswood Group, Kingswood House, 11 Prince of Wales Road, Norwich, Norfolk NR1 1BD. Tel.: 01603 284 284. Fax: 01603 768 310. Email: enquiries@kingswood.co.uk Website: www.kingswood.co.uk

The School Government Publishing Company Ltd – provides a list of Field Study and Outdoor Pursuits Centres: Darby House, Redhill Surrey, RH1 3DN. Tel.: 01737 642223. Website: www.schoolgovernment.co.uk/FSC/FSC.htm

National Association of Field Study Officers (NAFSO). An Organisation representing the professional body of people employed in field studies. Produces a journal and a number of other useful occasional publications. General enquiries to CEES, Stibbington Centre, Great North Road, Stibbington, Peterborough PE8 6LP. Tel.: 01780 782386. Website: www.econet.org.uk/nafso

Courses offering training in fieldwork skills for in-service teachers and trainee teachers: These are offered by several of the Field Studies Council's centres. A number of the courses for trainee teachers are part-sponsored by the British Ecological Society. More information can be obtained from the Field Studies Council's head office at the address given above.

Chapter 6

Learning science in a botanic garden

Sue Johnson

Overview

Botanic gardens have a significant role in developing scientific and environmental literacy. Mostly in urban areas, they provide a context for demonstrating historic and current sustainability. In addition, management of the botanic garden environment links aesthetic and scientific practices. Thus the potential for holistic teaching and learning is presented and, where hands-on experience is encouraged, young people encounter different learning styles. Regular visits allow plant study to be meaningful. Scientific models can be tested to show how vital plants are to human existence. Engaging with plants may also connect home- and school-constructed knowledge for many children.

Introduction

A botanic garden contains a range of ecosystems, is readily accessible because of its public nature and may be one of the few large, plant-rich locations in otherwise urban areas. Each of the 130 or more botanic gardens throughout the UK functions primarily as a resource to support the advanced scientific study of plants. Each one is unique, reflecting its location and ecology, its history and particular role, its size and the financial resources available to it.

A school visit to a botanic garden should be undertaken as an integral part of science education in its broadest sense. It is on the sharp interpretation of science, history, geography and other National Curriculum subjects that teaching and learning have become ensnared in the past decade. The demand for a body of knowledge to be taught and learned masks the interconnectedness of these 'subject domains'. Similarly, the outdated separation of informal and formal learning is joined in a continuum that is apparent in a botanic garden.

In botanic gardens science is put to work. It resembles little the science that is isolated and abstracted for the classroom. Instead it brings the true meaning of scientific literacy into focus. For a teacher with imagination, a botanic garden can begin to stimulate connections which encompass many subjects.

Botanic gardens can also help children with their understanding of how individual decisions have a significant effect on the environment, biodiversity, sustainability and cultural heritage, locally or globally (Figure 6.1). Through awareness raising and reflection, the experiences offered by a botanic garden can be linked with children's lives outside school. Students constantly interact with plant and animal science in a variety of contexts but may not see themselves in a bigger picture where their day-to-day decisions affect the systems on which plants and animals depend. For example, deciding whether to eat an apple or chocolate involves a choice that has local or global implications.

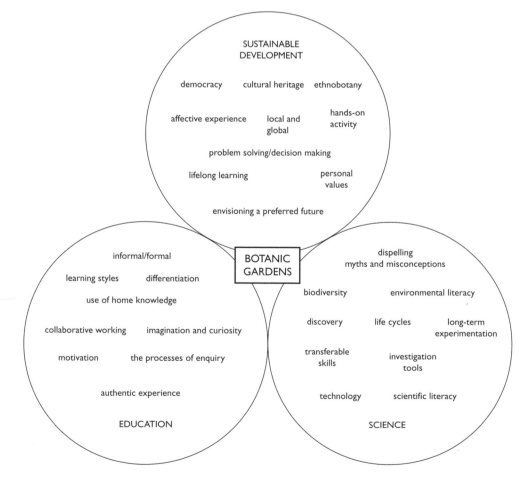

Figure 6.1 The aspirational concepts in the fields of sustainable development, education and science and their union in botanic gardens.

Life on earth depends on plants

One way of introducing the importance of plants to primary age children is to ask them to take a couple of deep breaths. The value of the oxygen that plants produce becomes obvious. Many children are not only unaware of the oxygen-providing value of growing plants but are also ignorant of the fact that plants provide many of the products they consume each day (Lewington, 1990). Botanic gardens have an advantage over local parks and gardens for fieldwork in that they display economically useful plants from almost every climatic region of the world.

In a walled garden near London's embankment, the Chelsea Physic Garden still grows examples of plants that seventeenth-century apothecaries studied there. Half of the 25 best-selling pharmaceutical drugs originate from plants. *Digitalis lanata* (woolly foxglove) is the basis of the heart medicine digitalis; *Ammi majus*, in the carrot family (Umbelliferae), provides compounds to treat psoriasis; angina and high blood pressure are both treated with derivatives from *Papaver somniferum*, the opium poppy (Minter, 1997). Such examples serve to explain why plants are so important in our everyday lives.

The Eden Project explains that rainforests have great untapped potential because fewer than 5 per cent of the plants in Amazonia have been tested for their medicinal uses. Plants used as dyes, insect repellents, beverages, preservatives, poisons, perfumes, etc. are known to the indigenous population (mainly to the women). Since these 'ill-educated people' in 'underdeveloped regions' have the knowledge of how to use the plants that grow around their homes, there are implications for ethnobotany. Scientific knowledge is not just that which is written down and it is not just Western and high tech. It is often preserved in a cultural heritage that people pass on. Their understanding is passed down through the generations by way of stories and apprenticeship.

A visit to the extensive herb gardens that most botanic gardens feature offers an opportunity for early years and Key Stage 1 children to see, touch and smell (and possibly taste under supervision) plants which are used to flavour food. The affective learning potential of herbs can be explored. For Key Stage 2 and 3 classes there may be an opportunity for children to learn how to take cuttings of rosemary, sage, lavender, etc. ready to start their own herb garden at school. Cuttings are a starting point for lessons on cloning for older students. It demonstrates a different method of plant reproduction from seed dispersal.

Of the 20 million households in Britain, 17 million have a garden so many children have contact with gardens and gardening. In my own research I found that culinary herbs are among the plants that children do grow at home (Johnson, 2001). Children might also have been taught the names of some herbs by parents, grandparents or other family members. If so, a bond between home and school knowledge is forged. As a way of learning it also mirrors how rainforest or other aboriginal people have passed on their knowledge through the generations. That it is mainly women who pass on insights about food and medicinal plants presents a chance to emphasise the largely unsung role of women in science. Extensive knowledge of herb use was still essential in Britain until about the mid-twentieth century. It may yet be important for today's children to know about the many uses of herbs because there are no certainties in their future. Visiting a herb garden allows the sensory stimulation of hands-on experience to be connected with the application of science and creates a potential link between botanic gardens and the school environment.

Physical encounters of this kind may be the style of learning appropriate to some children. Eyre and Marjoram (1990) argue that, without first hand environmental stimuli, 'creativity and the nature of enquiry and adventure will be inhibited in even the most able' (p. 73). Equally, a child's confidence in his/her own experience as a basis for learning may also be reinforced by recognition of familiar plants in a different environment – by their leaf shape, flower or scent – and knowing some of their uses.

At secondary level a visit can be used to stimulate a debate about whether medicinal plants should be harvested from the wild. The possible alternatives can be considered. Since botanic gardens were originally repositories for plants collected from the wild, the argument might extend to whether scientists today have the right to collect in a similar way. With around 320,000 species of plant on earth, does extinction of a few species matter very much? Now would be the time to introduce students to the Convention on International Trade in Endangered Species (CITES), which relates to the conservation of all endangered species including plants, and other legislation that protects the environment.

Underlying all such arguments are issues of sustainability, morality and ethics. Few plants in tropical regions have been thoroughly investigated for their medical, food or economic uses. Ways of making payments to people for their knowledge of how to use plants unfamiliar to Western scientists may in itself be a topic for debate. Controversial issues and awareness raising of plant science and future conservation offer opportunities to discuss potential careers at all key stages.

Authentic knowledge

To make any valid decisions that affect the natural environment requires knowledge, understanding and a willingness to engage with the underlying issues. To engage students with plants and foster understanding teachers will need to motivate them. If students become sufficiently involved with plants they might be convinced that it is essential for human survival to adopt positive environmental attitudes and behaviours.

One aim of all botanic gardens is to achieve future conservation and, by implication, sustainable development. To communicate the inferences of the vast reserve of raw scientific data generated by in-house researchers – botanists, plant pathologists, soil scientists, entomologists, meteorologists, ornithologists, etc. – educators join with their colleagues. By doing so, the work of botanic garden researchers can filter into schools. If this can happen in such a way that children engage in similar experiments, so much the better, however, using authentic scientific techniques is somewhat restricted in the current educational climate.

The average teacher wants to cover a specific National Curriculum science topic when taking a class or year group to a botanic garden. S/he brings a coach load of children, for the sake of economy, and divides them into groups each with an accompanying parent/adult. In general the coach arrives at about 10 a.m. The party needs 30 minutes for lunch and leaves at 2.30 p.m. During the day the children probably have to complete a worksheet about some aspect of plant science. The teacher will have devised the worksheet, with or without a pre-trip consultation with education staff at the garden.

Obstacles to an effective teaching and learning situation stem first from the cognitive frameworks that the children bring with them. In the classroom they develop a routine for lessons, some of which are derived from formalised teaching strategies. If the themes, sequences, interpretative materials or narratives used in the garden are outside these compartmentalised frameworks, children may not recognise the visit as a lesson. They might also disregard what they come to understand during the experience because it is their own construction of knowledge. Second, when the children tour the garden with an accompanying adult, the educational experience may be poor. The best that can be said is that individual children do relate some plants to their home experience (Johnson and Tunnicliffe, 2000). Third, plants are of no immediate importance to most young people. As with exhibits in general, young observers spend only a few seconds looking at a plant (Ballantyne and Uzzell, 1996). If a bird or squirrel comes along or there is a chance to shop, the plant is deserted.

School groups are unlikely to have a day full of stimulating activity at a botanic garden unless there is thorough planning.

Botanic garden educators aim to enrich each visit to counteract teachers' as well as pupils' lack of plant knowledge. Teachers who rely on textbooks for their lessons on plants leave themselves open to passing on misconceptions and misunderstandings, which, once established in a child's mind, are difficult to alter. How does anyone without hands-on experience know whether pictures of the 'bean in the jar' or any other plant experiment are correctly labelled? To bring a better understanding of plant biology and human dependence on plants, botanic garden educators find ways of introducing participation and connections that inspire children.

All botanic gardens provide interpretation boards or displays to inform the general public and children on school visits. Others have trails that require navigational skills and answers to questions. Learning from texts, even if botanic garden scientists write them, is no substitute for learning that can come from the element of 'scaffolded' questioning by an adult accompanying a group of children.

Children are curious and are full of questions about plants. How their questions are answered is very important. In-house education staff have the experience to pose questions that compel young people to engage with plants. With careful observation, use of the senses, possible prior knowledge or experience with plants and a willingness to participate in dialogue, children can find most of their own answers.

Teaching in botanic gardens is only effective if it brings about learning. A botanic garden offers opportunities for discovery, participation and motivation all underpinned by a memorable experience. If a lesson with these components also stimulates curiosity and an interest in knowing more, then learning is likely to be the outcome.

Botanic garden educators have knowledge of their garden at all seasons and can therefore provide plenty of sites for surveying work. They can also give students hands-on practice, use a broad range of investigation techniques, are able to discuss variables and propose recording methods other than writing. Whether they can use these different approaches to teaching depends on the class teacher. Being prepared to allow leeway for teaching that is different from standard classroom practice and outside the cage that has been constructed around rigid learning frameworks does not come easily when unadventurous options have met requirements in the past.

Currently, a teacher taking a party to visit a botanic garden accepts that it is necessary to take with him/her a group of parents or other adults for the required health and safety ratio. The adult to student ratio may prevent mishaps adequately but on its own does little to aid a well-constructed, informative day. To do so botanic garden teachers often use informed helpers. In some gardens there is team teaching and groups of children pass from one activity to another as they get involved in different aspects of a single topic. For example, at Wisley, soil days are on offer (Figure 6.2). At primary level, one group of children would work on the content of soil, feeling the texture, looking at jars full of soil and water where the particles have precipitated into layers according to their size, with humus floating on the top. Children can also sieve soil and note the proportion of particles at each size (Table 6.1).

The children can test the assertions made in Table 6.1. They can make predictions about particle size and the time it takes for a known volume of water to filter through soil columns (perspex tanks with a drain hole on one side at the bottom). The water is collected and the time recorded for each column. For secondary level students, the same exercises give them a basis from which to deduce the link between soil type and the crops which might grow well on it.

Ecosystem studies can start with an investigation of soil on site, so a second group activity is concerned with soil depth and profiles. Children would visit

Figure 6.2 A soils day at Wisley. Children examining soil particles using magnifiers.

Table 6.1 Soil particle size

Size of holes in sieve	Weight of particles caught in this sieve (g)
Large	
Medium	
Small	
Bottom container	

Note: Take some soil, preferably dry, and weigh it. Using a set of three soil sieves and the bottom container, sieve the soil through all of the sieves. Weigh what is left in the sieve with the largest holes and place it to one side. Repeat the weighing for the soil in the sieve with the medium holes. The finest particles are left in the container at the bottom. Complete the chart by entering the weights. Mainly medium-sized particles give the soil a good structure. Predominantly very fine particles mean that the soil will not drain well and will become boggy. If the soil is made up mostly of large particles, the soil will drain quickly and dry out easily.

holes dug in different parts of the garden to show a variety of soil profiles. Primary groups could measure and draw profiles and rub soil on the drawing to colour each horizon. They might also measure plant root length (seedlings, grasses, dandelions, other weeds and container-grown herbaceous plants or shrubs) to find out which parts of the horizon are reached by different plants, or at different stages of a plant's growth. Secondary groups would be asked to explain why there are horizons in the soil profile and make scale drawings. By looking more closely at root hairs using a hand lens, they might discuss how plants take water from soils. Botanic gardens can also show examples of plants which exhibit growth irregularities associated with inadequate supplies of soluble soil nutrients. Advanced level students could also consider the effect of temperature on water flow through plants and the resulting evapotranspiration.

Making compost is the third activity. Here, materials – paper, cotton, plastic, metal (with no sharp edges), vegetable peelings/fruit skins, twigs, woollen socks, egg shells (washed), cardboard, leather, etc. – are mixed. Using simple instructions, magnets, clothing labels, etc. children sort them into compostable and non-compostable categories. Secondary groups might be asked to do a similar categorisation and work together in groups to consider factors that might affect the time each item takes to decay. Here the science of materials is linked with natural processes.

A fourth activity is to load a compost heap. Barrows of leaves, bales of newspaper, cardboard, waste household organic matter, etc. are made available. Primary children could then be shown an older heap and, using a drain pipe in the heap, feel the heat at the centre (the pipe should be put into the heap during its construction and the compost end of the pipe should have a plastic cover).

Secondary groups might be asked to suggest reasons why heat is produced and how it might vary throughout the year. Make sure that children wash their hands well afterwards. A wormery provides an alternative study. Here questions might be about worm feeding habits and life cycles, maintaining the worm population and the probable content of the liquid waste produced. All of these elements are important for any terrestrial ecosystem study.

Older primary children could also record and identify insects in the compost heap to help them construct a food chain. Secondary students could, in addition, record fungi and use these observations, together with their sorting experience, to create a food web either on site or in follow-up work. Depending on the time available or the emphasis of the lesson, they might also judge the merits of different styles of compost bins and materials from which they are made based on their earlier work on decay rates, heat generation and seasonal variations. The children should wear disposable polythene gloves. If these are not suitable or available then ensure good hygiene by making sure the students wash their hands well afterwards.

The composting theme can be extended at lunch-time for any age group. The remains of lunch can be separated into compostable and non-compostable elements and there should also be a category for reusable items (Table 6.2). The compostable and non-compostable materials are weighed and each figure is divided by the number of people who had lunch. The results will show the average weight of lunchtime non-compostable waste each individual produces and the average amount each one could compost each day (but probably won't!). As an alternative, the party could be asked to bring a fully compostable packed lunch from which a list of compostable packaging materials can be made.

Whilst in the team-teaching soil activity there is the potential for differentiation of any of the scientific experiences, this lunchtime experiment is all

Table 6.2 What was wasted at lunchtime?

What organic material was left over?	What non-organic material was left over?	Weight of organic waste	Weight of non-organic waste	What reusable material is left to take home?

encompassing. Parents, children and teachers, whatever their age or ability, all eat lunch so this is an inclusive activity. If it is done on the picnic site it demonstrates that scientific thinking and experimentation are not confined to the laboratory or classroom. The weight of the compostable and non-compostable components of lunch also emphasises how easily decisions made in everyday life affect the environment and sustainability.

Taxonomy and classification

To fulfil their scientific purpose adequately botanic gardens only need to organise plants in serried ranks of labelled species. Fortunately, for centuries, horticultural skills have developed alongside scientific work in these gardens. All are beautiful, inspiring, cross-cultural environments in which age and ability are no barrier to learning. By being so they lend themselves to progression (Braund, 2001) in teaching and learning required by the National Curriculum. In science at primary level children start to study plants by naming their parts. Taxonomy is based on a difference in some part of a plant that distinguishes it from others that might look similar. The plant can therefore be classified as belonging to a particular species within a genus and family. Learning plant parts begins in the primary phase with the progression to taxonomy at Key Stage 2, investigation of local ecosystems at Key Stage 3 and environmental adaptation and evolutionary biology in Key Stage 4.

Beyond school, knowing how to identify plants is the first step in conservation of local flora and has implications for local cultural heritage. To make decisions about clearing land for road construction or house building, people need to be environmentally literate, which includes having some knowledge of plants.

Instead of being reductionist, with a single, simple plant diagram for the study of a flower, its leaf, stem, roots, etc., botanic gardens offer so many variations that the reason for naming plant parts has some meaning. Many botanic gardens offer a simple exercise for primary children based on leaves. Children are asked whether all leaves are the same. They do not have to write anything or carry a clipboard to test their prediction. Instead, on a small piece of card covered with double-sided sticky tape, they collect at least six different leaves. They can discuss their findings on site and take the card back to school as a record and stimulus for follow-up work. The leaves can also be laminated later and keep in good condition for 2 to 3 years. Starting at the primary level, leaf variation initiates an appreciation of biodiversity. Progression takes the same exercise but, for older pupils, relates it to the ecosystems from which plants with large or small leaves come. The reason why plants may have leaves of a specific texture and the variation in leaf colour in the autumn, or variation according to latitude and altitude (Capon, 1994), begin to be recognised.

For upper Key Stage 2 and secondary pupils, the arrangement of stigmas and stamen within a range of flowers can be observed and recorded. Groups of students each collect a different flower. They dissect it, stick each part of the flower onto a card and label the parts. The card can later be laminated and may be used to illustrate a key. These cards could begin an herbarium that will inform future students about our current environment – for them the environment of the past. The cards also show variations that each plant has developed in a part that is essential for reproduction. Such a task provides hands-on experience of collecting flowers, the intricate skill of dissection, identification of plant parts and evidence for a discussion of biodiversity.

Biodiversity

Species biodiversity is about the number of diverse species (species richness) and the number of individuals in any one species (abundance). Complete loss of a species causes a loss of genetic diversity and is permanent. The ability of a living organism to adapt as the world changes around it can indeed be a matter of its life or death. Exposing the magnitude of the problems humans are causing to the environment relies on those researchers, knowledgeable about world biodiversity, disseminating their work effectively. Invariably they do not (Soulé, 1988).

If children are to improve their understanding and skills in relation to biodiversity, it is essential to include a means of understanding and promoting positive action in the curriculum. They could follow botanic garden practice and grow plants of many kinds either in the school grounds or, where there is no land on site, grow houseplants in any light airy space in the school.

Making the focus edible plants brings the issue of genetic diversity and species abundance to a domestic level. To add this personal element children might grow food plants, either outside or on windowsills. Nurturing becomes a requirement, as does knowledge of which parts of these plants they hope to eat. If children can grow their own food, human survival becomes linked with the survival of edible plant species and illustrates in parallel the need for sustainable development.

At primary level the bean's life cycle is commonly drawn as a diagram. Some teachers grow beans indoors in pots and, if children are fortunate, they themselves may plant beans outside in the school garden. The latter only happens where the teacher has the knowledge, skill and land to do so. In a botanic garden there is the possibility of seeing at least one species of leguminous plant at some stage in its life cycle whatever the time of year. A number of botanic gardens still have order beds where plants of one family are grown in a single bed. All botanic gardens have many examples of the bean family in their vegetable gardens, flowerbeds and borders. A visit can certainly enhance the underlying biodiversity element relating to the bean-in-the-jar experiment.

Primary-age children can look for species abundance by identifying and counting the number of different members of the bean family in a vegetable garden. Noting the similarities and differences between peas and beans or runner beans and broad beans could be an additional challenge. Older students might do the same for a wider area of garden and record the habit (climbing, creeping, bushy, etc.) of plants within a family.

Follow-up work would be to consider why the species richness of the Leguminosae (bean) family is important to humans, how differences in morphology evolved and how and why species might be lost. How to conserve species abundance and richness to ensure genetic diversity is a difficult prospect for adults to address but there is no reason why this question should not be raised in schools.

Growing plants in one family is relevant to sustainability and using keys in school to recognise many of the species in that family growing in the local environment will eventually give the lesson personal meaning. Botanic gardens can assist with plant lists for easily cultivated members of a single family (e.g. Table 6.3).

Table 6.3 Plants in the Leguminosae family

Robinia, false acacia (*Robinia pseudoacacia*)	Broom (*Genista*)	Gorse (*Ulex*)
Vetch, e.g. horseshoe vetch (*Hippocrepis indigofera*)	Judus tree (*Cercis siliquastrum*)	Spanish broom (*Spartium junceum*)
Sweet pea (*Lathyrus odoratus*)	Sainfoin (*Onobrychis*)	Lucerne (*Medicago sativa*)
Erinacea (*Erinacea anthyllis*)	Restharrow (*Ononis repens*)	Birdsfoot trefoil (*Lotus corniculatus*)
White clover (*Trifolium repens*)	Red clover (*Trifolium pratense*)	Broad bean (*Vicia faba*)
Scarlet runner bean (*Phaseolus coccineus*)	Pea (*Pisum sativum*)	French bean (*Phaseolus vulgaris*)

Note: These examples are likely to be found in a botanic garden and are easy to grow in the school grounds.

At secondary level, nitrogen fixation is related to the bean life cycle topic. A bean, or other leguminous plant, can be dug up for students to see the nodules on its roots. Using a hand lens to view the root nodules teaches a valuable skill and adds to the experiences of the day. The observations made are directly linked with lessons on nitrogen fixation, soil fertility and crop rotation.

In a botanic garden students can investigate plant origins. They can see many leguminous plants growing in glasshouses that simulate tropical environments. The huge range of tropical leguminous plants exhibited in botanic gardens emphasises the importance of this family in those parts of the world where soils are generally poor and nitrogen-fixing plants are particularly important.

One botanic garden has included beans grown in a hydroponics unit in its repertoire of potential lessons. In the hydroponics unit bean plants grow without soil. This cultivation method can be replicated in schools. It has great potential for general growth experiments in primary schools. In secondary schools investigations involving growth rates and nutrient cycling are also possible. At both levels, a technique that is used on a large scale in desert regions can be demonstrated. Effective use of water to optimise crop yields may be of increasing importance for a sustainable future.

Taught in conjunction with soil science, a hydroponics unit can be used to show that nutrients from the soil are only needed in miniscule amounts and that the bean plant uses sunlight for growth, via photosynthesis. Letters to botanic gardens often contain the misconception that it is the 'food' in soil that makes plants grow (they do not mention photosynthesis). Teachers have to counter such misconceptions with authentic experience. Without the knowledge to do so, or means to demonstrate, ignorance persists for both the children and sometimes even the teacher. Practical experiments which have dramatic results – in this case many metres of root growth – are a move in the direction of a learning style to which some children respond well (Gardner, 1984). Made sufficiently inspiring it may even encourage an interest in plants and promote lifelong learning.

Lessons for all seasons

Winter

Despite botanic gardens being dynamic, with plants and wildlife that change constantly in response to season, weather, and even time of day, my research on schools visits to botanic gardens convinces me that most teachers perceive them as peripheral to the National Curriculum (Johnson, 2001). Usually schools visit on one occasion and only in the summer. In subsequent years they take a trip to a museum or an 'educational attraction'. Very few schools visit botanic gardens regularly and even fewer visit in the winter.

Primary groups

A stone slab lawn sundial, which uses the child as a gnomon, is laid out in the Birmingham Botanic Garden. It can be used in all seasons if the sun is shining and lessons on latitude, its effect on day length and how this can affect plant growth can follow.

Even in winter there are opportunities in all botanic gardens to identify and study tree buds, bark patterns, flowers that develop from bulbs, corms and rhizomes, alpine species and evergreens. Gathering evidence of biodiversity is not confined to the summer. Neither is study of the underlying principles of scientific modelling in, e.g. life cycles and adaptation. Both are illustrated in January and February when many flowers that bloom are sweet scented to attract the small number of pollinating insects flying in cold weather.

Slavishly following a scheme of work that takes little account of including the outdoor potential for lessons in any season is short sighted and counters teaching and learning for sustainable development and life in general. With sufficient warning, parents can dress their children appropriately for a day-long winter visit out of doors. Experiencing cold weather and walking are lessons in themselves especially for the many children who, because they are driven to school, have limited experience of both.

Even so, winter botanic garden lessons can be delightfully warm! In glasshouses, tropical plants can be maintained in temperatures around 20°C. Banana plants are commonly grown and provide an impressive example of an economic crop from the tropics, which the children themselves have available to eat all year round. At the same time these are plants that demonstrate the size of tropical leaves, their water shedding adaptations and how easily leaves are split by high winds.

A quick show of hands will confirm how many present eat bananas daily. A map, marked with the route many bananas take from the Caribbean, South America or even Asia to Britain, will show that bananas clock up 'food miles'. The effect on the atmosphere (airfreight) or the sea (container cargo) of transporting any crop may be broached. So too might the concept of every individual's 'environmental footprint' on the world – an especially relevant discussion for the winter months when so much of our food is imported.

Figure 6.3 An immersive experience in a tropical house.

In winter, children will have an immersive experience (Figure 6.3). The heat and humidity and the lush vegetation are as near to a tropical encounter as many children will have had thus far in their lives. The faint scents of flowers and wet earth fill the air. Some botanic gardens also have the sound of insects, mammals, birds, etc. in their glasshouses. Immersive conditions are less likely to be replicated in the summer when so many other people visit botanic gardens every day. The noise and jostling detract from sensory engagement. It is the memory primary school children take away from such an experience that is as important as the facts they discover.

Secondary groups

Secondary groups might make use of the glasshouses for half of their winter visit. They would look at exotic plants after a well-structured (and rapid) session of observations and recording of local plants that tolerate low winter temperatures. The differences and similarities should be quite obvious when the two environments are experienced in succession.

Again, bananas can stimulate debate about:

■ eating habits and how our eating decisions affect plant production methods;
■ the vulnerability of economic crops to inclement weather – banana plantations in the Caribbean can be devastated by hurricanes;
■ the variety grown – the British market favourite is Cavendish, a single cloned variety;
■ pests and diseases – an insect pest, a disease or fungus could easily wipe out the entire crop in the short term and possibly even the longer term;
■ use of pesticides and fungicides – relevant both to sustainable development and health.

The compass rose model (Figure 6.4) might be used to guide discussion of other tropical plants, some of which secondary groups might see in a botanic garden: plant life cycles, large-scale management of tropical crops, now and in the past, and the consequences of exploitation. Tobacco, sugar cane, cotton, coffee and cocoa are just some examples of plants that have had a dramatic influence on people (e.g. slavery, mass migration, smoking), the environment (e.g. pesticide use on cotton crops, land clearance for monoculture) and the pattern of world trade (from developing to developed countries, trade barriers, etc.). Who makes

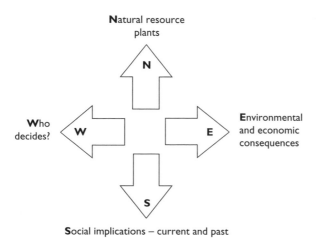

Figure 6.4 The compass rose model.

the decisions about intensification of farming and world trade, at both the macro- and micro-scale, is important in this dialogue.

Spring and autumn

In spring, classes can observe the variation in the timing of leaf growth, bud emergence and flowering that indicate differences between plants. Observation of plants over a number of years may help to indicate environmental change. Primary groups can touch both sides of a south-facing wall and feel the difference in temperature on each side whilst secondary groups can devise ways of measuring the same effect. Both groups can observe the effects microclimates have in a garden.

In the autumn, there is plenty of variation in seed dispersal methods to see. Collecting examples of seeds dispersed by each method provides yet another way of exploring plant diversity. Botanic gardens have a wider range of plants than school grounds or parks and so can offer a broader experience. Botanic garden staff have the experience to provide relevant explanations, especially of the more unusual methods of seed dispersal, e.g. the squirting cucumber (*Ecballium*). Children can devise their own experiments relating to seed dispersal. A change in leaf colour in early or late autumn shows how plants respond to local environmental conditions. Again, children can devise their own ways of recording leaf colour changes. Enquiry-based learning in each term and over a period of years may highlight time-shifts in leaf colour change.

Having a huge botanic garden collection of plants to visit regularly also allows individual plant preferences to be accommodated, e.g. cacti, grasses or insectivorous plants. Any inconsistencies observed in growth, flowering or other attributes will help to establish the notions that authentic knowledge comes from in-depth study over the long term and that science proceeds tentatively. Fostering long acquaintance with a plant can be encouraged in the local environment as an extension of work first undertaken in a botanic garden. Children may develop affective relationships with certain plants in this way. Such affective relationships may help these children to become intolerant of anything that contaminates or obliterates their treasured plants. Transmission of science as facts glosses over the personally discovered truths and motivations that inspire children to take pleasure in science and incorporate it into their daily lives.

The botanic garden ethos in schools

Stimulating an interest in plant study on a single day in a botanic garden is not going to make much difference over the course of a school year. If this is the sole visit in an entire school life then it will probably be insignificant in its effect. Teachers must not imagine that an isolated visit will do anything more than hint at the interconnectedness suggested in Figure 6.1. To perpetuate interest, schools could try to recreate themselves as botanic gardens have done.

Once just repositories for plant collections that invited the public to view, botanic gardens currently have a new function; they store a vast gene pool. They function on one level as a beautiful environment that is maintained by practical skills. Simultaneously they operate at a scientific level developing innovative techniques for growing, observing, recording and using plants. Schools could make the same sort of change when developing their school grounds.

Botanic gardens have accumulated knowledge and skills in horticulture, landscape design and landscape management. They could provide schools with the help they need to achieve low maintenance grounds with high learning potential (BGCI, 1994).

Links with scientists in a botanic garden might enhance school techniques for scientific enquiry in general and encourage the study of plants in particular. By following a botanic garden's holistic approach, schools could develop a programme of indoor and outdoor experiments, which, first, would be immediately valuable for scientific enquiry and assessment. Second, records taken each year (diaries, experiment results, dated photographs, etc.) would inform future generations so that long-term environmental change could be assessed. There are an unlimited number and range of possible teaching and learning scenarios and joint ecological or horticulture projects that might be attempted. Creative teachers are invited to explore the potential connections they could make with a botanic garden.

References

Ballantyne, R. R. and Uzzell, D. A., 1996 'Checklist for the critical evaluation of informal environmental experiences', in Filho, W. L., Murphy, Z. and O'Loan, K. (eds) *The Sourcebook for Environmental Education*, Carnforth: Parthenon Publishing Group, pp. 166–81.

Botanic Gardens Conservation International (BGCI), 1994, *Environmental Education in Botanic Gardens*, London: BGCI.

Braund, M., 2001, *Primary Plants*, Birmingham: The Questions Publishing Company Ltd.

Capon, B., 1994, *Plant Survival*, Portland, OR: Timber Press Inc.

Eyre, D. and Marjoram, T., 1990, *Enriching and Extending the National Curriculum*, London: Kogan Page.

Gardner, H., 1984, *Frames of Mind*, London: Heinemann.

Johnson, S., 2001, *Models of Gardening in Education*. Unpublished PhD thesis, Reading, University of Reading.

Johnson, S. and Tunnicliffe, S., 2000, 'Primary children talk about plants in the garden', *NARST Annual Conference, New Orleans 28 April – 1 May.*

Lewington, A., 1990, *Plants for People*, London: British Museum (Natural History).

Minter, S., 1997, 'Nature's pharmacy', *The Garden*, 122, 436–9.

Soulé, M. E., 1988, 'Mind in the biosphere', in Wilson, E. O. (ed.) *Biodiversity*, Washington, DC: National Academy Press, pp. 465–469.

Resources

Henry Doubleday Research Association (HDRA), Ryton-on-Dunsmore, Coventry CV8 3LG. Website: http://www.hdra.org.uk a website with many lesson ideas and a schools' network.

Education Department, Royal Horticultural Society Garden Wisley, Woking, Surrey GU23 6QB. Website: http://www.rhs.org.uk there is a schools membership scheme and regional INSET days.

Dr E Bower (Co-ordinator) (bgen@kew.org), Botanic Gardens Education Network, Museum No 1, RBG Kew, Richmond, Surrey TW9 3AB. To find the location of your nearest botanic garden and what it offers in terms of educational visits.

Chelsea Physic Garden, 66, Royal Hospital Road, London SW3 4HS. Website: http://www.chelseaphysicgarden.org.uk has resources for lessons.

Thrive – its model gardens have special facilities for children with disabilities of any kind. Website: http://www.thrive.org.uk

Biotechnology and Biological Sciences Research Council (BBSRC). Website: http://www.bbsrc.ac.uk For follow-up work and resources.

http://www.wormdigest.org/crittergallery.html Inhabitants of a compost bin.

Chapter 7

Learning at zoos and farms

Sue Dale Tunnicliffe

Overview

A zoo or farm visit is one of the few opportunities children have to encounter animals other than pets and everyday species. Pupils spontaneously notice obvious features and behaviours and name to their satisfaction the animal viewed. Listening to what groups say reveals their baseline knowledge and interest. Teachers can use this information to develop meaningful work, including science observations and enquiry. Farms provide a more informal opportunity for learning and a greater opportunity to find out about the use of animals by humans for food and other domestic purposes. Religious, cultural and dietary beliefs of pupils must be considered.

Children and animals

Animals are part of a child's experience from earliest days. However, very often, these animals are not living but are images created by toy manufacturers, and artists who create nursery decorations, TV cartoons and book illustrations. Children may come across animals such as dogs, cats and pigeons as pets at home or school, and invertebrates such as flies, slugs, snails and worms in the course of their everyday lives from their early years.

Animals in zoos and farms often provide members of the public with their only opportunity to see living animals other than everyday ones. Schools and parents think of zoos and farms as appropriate venues to take young children, pre-school and Key Stage 1 (5–7 years), in particular. Pupils talk when they visit zoos and farms. Our role, as teachers of science, is to find out what they talk about and direct the talk towards learning science. Farm visits are best for focusing on the nature of animals, particularly mammals, and their main characteristics. Zoo visits can focus on biodiversity, keys, adaptations and behaviours as well as enquiry science. For guidance on health and safety precautions you will need to refer to published guidance (see Resources box at the end of the chapter).

The 'animal as an exhibit' is different from seeing an animal at home, outside or at school. Zoo animals are meant to be seen. Farm animals can be seen but are not exhibited in the sense that zoo animals are with specially designed enclosures, often with backdrops and labelled.

There are four areas of knowledge and interest about animals which adults or children bring to looking at an animal exhibit and about which they may spontaneously talk:

1   A working understanding of the term 'animal'. The term is used most frequently by English speaking people to refer to mammals alone.
2   A working categorisation of animal specimens; in other words, a functional everyday taxonomy. Visitors are able to group the animals and relate observed specimens to other actual animals and those which they recall in terms of their everyday taxonomy. If the children or adults have been taught zoological taxonomy at school, such knowledge may be used within their conversations.
3   A knowledge of the structures and behaviours of animals, derived from the everyday experiences of the visitor and from science work at school.
4   An inherent curiosity about individual animals. Questions and comments about the authenticity of a specimen, its human associations and the unique personal links which animals evoke for each visitor are likely to form part of the spontaneous conversations. Often children and teachers will relate the animal to a story or other relevant activity across the curriculum.

Scientific concepts are developed through formal 'school type' dialogues between the child and teacher. Teaching strives to develop the personal ideas of the children. Skilled teachers help learners to reorder their previously learned knowledge and many adults follow such a course of action instinctively.

What do children notice?

In looking at live animals, children are particularly involved in:

■   the use of everyday language to verbalise the science concepts in their own terms;
■   egocentrism;
■   anthropomorphism.

Analyses by me of the content of the spontaneous conversations of primary school children at a zoo showed that 60 per cent of conversations held comments about the features of the exhibit other than the animal specimens, such as: the exhibit furniture, the setting, the trees and the rocks. Children subsequently used this descriptive information to define where the animal was. They then went on to name the animal, describe it or its behaviour, when noticeable. First-hand observations provide an experience which can be used to develop the ability of pupils to recognise parts of the body of animals, identify typical behaviours and group animals according to easily observed features. Teachers (and well briefed chaperones) can draw attention to the attributes of the animals used for allocating the animal to its zoological group – characteristics like the different body coverings of mammals, birds, reptiles and fish. Alternatively, tell children the name of the animal and its grouping and ask them to work out some of the reasons for the categorisation using features that can be seen. The visit can consolidate work already performed in school.

What attributes do children spontaneously notice and comment upon? Looking at the body parts and the behaviour of animals, such as the way they move around, are prerequisites for being able to categorise. For example, two 8-year-old boys had been asked by their teacher to look at each animal and say what it was and what class of vertebrate it belonged to, giving a reason.

Boy 1: That's a lizard.
Boy 2: It's a reptile because it has scales and a dry skin.

Children, like all people, have a need to categorise what they look at, and animals are no exception. Once children have spotted an animal they spontaneously allocate it a name. These names may be ones the children remember, or, alternatively, they may work out a name for the animals using recognisable features of familiar species that seem similar.

The names which children use tend to be the everyday names so, within a zoo the children use their existing knowledge of biodiversity to identify the animals. The teacher can use the opportunity to build on pupils' existing knowledge. A 6-year-old boy looking at an okapi remarked 'Look! That's half giraffe and half zebra!'

Anthropomorphism is the term used to describe the interpretation of the structure and behaviour of other animals in human terms. Children (and adults!) frequently use anthropomorphic explanations as illustrated by the following conversation from Year 6 children looking at a gorilla.

Boy 1: I think he's feeling ill.
Boy 2: He sits so still he is bored.
Boy 3: Oh, look at that one!

Comments about animals' bodies fall into four categories:

- the front end (head and sense organs), e.g. 'They have a small nose and a small mouth';
- the body dimensions (shape, size and colour), e.g. Year 4 boys at cotton-headed tamarins 'That is a baby'. Teacher 'Why?' Boy 'Because they are small';
- unfamiliar bits, e.g. horns, sex and reproductive organs. For example, Year 2 child at chimps 'Look at its pink bottom!';
- disrupters which break the pattern of familiarity, e.g. tails and legs. For example, Year 6 girl at elephants 'It's putting its tongue, I mean its trunk, in its mouth!'

There are also four categories of behaviours which children talk about:

- movements, e.g. Year 2 girl 'Aren't they cute? Look at them running round and round and around!';
- their position in the enclosure, e.g. Year 1 boy 'Up there!';
- feeding, e.g. Year 6 girl at elephant 'Look, it's eating a branch!';
- attractor behaviours (activities other than locomotion which draw attention of visitors, e.g. excretion, play). For example, Year 6 girl 'Look at the elephant, it's doing a wee'.

The age of the children looking at the animals affects their interest and thus what they say and what their teachers say. There is, for example, a greater interest in colour shown by children less than 5 years old and in shape by older children. Groups containing older children spontaneously comment on feeding behaviour significantly more and generate more emotional comments. Younger children make significantly more comments categorising the animals, allocating a 'category' name to the animals, using terms such as 'bird' and 'fish'. Such information provides a basis for relevant activities.

The gender of the child also affects their comments to a certain extent. Overall, there is remarkable similarity in conversational content of boys and girls. However, groups with only boys name animal specimens more whereas groups with only girls make more emotive comments.

Responses to animals through children's senses and emotions

Exhibits with lots of species confuse the children, so choose to look at exhibits with one type. Farms are excellent for this, where the children can focus on one species, e.g. cows, looking for the features or behaviours you want them to.

You may want the children to observe the animal through a variety of senses. Some kinds of animal are better than others for this. This approach is particularly important for children with some form of learning difficulty. For instance, visually impaired children respond particularly well to domestic animals which can be touched. For this reason a visit to a farm or a children's zoo can be ideal as it provides greater hands-on opportunities. Sounds, of course, can be a focus of a visit as can smell.

Farm animals elicit predominantly emotive responses from school groups but fewer comments about behaviours. In the spectrum of companion animals, which runs from free-living wild animals to pet animals kept at home, farm animals are nearer the pet image than are zoo animals. This may account for the more affective emphasis of farm comments. Farms often provide opportunities for handling animals (Figure 7.1) which leads to many comments! Ensure that hand-washing facilities are *readily* to hand and used immediately after animal handling. Adequate supervision is essential with very young children, who may put fingers in mouths before there has been the opportunity to wash them.

Labels provided in zoos are seldom read them by visitors. A 'talking human' is a more effective way of giving information, while guided tours, as long as there

Figure 7.1 Child at a city farm weighing a chicken.

are only a few children per adult, can be very effective. Some educational farms provide information through farm teachers.

During school visits teachers and chaperones can act as label readers and repeat the contents to the children. Children can be encouraged to read the labels for the group and getting them to design labels for certain animals is a useful language activity.

What do your pupils say?

Try listening to what your pupils say. You can tape their conversations and play them back. If you listen to what your pupils spontaneously say about animals in a zoo or farm you can gain useful information for planning your teaching. Find out:

- whether there is a universal pattern to comments about animals;
- whether the animal as an exhibit rather than free living – like in school grounds – make a difference;
- whether the pupils ask for information or use that provided by the zoo (or you) or interpret the animals from their existing knowledge and experience.

You can type pupils' conversations out or you can fill in a summary chart like that shown in Table 7.1. You can devise your own, including categories about which you want to know if the children talk.

Chaperones – other adults leading a group

Briefing other adults

The pupils may have a guided talk, lecture or interactive session in an education department. Even so you need to tell the other adults with you about the aims and objectives of the visit. If possible, provide these adults with background information and brief them on the focus of observations as children's attention needs to be drawn to the relevant features which are the basis of zoological knowledge.

You should warn female adults who are visiting farms at lambing time about the possible risk of disease transmission to those who may be pregnant.

Brief the adults on the names that you would like the children to use, bearing in mind the names which the children are likely to use spontaneously. For instance, if your project is on cats, suggest that the dialogues with children

Table 7.1 Tunnicliffe conversation observation record (TCOR)

Location	Animal 1	Animal 2	Animal 3	Animal 4	Animal 5	Totals
Animal being observed.						
Educational task set.						
Age of pupils.						
Orientation to animal. E.g. 'Where is it?' or 'It's up there'.						
Comments/questions about animal's name. E.g. 'What is it?' or 'It's a lion'.						
Comments/questions about body. E.g. about colour, legs, tail, size.						
Comments/questions about behaviour. E.g. 'It's sleeping'.						
Comments/questions about other biology ideas such as adaptation, predator/prey.						
Comments/questions from other areas of curriculum besides science. E.g. maths, language, geography.						
Comments in human terms. E.g. 'It looks like granddad', 'It's having breakfast'.						
What will it do to me? E.g. 'It's dangerous!'						
What can I do to it? E.g. 'It would make a nice coat', 'I'd fight that tiger!'						
Affective comments about the animal. E.g. 'I like it', 'It's cute', 'It stinks', 'Ugh!'						
Comments/questions about animal's natural environment. E.g. 'Where does it live in the wild?'						
Comments/questions about its survival. E.g. 'Is it an endangered animal?'						
Other comments/questions about the exhibit. E.g. about the rocks, trees, cage, enclosure, field.						
Comments about or in response to the signage. E.g. 'Read the sign' or 'Answer the sign'.						
Did they mention their sense of sight?						
Did they mention their sense of smell?						
Did they mention their sense of hearing?						
Off topic comments/question. E.g. 'What time is it?', 'When is lunch?', 'I want to go to the shop'.						
Management. E.g. 'Stop it!', 'Let's go.'						
Others not covered above.						

Note: For each conversation at an animal tick in one column if a topic is heard. Only tick once if a topic is heard. This is not a count of the number of times in an exchange but only the number of exchanges that mention a topic. Start a new column for each new animal.

should begin with the familiar term 'cats' and develop the use of scientific language from that point by introducing the levels of grouping and then their names.

Effect of presence of adults

The adult with whom children look at the animals is important; they can affect the nature and content of conversations. If the children are being taught at the exhibits it is to be expected that the conversations will be characterised by particular conversational forms between pupil and teacher where the teacher asks a question, the child responds and the teacher closes the conversation and moves on to another teaching exchange.

Often, when an adult is not 'teaching', the children lead the conversation. Some adults try to bring back the children's focus to a teaching point, often unsuccessfully as in the following conversation with a 7-year-old girl about a gorilla.

Girl: Their hands are like ours.
Adult: If you look closely, they haven't got hair on their palms or fingers, have they?
Girl: Oh look at that baby!

Children-only groups

The conversations of children-only groups are predominantly of an observational or commentary nature. They contain fewer management or social references, reflecting the perception identified amongst children that adults who accompany school groups are dominant and managerial. The presence of any adult also focuses the conversations more on facts and relevant observations.

In view of the burden of care for the children carried by the adults participating in a school visit, it is not surprising that conversations of groups with chaperones contain many management or social references. Chaperones use the names with the children more than teachers do, probably to control the group and establish social dynamics with the children to whom they are often strangers and with whom they are unlikely to share a rapport. On the other hand, the presence of a chaperone may facilitate the exchange of social information between children more than in groups with a teacher. The following exchange amongst a group of 5-year-old children with a chaperone is typical of the social nature of the conversations of chaperoned groups in a zoo.

Adult: Look at this one. Look up there. Look in the branches!

Girl: Mum, Peter pushed me.

Adult: Oh, he didn't mean to, did he? He's got to see well so that he can tell his Mummy about all the wonderful things that you see.

Children talk more about physical features and behaviours when they are with their teacher. Such observations are an early stage in the acquisition of classification and the features used in compiling categories, so it is important that the children do particularly attend to these features. So, if you want your pupils, who are not in your group during the visit, to notice particular things they need a well-briefed adult with them. Frequently chaperones and teachers use questions to ensure that children are able to view the animal in the exhibit.

Naming is one of the main things mentioned by all pupils. The allocation of specimens to a category, e.g. class or order, occurs in all three types of groups: pupils only, pupils plus teachers, pupils plus chaperones. The *everyday* labelling word, e.g. beetle, has a dual function. It is also the name of a category, e.g. the order Coleoptera or beetles. 'Beetle' is the noun used by the pupils, not because of the possession of zoological knowledge, but because of everyday knowledge. In the following example of conversation between two 7 year olds the animal being categorised was actually a locust.

Boy 1: There's a little beetle.

Boy 2: See its head with its eye and the enormous body?

Farm conversations

In conversations among primary children at a farm, unlike that at a zoo, I have found there are no significant differences between any category of conversations between the age groups. Farms, where the animals are not exhibited, generate significantly more affective attitudinal comments than do zoos.

It is particularly important for farm visits where there are pigs to be aware of cultural and religious taboos about animals and not, for instance, expect Muslim pupils to talk about and carefully observe pigs.

Comments at farms are often of an everyday nature. Pupils notice things about the animals which relate to their own experience, often whilst a teacher is trying to give information, as did the 10 year olds in the following conversation:

Girl: They have earrings, they have earrings (these were in their noses).

Farm teacher:	Look at their feet. Are they like ours?
Girl:	No they have hooves don't they?
Boy:	They have earrings.
Farm teacher:	Do you think their stomachs are like ours?
Boy:	No.
Boy:	They have big eyes.
Farm teacher:	Yes they have big eyes.
Girl:	They have something on their ears.
Farm teacher:	They have four stomachs.

Maximising the educational value of visiting a zoo or farm

Liase with the education officer at the site you wish to visit. They often provide planning material and welcome a visit from you to discuss how to make the most out of the pupils' visit.

Plan to study aspects of the animal that the children are more likely to notice such as:

- how do the animals communicate?
- what sense organs do they have and what is their position and function?
- what foods do they eat? It helps here to get the pupils to look at the mouth of the animal, the location of its eyes and the type and position of its teeth.
- what body parts do they have which are adapted to the animal's natural habitat? For example, a camel's feet for walking on sand; the streamlined body of a seal for swimming.

For infant children, it is a good idea to look at the body shapes and sizes of animals in terms of a standard benchmark such as the children themselves! Alternatively, work on body coverings which can also include texture, colour and function as well as seasonal changes. The following conversation is of a pre-school group and their teacher who was teaching the children about the characteristics of birds. The group were at the penguins.

Girl 1:	Ah.
Teacher:	What colour are they?
Girl 1:	Black and white.
Teacher:	What is their body covered with?
Girl 2:	Feathers. They are birds.

Secondary pupils usually have defined tasks linked to the syllabus which they are following and related to a session at the educational centre. Spontaneous conversations tend to be similar to those of the younger children although with more emphasis on reproduction. Many secondary pupils visit a zoo to debate the issue 'Why zoos?' The visit very often changes their views and leaves them feeling positive about zoos. There are very few spontaneous conversations at any age group about conservation issues.

Other factors related to pupils' behaviour also affect the conversational content. Social interactions between pupils generate other comments, hence conversations, unrelated to the animal exhibits, while other needs of visitors generate conversation and movements. Unfamiliarity of a site has an effect on the movements, other behaviours and thus conversations of visitors, although research has shown that the use of pre-visit preparatory material (advance organisers) helps structure the visit for pupils and makes the visit more meaningful and efficient in terms of directed movements. There are three main advanced organisers: maps; overviews of what can be seen; and conceptual pre-organisers.

You may hear reference to pre-visit use of these in school when the pupils are talking. For example, an 8 year old said at the golden lion tamarins that he knew them because he had read about them before he came, using a book at school.

The way visitors spend their time, and hence the pattern of their movements and thus the content of their conversations about the exhibits, is related to the stages of the visit. Pupils need an orientation time before setting off on the focus of the visit, unless they have visited the site before and are familiar with it. Alternatively, pupils need a wind-down time and then a leaving phase (shop visit and so on). Educational tasks should be planned. You may book a session with the education staff of the establishment and use their talks and activities. You may decide to design your own activities. However, the pupils cannot focus on a task all the time and need an orientation time, a task-focused time, a general look around time before winding and leaving. Without a task school children, when in groups without an adult, become 'wanderers', without a focused occupation. Remember, both pupils and adults are likely to alter their behaviour as they become tired.

The structure for the 'intensive looking' or task phase is frequently provided by prepared worksheets. The conversations between pupils when well-designed worksheets are in use would be expected to reflect a higher number of references to both attributes of animal specimens and the names of animals as pupils seek the 'answers' using the text on the worksheets and the labels at the exhibits as prompts and sources of information.

Worksheets and other participatory activities

There is debate about the use of worksheets. You will have to decide whether a worksheet will serve to focus the attention of your pupils on what you want them to look at and explore at the zoo or farm, or whether using a worksheet will impede their learning. Some worksheets are little more than tick sheets and hardly require the pupils to look carefully at exhibits. Collaboration between groups often results in pupils copying the answers without actually looking at the animals. Sometimes chaperones feel it is their role to find the answers and give them to the children. The worksheet effectively becomes an exhibit and the real exhibits are ignored.

On the other hand, worksheets which require the children to look carefully at the animals and perhaps complete a drawing by sketching a particular aspect of the animal in response to a guiding question can be very effective in helping children find out more information. Such interactive worksheets can lead pupils into looking at animals with a purpose. An extension of worksheets with words and drawings to complete through observations is drawing whole animals. Drawing is an important part of science and drawing at first hand from specimens is a key skill in biology. An extension of drawing animals is to provide pupils in groups of two or three with a disposable camera. Invite the pupils to take photographs of animals which interest them. The groups have to keep a log of which animals they chose to photograph and give their reasons. This activity can be broken down into giving one pupil alone a camera and asking that pupil to photograph three animals of their choice. The pupil then passes the camera on to another child in the group. Alternatively, each pupil in a group can have a number of frames to use and they can use them whenever they choose during the walk round the zoo or farm.

Tasks for pre-school and Year 1

The main aim with pre-school and Year 1 pupils is to raise their awareness of animals and help them to begin acquiring the skills of observation which can lead to groupings. Try making a 'zoo kit' with them before they come on the visit. They can use this in pairs or one-to-one with an adult during their visit (Figure 7.2).

Visit the zoo or farm and make a map of the route you suggest the children take. Plan your own route. Provide a map/list for helpers. Some of the animals in zoos relevant to the zoo kits are flamingos, lions, tigers, penguins, elephants, the Children's Farm animals, the Reptile House or Tropical House for some colours and textures, zebras, camels and giraffes for patterns. You might like to plan

Zoo kit teacher's notes

Objectives:
Children will observe, using hands-on materials, the colour, pattern, shape and size of animals, as well as developing their knowledge of animal kinds and associated language skills.

Suggested contents:
A container – a bag or box. In each of the bags or boxes there should be:

- A cardboard Eye Spy tube (kitchen paper tube)
- A magnifying sheet or handlens
- A set of colour cards
- A set of pattern cards
- A toy farm animal
- A toy zoo animal
- A touch, feel and talk card (containing, for example, a piece of fur and a bit of lizard skin).

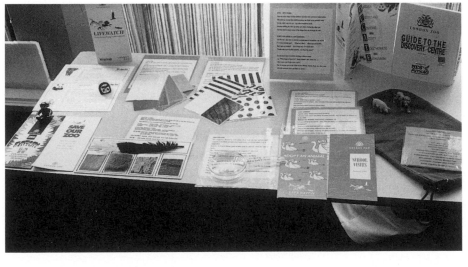

Figure 7.2 The contents of a zoo kit.

such a route, mark it on the map and give a copy to groups of children as practice at map reading.

Preparation and follow-up activities for zoo kit

Before you visit

Develop the relevant vocabulary for colour, pattern, shape and size. Children should know the words black, white, striped, spotted, rings, plain, patterned, grey, brown, red, green, blue, yellow and pink. Practise describing plain and patterned things in the classroom using colour words. Develop the vocabulary for textures – hard, soft, dull, shiny, warm, cold, rough, smooth and soft. Practise describing familiar items in the classroom using these descriptive words.

Introduce pupils to the shapes and names of some of the animals they will see during their visit, especially the ones noted in the suggested route. Use toy animals, templates, jigsaws and books as well as slides, videos and CD roms.

Play observational games in the classroom such as I-spy. Try I-spy colours, shapes, patterns. Use your hand clap as a time measure: 'How many circles can you find between my hand claps?' Play matching words to patterns, words to shapes.

Practise with the children using a hand lens or magnifying sheet so that they know what it does. Look at print as a practice. They can look at their own skin as part of the zoo activity.

During your visit

Design each activity with a card for the adult to read with suggested activities and dialogue for the chaperones to follow if they wish.

After your visit

- Paint patterns and shapes which the children saw.
- Model the animals the children looked at from clay or other materials.
- Make a word mobile, an animal mobile.
- Write an animal poem inside the outline shape of a particular animal, e.g. snake and elephant.
- Make a collage.
- Plan and construct a model of the zoo.
- Make an animals touch tray with everyday things which feel like the touch, feel and talk card.

Farm activities

A 'farm kit' can focus on coverings – hair and wool. It can focus on patterns if there are animals with distinct colourings, such as hens, sheep, cows and pigs or on shapes and smells. Use farm words and incorporate animal noises into your activities, for example, those of cows, chickens and sheep. Be aware that Muslim children do not discuss pigs.

Design some open-ended questions to which the answers may be found by making first-hand observations at the zoo or farm. An example is given in Table 7.2. Provide pupils with such a sheet with their own task/question/challenge inserted. They would then insert answers to the rest of the categories. This activity is suitable for primary and secondary children depending on the task/question/challenge you set.

Table 7.2 Animal science enquiry

	Example 1	*Fill in your own*	*Fill in your own*
Task/question/ challenge.	Do all mammals have external ears?	Which of the animals have black and white stripes?	
Main science idea.	External ear flaps are a mammalian characteristic. (Seals are an exception.)		
Main enquiry skills.	Observing, recording, inferring.		
Thinking stage ■ What is already known?	Human beings and some animals like cats have ears.		
■ What has to be found out?	Which mammals have ear flaps?		
■ What will we do to find out?	Make list of mammals we see in the zoo; observe whether each one has ear flaps.		
■ What do we think we will find out?	We think all the mammals will have ear flaps.		
Planning stage ■ Each pupil's role or task in the enquiry.	■ Map reader. ■ Observer. ■ Recorder.		
■ Resources needed for the enquiry.	■ Clip board. ■ Pencil. ■ Record sheet. ■ List of animals. ■ Map of zoo.		
■ Step-by-step action plan.	■ Find location of animals to be observed and plan route. ■ Go to exhibit and find animal. ■ Make and record observations. ■ Repeat for each succeeding animal.		

Table 7.2 (continued)

	Example I	*Fill in your own*	*Fill in your own*
■ Observations to be made.	Look to see whether there is an ear flap.		
■ Type of recording sheet. How will records be made?	List of animals to be observed and space to check whether ear flaps have been observed.		
Results – what did we find out? What observations were made?	■ Lion had ears. ■ Elephant had ears. ■ Seals don't have visible ears. ■ Etc.		
What do these observations tell us?	All land mammals observed had external ears.		
Have we answered the original question/ task/challenge?	Yes.		

Older pupils can use the above suggestions. Zoos provide worksheets for particular topics. Ask the education department what they can offer in the topics in which you are interested. Here is a Key Stage 4 example based on a suggestion from Jersey Zoo.

Plan for a Key Stage 4 visit to a zoo

This is based on material from Maggie Esson, Jersey Zoo: scientific enquiry – investigative skills – science Key Stage 4

This workshop can be run entirely at the zoo over half a day or can be started at the zoo on a shorter visit and concluded in school. Choose the animal which you wish to investigate.

Aim: Explore ways in which ideas can be investigated using scientific knowledge and understanding and identify key factors to be taken into account when collecting evidence.

Objectives: Using a group of sociable zoo mammal species, chosen by teacher or pupils, pupils will:

■ plan a strategy to measure the behaviours of a mammal species;
■ consider the benefits of behavioural enrichment on mammal behaviour;
■ carry out an initial investigation and make predictions;

- design and present environmental enrichment devices;
- collect evidence to support predictions.

Plan: Present, in education department, information on the role of zoos in the twenty-first century, including the importance of psychological well-being of captive animals. Show comparative slides or images of zoo history. Discuss needs of social animals. Visit the enclosure and have a question-and-answer session with keeper. Return to the classroom and explore the challenge question and brainstorm how to answer it. For example, how can a zoo actively promote appropriate behaviours in the chosen animal and measure those behaviours? Discuss a list of behaviours that could be measured. Introduce environmental enrichment as a tool for promoting interest, challenge, exploration and psychological well-being. Use slides of different species and enrichment as examples.

Activity: Period of self-directed learning as pupils work in pairs to research and predict likely changes in behaviour that environmental enrichment could stimulate. Pupils go on to design an activity and visit enclosure to collect data to record observed behaviours. On returning to classroom results are discussed and ideas for further work, such as designing and making enrichment behavioural artefacts, are discussed. Zoo educator discusses the project ideas and provides further relevant information. The artefacts are made and taken to the enclosure where the animals are observed interacting with them.

Presentation and discussion: Students present their findings and summarise results. They decide whether findings support initial ideas and reflect on appropriateness of strategy. (This activity can be completed in school, with students developing presentation skills including use of diagrams and charts and demonstrating ICT skills.)

Further reading

Bell, B, 1981, 'When is an animal not an animal?', *Journal of Biological Education*, 15(3): 202–18.

Falk, J. H. and Dierking, L., 1992, *The Museum Experience*, Washington, DC: Whalesback Books.

Falk, J. H. and Dierking, L., 2000, *Learning in Museums*, Washington, DC: Whalesback Books.

Hein, G., 1998, *Learning in the Musuem*, London: Routledge.

Tunnicliffe, S. D., 1996a, 'Conversations within primary school parties visiting animal specimens in a museum and zoo', *Journal of Biological Education*, 30(2), 130–41.

Tunnicliffe, S. D., 1996b, 'Talking science at animal collections', *Primary Science Review*, 45, 24–7.

Tunnicliffe, S. D., 1998a, 'Boy talk: girl talk – is it the same at animal exhibits?', *International Journal of Science Education*, 20(7), 795–811.

Tunnicliffe, S. D., 1998b, 'Down on the farm: the content of conversations generated by schools viewing live animals as exhibits and on a farm', *Journal of Elementary Science Education*, 10(1), 1–17.

Resources

Refer to published guidance on farm and zoo visits, including the most up-to-date information from the DfES, as well as 'Pupil Visits to Farms: Health Precautions' (1997) and 'Avoiding Ill Health at Open Farms – Advice to Farmers (with teacher's supplement)' HSE, 2000, AIS No. 23, HSE Books.

When planning your zoo or farm visit you need to identify what the visit can offer to the curriculum/syllabus to which you are working. Websites can be a useful source of information.

You can get a list of Zoo Federation members for the UK and Northern Ireland. Tel: 020 7586 0230. Fax: 020 7722 4427. Email: fedzoo@zsl.org For up-to-date information about farms try http://www.farmgarden.org.uk or www.farmsforteachers.org.uk You could also try the English Tourist Board. They have a list of farms open to the public on their website www.travelengland.org.uk Try a search by name for a zoo near you.

The website for the American Zoo Association, www.AZA.org, will lead you to many zoos in the USA with a great deal of relevant information.

Chapter 8

Learning science at museums and hands-on centres

Martin Braund

Overview

The range of provision for learning science in museums and hands-on centres and galleries (HOCGs) is reviewed. A contextual model is used to help understand the nature of learning in these places. The special place that handling objects plays in educating in science is described. A brief overview of some important aspects of research in museums and HOCGs acts as a prelude to describing actions that teachers might take to improve experiences for pupils.

Introduction

Museums have a long educational legacy and connection with learning science. The world's first museum is reputed to have been constructed by Ptolemy I in Alexandria in 290 BC. It was established as a centre for learning dedicated to the 'muses', daughters of Zeus who presided over the arts and sciences. In England the first recognisable museum with its own dedicated building was the Ashmolean in Oxford. It was established in the late seventeenth century as a centre of academic activity in the sciences within the University of Oxford. Today, the museum sector in the UK constitutes a large network of varied providers giving access to exciting, challenging and stimulating opportunities for pupils to embellish, enrich and extend the more formal learning of science that takes place in school.

Providers for science learning include the large national museums such as the Natural History Museum and Science Museum in London and their regional outposts, museums dedicated to scientific or technological themes and science galleries within general museums. In the last 20 years there has been a growth in what has been called 'hands-on centres'. These provide for a much higher degree of interaction with exhibits than is generally found in more traditional museums and galleries. Visitors are encouraged to touch, explore, investigate and bring about change through personal interaction with exhibits. The depth of interaction ranges from mere button pushing so as to operate a machine or process to a deeper involvement via personal experimentation and problem solving. Interaction often entails substantial thought about the underlying science, and collaboration and conversation with others helps to consolidate and deepen the learning. Hands-on provision in the UK covers a wide range: from small clusters of exhibits, e.g. in visitor or interpretative centres, through interactive galleries in larger science museums, e.g. 'Launchpad' within the Science Museum in London and 'Xperiment' within the Museum of Science and Industry in Manchester, to purpose-built science centres such as Techniquest in Cardiff and Explore@Bristol. The diversity and quality of what is on offer has been extended through £1 billion of funding from the Millennium Commission. There is now a science centre, interactive gallery or museum featuring an aspect of science within reach of most centres of population in the UK. The ECSITE-UK website gives details of location, type of provision and what is on offer (see Resources box).

It is not difficult to justify what pupils gain from studying science in these places. Museums and hands-on centres and galleries (referred to as HOCGs from now on) have a very special place in educating school pupils in science because they:

- provide a special and different environment to schools in which pupils are motivated often through handling real or newly encountered objects or by interacting with hands-on exhibits;
- enable physical or manipulative access to concrete examples or simulations of abstract scientific phenomena and concepts (some of these phenomena cannot be easily or economically reproduced in schools);
- provide for interaction with exhibits that allows pupils to apply and use key scientific process skills such as questioning, predicting, observing, problem-solving, comparing, investigating, hypothesising and considering evidence, in new, interesting and challenging situations;
- provide places where pupils can learn to place scientific phenomena and concepts within everyday contexts;
- enable access to rare or otherwise inaccessible artefacts, specimens and systems;
- allow pupils to understand scientific discovery, technological development or key relationships by arranging artefacts, specimens and systems within historic or connected sequences;
- provide access and understanding of the inner workings of machines or systems, allowing pupils a window through which they can see inside scientific and technological 'black boxes';
- offer an opportunity to shape and develop pupils' attitudes to science and, in a wider sense, to learning itself. Specifically, pupils develop attitudes that are important in studying science such as curiosity, open-mindedness,

critical reflection, creativity, inventiveness, respect for evidence, co-operation, perseverance, toleration of uncertainty and sensitivity to the environment;

■ provide a secure and stimulating environment in which science is viewed and learned with a sense of awe and wonder.

Understanding the nature of learning at museums

Falk and Dierking (2000) have devised a model that helps us understand the learning that takes place in informal settings. They call this a 'contextual model' and have applied it in situations where learners have an element of free choice in what they do. Whilst pupils on school visits to museums may be more limited in the amount of free choice activity they engage in, the model is very helpful in shedding light on the nature of the learning that takes place. There are three aspects to the model, all of which interact when pupils visit museums and HOCGs. Figure 8.1 summarises the key features of the model.

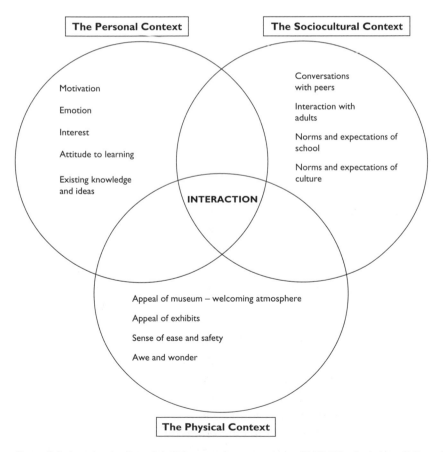

Figure 8.1 A contextual model of learning in museums and HOCGs (based on Falk and Dierking, 2000).

The personal context

Falk and Dierking identify four aspects of the personal context as they affect the museum visitor:

1   Learning flows from appropriate motivational and emotional cues.
2   Learning is facilitated by personal interest.
3   New knowledge is constructed from a foundation of prior experience and knowledge.
4   Learning is expressed within appropriate contexts.

Museums are rich and stimulating environments. They can and should be joyful places for learning to take place, free of the shackles that the more formal settings of the school curriculum, classroom and laboratory almost inevitably require and impose. In this sense a visit to a museum or HOCG is packed with emotional and motivational cues that act as a prelude to engagement.

When pupils visit a museum the teacher assumes or hopes that they will be interested in what they will see. Pupils' motivation may be *extrinsic* or *intrinsic*. Extrinsically motivated pupils want to learn so that they will do well in school. Intrinsically motivated pupils engage in learning for its own sake; they are the ones most likely to interact with exhibits from the outset and to pursue personal learning agendas. Ideally, the learning that takes place on a well-organised school visit facilitates both modes.

Pupils rarely interact with exhibits or displays knowing nothing at all about them. Their knowledge may be limited or partly formed from contacts with school-based sources or absorbed from other informal or home-based learning such as films, TV and video. In the last 25 years a dominant view has been that pupils *construct* understanding of science through an interaction between their existing ideas and new knowledge or experience. This constructivist notion of learning recognises that pupils' ideas are often in conflict with the science we want to teach and that the processes through which they integrate new experiences to bring about change in thinking can be slow and complex. A museum can provide exciting, unusual and dynamic experiences that help to bring about change, though like many learning experiences in school, it is unlikely that any one event will result in major new understanding. The following example helps illustrate this point.

An exhibit in Explore@Bristol requires pupils to mount a cycle and pedal as hard as they can. The cycle wheel is connected via dynamos to a number of output devices: a fan, various coloured lights and a beacon. There are a number of switches each controlling an output device. The harder you pedal the more energy is transferred to the outputs; the more devices that are switched on, the harder it becomes to pedal. The underlying scientific concepts of the exhibit are energy transfer and in particular energy input in relation to energy requirement (the effort required in pedalling is proportional to the energy required by the output devices). As a quality learning experience of science it has much to offer. It requires the pupil to use many senses and involves personal actions and decisions that might lead to deeper thinking. The ability of this one-off experience to improve pupils' understandings of the scientific concepts is, however, debatable. We know that pupils have many misconceptions about energy – for example, many think of energy as a substance, consumed in transfers from one form to another (for a review of pupils' misconceptions in this and other areas of science, see Driver *et al.*, 1994). The museum experience cannot on its own hold out any more hope of bringing about change in pupils' understandings than activities in school physics lessons can. Indeed, the experience might even reinforce the misconception. The important point is that it adds significantly to the teacher's repertoire of explanation. The teacher's job back at school is to draw on this and other teaching in physics so that learners can make the most of the new, graphic and enjoyable example experienced at the museum, so helping them to construct new meanings and understanding. In this way the museum experience can be seen as a constructivist one (Figure 8.2).

Figure 8.2 Pupils interacting at an exhibit on bridge design at the hands-on centre Explore@Bristol.

The sociocultural context

What we learn in any situation is often mediated through our gestures and by conversation with others. The ways in which we act in and react to different learning situations is a product of our culture. Our culture and society and the ways in which we have been brought up impose a set of social norms setting expectations and rules about how we might behave in different situations. School groups are an example of what Falk and Dierking call a 'community of learners'. The norms and expectations of this community and the resulting ways in which they act in museums may be quite different to other groups, e.g. families. Watch a school group going around a hands-on science centre or gallery and look at the range of social behaviours that you can see. Individuals and groups behave differently according to a mixture of influences. What seems at first quite chaotic may be just part of a natural social adjustment to a new learning environment. At some stage conversations may take place either between the pupils in a group or with adult helpers, teachers or museum 'explainers'. These conversations are a vital part of the culture of learning at museums and make a key contribution to the outcomes. As we shall see later, there are clear messages for teachers here about how they might help or hinder the learning process by the effect they can have on the sociocultural context.

Young children benefit from a chance to engage in group play and some museums provide a chance to do this whilst learning something about how their society is organised and functions. At Eureka, for example, children can engage as groups with a number of familiar and unfamiliar settings in spaces arranged around a 'city square'. In the garage they choose appropriate clothes, don overalls and then explore the workings of a car, choose and change tyres and fill the car with imaginary fuel. In the supermarket they select food items, fill a shopping basket and then visit the checkout, working out the appropriate amount of money to give the cashier.

More conventional galleries in museums tell stories or place exhibits in sequences that help pupils make connections between them. For example, a popular exhibit with school visitors to the Castle Museum in York explains the history and technological development of the flushing toilet from its humble origins to the design developed by Thomas Crapper. In this way the museum helps pupils think about the everyday applications of science and technology through stories about their histories. Museums may also use actors playing the parts of great scientists. Pupils are encouraged to converse with characters so that they actively engage in stories about scientific discovery.

The sociocultural context of learning at museums is dependent to a large extent on how much people are stimulated to engage in the first place. This is connected with the environment they encounter or what Falk and Dierking call the 'physical context'.

The physical context

People's memories of museum visits refer strongly to the sights, sounds and even smells encountered. Specific details are remembered even after a considerable time (Stevenson, 1991). The environment of the museum or HOCG has a significant impact on the quality of the experience, and hence the amount of engagement and learning that takes place. Some of the great national and regional museums constructed in the Victorian age of museum building in the second half of the nineteenth century were designed as monuments to culture and scientific advancement and to house the new and impressive collections of the time. They represent daunting yet awe-inspiring experiences for children. I can still remember my first visit to the Natural History Museum in London as a child of 9. I was in awe and wonder at the sight of the huge blue whale hanging from a giant, lofty ceiling and the *Diplodocus* skeleton soaring above me in the entrance hall. But at the same time I was overawed and rather intimidated by the physical size and space of the building. It is no wonder that children and adults sometimes refer to museums as off-putting places that remind them of dusty, hushed and sombre cathedrals. Perhaps the environment itself triggers a set of sociocultural norms dictating our behaviour in such places. We expect ourselves and our pupils to behave in a reverent and subdued way. This is rarely conducive to learning. Far better to hear the chatter of pupils talking about what they see and experience and whoops of delight as they try or discover something new.

Science museums and galleries today have invested a great deal of effort in designing exhibits that appeal and attract. Many, such as Techniquest and Eureka, use bright primary colours and place buttons and levers at child height to attract attention and remove barriers to interaction. The whole sense is one of a comfortable, safe and friendly environment in which reluctance to act and engage and reticence about 'having a go' are dispelled.

Museums provide a physical space in which artefacts, specimens and exhibits are related to themes and aspects important to understanding science and hard to replicate in the classroom. Exhibits and the way they are presented put science and technology firmly into social, industrial and historical contexts. As such, they make a welcome contrast to the more abstract and de-contextualised learning that unfortunately characterises much of school science.

An object lesson in learning in science

Before considering research evidence that might help teachers to capitalise on museum visits, it is worth looking at an aspect of museum work that makes an important contribution to scientific experience and learning at any age. The handling of specimens and manufactured objects (artefacts, as many museum educators call them) has been a tradition in museum education in the UK for some considerable time. 'The object lesson' became a paradigm of museum education in the early twentieth century. Pupils were allowed to touch and often told to describe and draw a range of unusual specimens and objects, often to enhance the curriculum areas of nature study, art and English.

Looking at objects in glass cases might raise questions about them but sight is a rather distant sense and does not open up possibilities that handling provides. Handling should stimulate questions and speculation, e.g. about where the object came from, what it is composed of, how it relates to other objects or to the environment. Figure 8.3 shows how lines of questioning about an object, in this case a fossil ammonite, might be developed.

Handling invites the pupil to explore with a degree of freedom using a number of senses. Handling enables holistic learning. Hooper-Greenhill (1991) defines holistic learning as: 'to know things in relation, to understand how parts relate to the whole' (p. 102). In this way the fossil ammonite is questioned in terms of its possible relationship to other animals and plants, to the environment in which it lived and to the processes through which it was fossilised.

In one recently opened museum, the 'Wildwalk' in @Bristol, there is an opportunity to handle and question specimens through macroscopic and

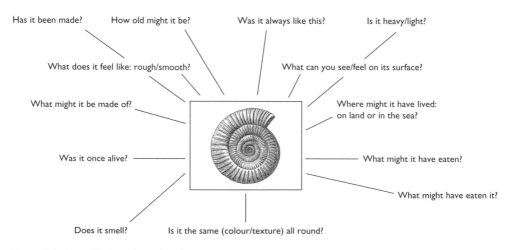

Figure 8.3 Questioning objects and specimens.

microscopic observation within a sequence explaining the evolution of life on earth. Object handling thus contributes to a more holistic learning experience where the 'object lesson' plays a part in a larger experience of learning about evolution.

Sight can be a dominant sense and of course for some pupils it may be impaired. Removing it and challenging pupils to guess or work out what an object might be is often a worthwhile experience. A common experience at museums and HOCGs is for pupils to work out what objects might be from touch or smell. At Eureka, pupils are encouraged to feel the shape, texture and temperature of common kitchen utensils placed inside kitchen drawers. In some interpretative centres pupils might be asked to lift a flap and to feel the skin of an animal and work out what it might be.

In some galleries, e.g. 'Things' at Eureka, objects are fixed to open displays so that they can be touched and felt even though they cannot be removed. This provides a sort of half-way house but can end up being a frustrating experience for some pupils. In the Natural History Museum in London the handling of some real specimens in the museum is also linked to a virtual version on a website called 'Quest' (see Resources box). The Quest website has been designed more as a challenge for pupils and as a taster of what can be done rather than as a replacement for handling real objects. A number of on-line tools are available to carry out virtual explorations of objects. In the example shown in Figure 8.4, a sample of 'brain coral' is shown with a section that has been magnified to give some idea of the surface structure that would be visible with a magnifying glass.

Finally, it is worth noting that many museums provide an outreach service so that objects, specimens and experiments can be borrowed from the museum and used in school to enhance science lessons. Activities from Techniquest come in kit form with instructions and supporting materials for teachers. These relate to concept areas such as light and colour, forces or more specific themes and topics such as animal skulls.

How pupils learn at museums: what research has to tell us

Over the last three decades there has been a substantial amount of research carried out in museums and HOCGs. Although much of this has been concerned with evaluating the impact of museum, gallery and exhibit design on the behaviour of a range of visitors, there is a significant amount that we now know about how pupils interact and learn. The intention here is to give a very brief overview of some important findings for teachers and other professionals to

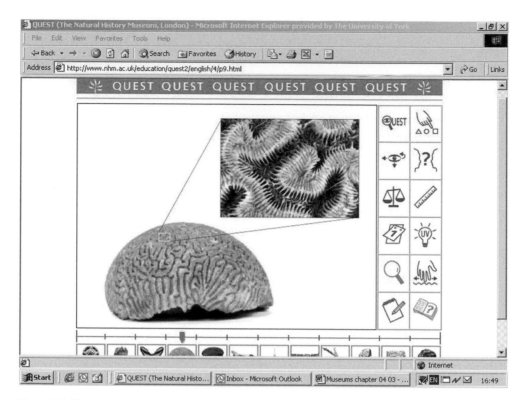

Figure 8.4 The virtual environment used to investigate objects on the 'Quest' web pages of the Natural History Museum's website.

consider. There has been a number of succinct but quite detailed reviews of the literature on museum research and the reader is referred to these for a fuller treatment (see McManus, 1992; Dierking and Falk, 1994; Rennie and McClafferty, 1996).

Research is considered here in three main areas:

1   research on the impact of museum experiences on learners;
2   research on the ways in which school-aged pupils behave and converse;
3   research that examines the level of interaction at HOCGs.

Impact of the museum experience

The number of research studies providing evidence of improved knowledge and understanding of science following visits to museums or HOCGs is limited. However, Dierking and Falk (1994) quote studies that have detected improved understanding of concepts as measured on pre- and post-tests in physics following museum visits. It is far more common, however, to find studies in research reviews (e.g. Rennie and McClafferty, 1996) showing that museum experiences have a major impact on pupils' attitudes to learning science. In their substantive review of research in science centres, Rennie and McClafferty include a quote that sums up the position of many researchers: 'the key question is not: do people learn science from a visit to a science centre?, but, do science centres help people to develop a more positive relationship with science?' (p. 83).

Visits to science museums and HOCGs can have a deep and long-lasting effect. Stevenson (1991) studied visitors to the Science Museum in London and particularly to its hands-on gallery 'Launchpad'. Family groups were observed interacting at the museum and then questioned as to what they could remember 2 weeks and then 6 months later. Stevenson found a surprising level of detail in the memories of both adults and children with a substantial number of responses relating to the science ideas that exhibits had dealt with.

Learners' behaviours and conversations

Much of what is known about the learning behaviours exhibited by children when they visit museums comes from studies of family groups. Less is known about the nature of interaction and conversation amongst school groups though this is an area that is now receiving some attention. We know that family groups often behave in quite similar ways in a number of different types of museums and galleries. The agendas for family visits are often set by parents according to their interests or what they perceive the interests of their children to be. Adults in family groups generally interact less in the physical sense, probably because they are more likely to have adopted a 'don't touch' mode of working (Dieking and Falk, 1994). Stevenson (1991) compared groups containing children with adult-only groups interacting in the 'Launchpad' gallery at the Science Museum in London and found that groups containing children engaged in more 'play' with interactive exhibits but were less likely to read text and instructions unless prompted to do so by an adult. Interestingly, Stevenson also found that the duration of conversations and the time that groups spent interacting with exhibits declined in the order:

family groups > children-only groups > teacher–pupil groups.

This supports the idea that teachers may actually discourage sustained interaction and dialogue with obvious consequences on the quality and quantity of learning that occurs.

More recently, analysis of conversations of family and teacher–pupil groups at the Natural History Museum in London showed little differences between the two groups in the quality of conversations about preserved specimens. Pupil–teacher groups did, however, make more emotive comments and engage in more conversations about body parts (Tunnicliffe *et al.*, 1997). The authors go on to criticise teachers accompanying school parties, claiming that they must take more responsibility for developing the educational potential of visits.

Levels of interaction

The problem with much research on the outcomes, i.e. 'learning' that may or may not come from 'interaction' with exhibits, is that these outcomes are typically judged against a number of indicator behaviours that are predetermined for each exhibit. This may lead to a checklist approach that tends to ignore the individualistic nature of learning and hence the role of the experience in interacting with an individual's existing knowledge in the construction of new meanings and understandings (i.e. it is not sympathetic with the 'constructivist' concept of learning mentioned earlier in this chapter).

Recently, Barriault (1999) has produced an analytical framework, derived from observing interactions at two centres in the UK and Canada. This has resulted in the grouping of behaviours into three levels according to her perception of the 'depth' of learning that occurs. Barriault's framework is reproduced as Table 8.1.

Initiation behaviours (doing, watching others engaging, information/assistance offered by others) all help school pupils feel safe and help them take the first steps to a more meaningful learning experience. They allow pupils to 'test the waters'. Many HOCGs now use 'explainers' to help pupils take these first steps. The net outcome of transition behaviours is a more committed and motivated individual able to progress to a higher degree of thought through investigation

Table 8.1 Learning behaviours and depth of learning at hands-on exhibits

Learning behaviour	Depth of learning
Doing the activity Spending time watching others engaging in the activity Information or assistance offered by staff or other pupils	Initiation behaviours
Repeating the activity Expressing positive emotional response in reaction to engaging in activity	Transition behaviours
Referring to past experiences while engaging in activity Seeking and sharing information Engaged and involved: testing variables, making comparisons, using information gained from activity	Breakthrough behaviours

Source: adapted from Barriault, 1999, p. 2

and improved reflection on outcomes. The pupil feels comfortable and eager to engage further.

Each of the examples of breakthrough behaviours given by Barriault acknowledges the relevance of the activity and learning gained from it for the individual. Further interaction, including the testing out of variables, is an indicator of deeper learning as is the seeking and sharing of information from or with others.

Research, such as the few studies cited here, together with the contextual model of learning discussed earlier, help us to understand more about the ways in which pupils behave, converse and interact when they learn science at museums and HOCGs. These messages are developed in the next section in order to generate guidance that should help teachers and others maximise the potential for learning at museums and HOCGs.

Supporting and improving interaction

The role that the teacher and school can play in maximising what pupils get from a visit to a museum or HOCG is part of what I call the 'experiential sandwich'. The school and teacher provide the bread and the visit the filling. The information in the box on the following page sets out what the teacher might usefully do before, during and after a visit.

The teacher must first decide if she/he wants the experience of a visit to be anything more than just a fun day out – not that there is anything wrong in this. If the visit is to contribute meaningfully to pupils' learning of science within the curriculum framework of the school then, as in most teaching, there is no easy shortcut to thorough preparation for pupils' learning. One way of enhancing learning from the visit is to consider the support that should be provided. Support can be provided through questions or mini-trails that prompt pupils' interaction and so encourage the sorts of transition and breakthrough behaviours described by Barriault. It may be appropriate and useful to share these with adult helpers who will accompany the trip. Ways of doing this have been described by Braund (2000) but materials to help teachers do this also feature in guidance notes issued for teachers and parents by many museums and HOCGs.

There is a fine line between giving enough prompts and guidance and a 'death by worksheets'. We have to remember that the main contribution that museums and HOCGs make to learning science is that they engender positive attitudes to learning science and hopefully make the pupil want to know more. They are

Getting the most from your visit to a museum or hands-on centre

Before you go:

■ Think about the purpose of your visit and its position in your scheme of work. Is the visit to give general experience and stimulation as an introduction to the topic? Is it to support specific learning of certain concepts? Is it to consolidate teaching that has already taken place?

■ Visit the museum, or if you can't, visit its website or talk with someone who has been before.

■ Plan for what scientific concepts and skills should be met before the visit and what should be followed-up back at school.

■ Decide what part of the exhibition or what exhibits will form the focus for learning and/or whether your pupils need to follow a set route or sequence.

■ Find out what facilities and services the museum offers, e.g. whether the museum has 'explainers' to assist pupils, a classroom where work can be followed-up or workshop activities led by the museum's education service. Decide how you will use these services.

■ Find out what additional adult support is available and can be provided for the visit, e.g. parents, student teachers, etc.

■ Decide how adults might be informed and supported so that they can offer help to pupils at the museum, e.g. devise prompt sheets or use ones provided by the museum.

At the museum:

■ Provide some time and space for pupils to orientate themselves and 'play'. This allows the class to have some free exploration time and to dissipate some of their initial 'energy'.

■ Tell the class what you expect them to do. It is usually better for pupils to work in pairs or small groups so that social interaction at exhibits can occur.

■ You may want to offer some limited guidance or prompts, e.g. by way of a 'trail card'. Record experiences, e.g. by taking digital photographs or making a video.

Following your visit:

■ Ask pupils to tell you what they remembered most from their visit. What were they impressed by? What new things did they learn?

■ Allow pupils to develop their learning by broadcasting their experiences to others. You could ask them to do this by preparing and sharing posters and displays or by giving a presentation.

■ Use activities and practical tasks that enhance and develop the learning experiences at the museum. Avoid trying to replicate what they did at the museum.

■ Refer back to experiences at the museum, not only in the topic but in future lessons as well. This helps pupils to value the experience and to consolidate learning by integrating gains from the informal situation in the museum with the more formal learning in school.

categorically different places to schools and so to use school strategies such as filling in worksheets or didactic teaching in front of exhibits in an unthinking and unsympathetic way denigrates the educational potential and defeats the prime objective of the visit.

Conclusion

In this chapter I have explored the potential of museums and HOCGs for pupils learning science. We have considered the ways in which the places themselves and interactions in them, physical, inter-personal and emotional, can contribute to and sometimes hinder outcomes. The museums sector as a whole and provision for schools continue to expand. The sector is a key player in the leisure and tourism industry. Museums have roles to play as academic institutions and in the conservation and preservation of historic and scientifically important artefacts. Sometimes these different roles compete, but the emphasis of responsibility has shifted significantly in the last few years towards that of education and learning. The government agency for museums archives and galleries called *re:*source (see Resources box) has recently issued a framework called *Inspiring Learning For All* that should go some way to helping providers plan and evaluate the contributions that they can and should make to learning.

Museums and HOCGs are also key players in the continuing professional development and initial training of teachers. Many provide workshops, either in-house or through outreach programmes, that address gaps in teachers' subject knowledge as well as providing ideas for teaching activities and investigative work. Teachers can glean useful and new ideas from visits to museums. The work that goes on in communicating often complex science to a mass audience acts as a source of ideas that the teacher can adapt for her/his classroom. We must remember, however, just as the museum should not replicate the classroom nor should the classroom seek to replicate the museum. Museums and HOCGs are a key resource and should be used more, especially by secondary schools. If the learning experience is properly planned and supported as part of an appetising experiential 'sandwich' then it represents high quality learning and value for money. Used in this way, visits make major contributions to pupils' motivation and so to their wider desire to learn more science. If results in tests and examinations is the issue, and unfortunately it often is, then the experiences gained will surely play a part. After all, motivated and interested learners tend to do well in school.

References

Barriault, C., 1999, 'The science center learning experience: a visitor-based framework', *The Informal Learning Review*, Informal Learning Experiences Inc. http://www.informallearning.com/archive/1999-0304-c.htm

Braund, M. R., 2000, 'Enrichment beyond the classroom', *Child Education*, 77(7), 58–9.

Dierking, L. D. and Falk, J. H., 1994, 'Family behaviour in informal science settings: a review of research', *Science Education*, 78(1), 57–72.

Driver, R., Squires, A., Rushworth, P. and Wood-Robinson, V., 1994, *Making Sense of Secondary Science: Research into Children's Ideas*, London: Routledge.

Falk, J. H. and Dierking, L. D., 2000, *Learning from Museums*, Walnut Creek, CA: AltaMira Press.

Hooper-Greenhill, E., 1991, *Museum and Gallery Education*, London: Leicester University Press.

McManus, P. M., 1992, 'Topics in museums and science education', *Studies in Science Education*, 21, 160–82.

Rennie, L. J. and McClafferty, T. P., 1996, 'Science centres and science learning', *Studies in Science Education*, 27, 53–98.

Stevenson, J., 1991, 'The long term impact of interactive exhibits', *International Journal of Science Education*, 13(5), 521–31.

Tunnicliffe, S. D., Lucas, A. M. and Osborne, J., 1997, 'School visits to zoos and museums: a missed educational opportunity?', *International Journal of Science Education*, 19(9), 1039–56.

Resources

Museums and HOCGs mentioned in this chapter

Explore@Bristol (the science centre is part of a group of visitor attractions that include an Imax cinema and 'Wildwalk' collectively known as @Bristol) Anchor Road, Harbourside Bristol BS1 5DB. www.at-bristol.org

Techniquest Stuart Street, Cardiff CF1 6BW. www.techniquest.org

Eureka! The Museum for Children, Discovery Road, Halifax HX1 2NE. www.eureka.org.uk

The Science Museum (contains the hands-on gallery 'Launchpad') Exhibition Road, South Kensington, London SW7 2DD. www.sciencemuseum.org.uk The Science Museum in London is one of a family of museums that includes the Museum of Photography in Bradford and the National Railway Museum in York

York Castle Museum, Eye of York, York YO1 9RY. www.yorkcastlemuseum.org.uk

The Natural History Museum, Cromwell Road, London SW7 5BD. www.nhm.ac.uk

See also www.nhm.ac.uk/education/quest2. This gives access to the 'virtual handling' activity referred to on pages 121–2.

Museum organisations and gateway sites

re:source www.resource.gov.uk This is the website of the Council for Museums, Archives and Libraries. Updates and documents on learning in museums including *Inspiring Learning for All* (2003) can be downloaded from the site.

ECSITE-UK www.ecsite-uk.net This site represents over 80 HOCGs and museums in the UK and provides a 'gateway' to their websites.

The Campaign for Learning in Museums www.clmg.org.uk An organisation set up by leading museum professionals. Deals with the latest debates and news on learning developments in the UK.

Chapter 9

Learning science at industrial sites

Joy Parvin and Miranda Stephenson

Overview

The chapter is divided into three sections. The first section looks at the general reasons why industrial companies host visits from students and younger pupils at their sites. Some hints are given to help open the company doors to teachers and their classes. The second section focuses on an in-depth primary school case study, *Children Challenging Industry*. The final section looks at the benefits of taking older students out into industry. The principles and practicalities described in the final section are equally applicable to primary school visits.

The industrial perspective

Industry and education

In the UK there is a long history of support from the manufacturing industry for science education in schools. This chapter will look at the general principles concerned with taking parties of school pupils and students out into industry, considering the benefits and the practicalities for doing so. Before delving into the details, it is helpful to understand a little about how industry operates. This will give some useful background information to those new to taking young people out to a manufacturing site, and ammunition to those trying to persuade companies new to the idea of opening their doors.

So what is happening in the UK? The following summary draws on three studies of industry-education practice conducted by the Chemical Industry Education Centre (CIEC) and commissioned by three organisations representing various sectors of manufacturing industry. In each case, the commissioning body was keen to discover what their members were doing to support science education in schools and colleges (see Stephenson and Wingfield, 1998a; Hubbard and Stephenson, 2000; and Stephenson and Wingfield, 1998b for full details).

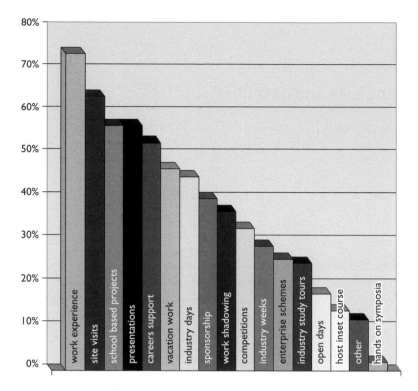

Figure 9.1 Educational activities supported by the chemical industry in 1999.

Evidence has suggested that significant numbers of sites in each of the three sectors of chemical manufacturing (chemicals, pharmaceuticals and polymers) are supportive of schools/college work. The range of activities they provide is shown in Figure 9.1.

Figure 9.1 shows that site visits are one of the more popular activities provided by industry. However, companies tend to impose constraints on those they will let through the gates. Geography, group size and age-range are three critical factors that teachers need to overcome. These will be dealt with later in this section. Let us look first at why companies are involved at all with science education.

Reasons for industrial support

The three main reasons are:

- recruitment
- contributing to the community
- enhancing reputation.

Recruitment

The chemical and pharmaceutical industries are particularly good at engaging with school students. The polymer industry at the time of its audit in 1998 was concerned with the challenges of recruitment as it was beginning to recognise a serious shortage of good quality recruits to the industry (Stephenson and Wingfield, 1998a; Hubbard and Stephenson, 2000). The study showed that the polymer industry was unfamiliar to students and consequently many failed to consider the sector as a career option. The students questioned in the study had invariably stumbled into the industry accidentally rather than as a considered choice.

The chemical sector also complained that students of insufficiently high quality were being attracted to it. At a time when it was concerned to increase innovation and competitiveness this was seen to be a serious problem. The pharmaceutical industry alone appears to have the 'right' image with young people and is therefore able to attract sufficient recruits of the desired quality.

Contributing to the community

Increasingly, manufacturing industries are taking their role in their immediate community more seriously. Thus programmes such as Responsible Care (see Resource box), which is a requirement for membership of the Chemical Industries Association, demand that companies take a proactive interest in supporting and reporting to their community. Schools are seen as part of this community work, and thus companies will often be sympathetic to requests from local schools for assistance. This can be quite broad, from providing football strips to refurbishing laboratories. It is worthwhile remembering, however, that for the majority of company sites, the budget for schools will come out of their community budget and so it tends to be small. It may, however, be large enough to cover the costs of hiring a coach to bring the school party to the site, which is often too great a cost for school budgets. A more significant contribution by industry is the time and effort a company is prepared to make in tailoring a visit by a school/college party to meet the curriculum and educational needs of the teacher and their students. Teachers should appreciate this, if they wish the visit to be a success.

Enhancing reputation

The chemical sector conducts an annual survey of society's perception of them compared with other industrial sectors (MORI, 2003). This survey shows that the chemical sector has a poor reputation, being third from bottom, with tobacco and the nuclear industry being the only sectors below them. The pharmaceutical industry fairs much better. The polymer industry is not identified in the survey but acknowledges that its reputation is poor as it is largely associated with cheap products and litter.

A good reputation grows from familiarity, trust and perception of safety. The more dangerous an industrial sector is considered to be, then the harder it has to work to show that it operates responsibly and safely. Educational activity is seen as a route to increasing young people and their teachers' familiarity with the industry, what it does, how it operates and the contribution it makes to society and the economy. When the relationship has been sustained over a period of time, then trust is established which in turn leads to a better reputation for the company involved, and potentially for the industry as a whole. Thus, understanding these three driving components to reputation can help to negotiate your way into a company.

Constraints applied by industry

Geography

Companies are now tending to focus on schools in their immediate locality. This can make it very difficult for schools and colleges in rural or urban regions to find a suitable company to visit. Schools prefer companies closer to home to save time and expense. So, although chemical and pharmaceutical companies may be hard to find, it is possible to make use of other types of manufacturing industries such as those found on local business parks and industrial estates. Teachers from the Salters Advanced Chemical course (Burton *et al.*, 2000), an advanced level course which recommends visits to industrial sites that make use of chemistry, use the following range of industrial sectors for their site visits:

- agrochemical/agricultural materials
- breweries
- construction and allied industry
- cosmetic industry
- fine/speciality chemicals
- paints and resins
- paper industry
- pharmaceuticals
- polymer industry
- steel industry
- utility industries.

Selecting a site to visit can be the hardest challenge. There are various organisations and websites that can help (see Resources box).

Many teachers strike lucky by finding a company through the parents of students or the partners of colleagues. These personal contacts are most important, as they give direct access to the company and via a person who has good reason to want the tour to be successful.

Group size

There is no evidence that suggests large companies are more open to site visits than smaller companies. However, small companies, that is those with less than 70 employees, tend to prefer small groups. In the main, companies that are open to take visits try to accommodate the teachers' needs. Thus if they cannot accommodate a full class of 30, they will often be prepared to have the class visit on two separate occasions in groups of 15. Although this makes for a little extra work, if the company is meeting all the other requirements, it is probably worth doing.

Age group

Most companies are now open to taking groups from both primary and secondary schools. The next section, that describes the Children Challenging Industry project, gives detailed accounts of successful visits by primary-aged children to industry. Sometimes companies plea that they only have insurance to cover visits from students aged 14 and above because of the nature of the work that goes on at the site. There is no evidence to suggest that this has been imposed on the site by insurance companies, as many companies that are considered to be high risk sites (COMAH sites), for all the reasons expressed above, nevertheless open up their site to primary schools, as Figure 9.2 clearly shows.

Occasionally a company will impose the need to keep the pupils or students on a coach to go around the site – for safety reasons, but one of the studies in the next section shows how a tour from a coach can be made very enjoyable and informative.

The next two sections show that a properly planned and prepared visit can be of enormous benefit to students and pupils.

So it is worth overcoming the initial obstacles and taking young people out to see science in action. But remember, once a good relationship with a site has

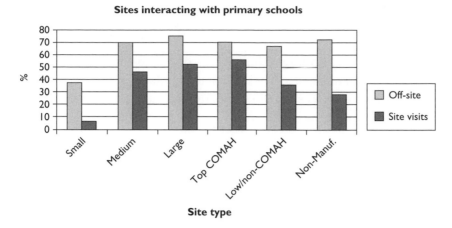

Figure 9.2 Data provided by the Reputation Advisory Group, Chemical Industries Association.

been established it is worth cultivating by giving constructive feedback and, of course, thanks. The next section is concerned with the Children Challenging Industry programme, a national scheme. The final section examines site visits for older students. These two sections give teachers and those in industry the opportunity to consider the principles of site visits across the full age range.

A primary science–industry project: Children Challenging Industry

Background to the project

Teacher confidence and knowledge has improved since the inception of the National Curriculum (Roberts, 2002). However, a great deal of support is still needed for teachers to feel wholly confident and competent to teach science, especially to the levels required of 10–11 year olds. In addition, industry–education links are sporadic in primary classrooms today. Few schools have a policy on industry links (Parvin, 1999), and the foci on numeracy, literacy and ICT training in recent years have put such links even more firmly at the bottom of the agenda.

Why are such links important? The industry's reasons for links with schools have been discussed in the previous section. For schools, the key reason for forging links and partnerships with industry is to show the relationship between classroom science and the 'real world'. As the worlds of the chemical industry and primary schools are very different, it is often difficult for these partnerships to become established, without the advice and support of an intermediary. Hence, the Children Challenging Industry (CCI) project was born.

The Children Challenging Industry project

The project, started in 1996, and still continuing in the north of England, resulted from collaboration between a small chemical company (Thomas Swan & Co.) and the Chemical Industry Education Centre (CIEC). The chemical industry, as a whole, has long-suffered a poor public opinion and perception and Tom Swan, company owner, wanted to inspire young children by demonstrating exciting science in action. The experience of CIEC, coupled with Tom Swan's enthusiasm and company sponsorship, culminated in a highly successful model for industry–education links, Children Challenging Industry (CCI). The aims of the project are:

- to improve primary school pupils' perception of the science-based manufacturing industry and its relationship with science;
- to enthuse children for science;
- to provide in-service training for teachers in aspects of the National Curriculum for science, focusing particularly on investigative science.

These aims are achieved by individual teachers and schools, by groups of schools with a common interest, or on a regional basis. In the CCI model, a trainer works in partnership with schools and companies in a designated region. Trainers have a strong background in teaching and/or training in primary science, and the ability to establish effective links with organisations that support industry links with schools (such as Business–Education Partnerships).

Each of the three programme elements shown in Table 9.1 will now be expanded upon in turn, to establish the principles of CCI.

Table 9.1 Elements of the Children Challenging Industry programme for schools taking part

Programme element	For teachers	For pupils
1. Training session for whole school staff	60–90 minutes on industry-linked science investigations for 4–11 year olds	
2. Up to 3½ days of science investigations (1 per week) set within an industrial context	Where possible, these sessions are given by an advisory teacher, thus providing classroom-based training for 1–2 teachers in each school	A class of 7–11 year old pupils carries out science investigations within an industrial context
3. An industrial visit	The visit closely links with the classroom investigations	

Training session for the whole school staff

When trying to establish a way of working in a primary school, in which all teachers usually have responsibility for teaching the science curriculum, it is important that the whole staff have access to the information. This training session therefore aims to introduce all the staff to the idea of teaching science through industrial contexts, or to further develop or enhance on-going links of this nature.

Classroom investigations

The training in classroom investigations has proved to be an invaluable tool in supporting teachers in relation to the National Curriculum for Science, and investigative aspects in particular. Until 2003, the emphasis of end of Key Stage 2 tests was on the 'knowledge' components of the science curriculum, and not on investigational skills and processes. Therefore, investigational activities have been welcomed in the CCI project by teachers and pupils alike as refreshing and motivating. With the test changes implemented in 2003 (DfES, 2002) CCI has proved increasingly popular, as teachers look for additional support in teaching investigational skills such as planning, predicting, measuring and evaluating data.

Many schools take part in the CCI project primarily for the science support. The industry link is an added bonus. However, once the class has completed its project work, including the site visit, the majority of teachers are keen to repeat and develop the industry link with their class, and other classes, as the benefits of such a link becomes clear (these will be described later).

Several sets of classroom investigations are available for teachers to choose from when taking part in CCI. These sets, or 'topics', are characterised by:

- an industrial storyline;
- practical hands-on approach to science;
- simple equipment available in primary schools (or collectable by the pupils, such as plastic bottles, drinks cans);
- detailed guidance for the teacher on how to carry out each investigation;
- a wide range of suggestions on how pupils can discuss and record their investigations.

One example of a topic, and its links with industry, will be described. This topic is 'Water for Industry', and consists of a series of five science investigations. Through these investigations, the industrial storyline unfolds, and the children's investigational skills are developed. Most manufacturing sites use water for heating and cooling, and this forms the context for this topic. Following a fictitious letter from industry, asking pupils to investigate some problems that the company are having, pupils carry out a series of investigations, gradually developing their investigative skills and ability to work as part of a team (and thus modelling the way in which industrial teams work together). These investigations include: selecting the most appropriate material for a water pipeline, exploring a range of sealants to join sections of pipeline, filtering a 'muddy' water sample, and learning about heat exchange as a method of cooling.

The importance of these investigations to industry can be further demonstrated by obtaining additional materials from local companies. Company personnel can be asked to provide photographs, video footage of industrial processes and samples of kit demonstrating aspects of their work linked to the school topic. For example, photographs of scientists at work in the laboratory, ideally carrying out tasks similar to those of the pupils, such as heating, cooling, mixing and filtering. The images and samples should show pupils that the equipment used by professional scientists is not too dissimilar to their own. Highly technical equipment is also used in industry, but this is mystifying to the pupils, and can develop pupils' perception that science is either very difficult or magical. Similarly, photographs of process equipment opened for cleaning (such as huge mixing vessels, filters, cooling equipment) can demonstrate laboratory equipment scaled-up. Many companies have aerial photographs of their sites, and these can give pupils an idea of the size of the site, and how the land is used for many different functions such as: office space, different production areas, large storage tanks (known as 'tank farms'), laboratories, heat and power production and water treatment.

Samples from the site, such as small pieces of equipment, are also useful when carrying out classroom activities. For example, a company could make a small section of pipeline containing three to four different methods of joining sections of pipe together, to follow on from the sealants activity described above. A range of filters used on-site, or samples of products in small jars can be provided. Intermediate products are a revelation to pupils who think a company puts ingredients (or raw materials) in at one end and gets a finished product out at the other end. The idea that a company might make lots of 'in-between' products for a wide range of end-products is fascinating to them. For example, one company describes its product to children as 'an important ingredient that goes on to be used in the glue at the end of a Mars bar wrapper'. Companies manufacturing intermediate chemicals and materials (chemical, pharmaceutical, polymer companies among them) are common across the UK, and provide a wonderful science link for primary-aged pupils.

Site visits

Ideally, a school working through this science–industry project, would follow the classroom investigations with an industrial visit. The advantages of culminating the programme with the site visit are that the children go to the company with some prior knowledge of the company and what it does. Children are curious to find out more about how their classroom investigations relate to the company's work and they are confident enough to ask questions of the company personnel (based on their own recently acquired knowledge). The company personnel are always impressed and surprised by the children's knowledge and their mature level of questioning.

The occurrence and success of the visit will depend largely on enthusiasm from both the company and the school, and on good forward planning. In addition, site visits are most successful when company personnel have received training on how to carry out a 'tailored' visit for primary-aged children.

Once trained on effective language, curriculum requirements, interactive talks, appropriate and relevant areas of the site, and specific links with classroom topics, the company plans their tour – in conjunction with their educational partner. The duration of the tour is generally 2 hours, and engages pupils in as many of the following as possible:

- A brief introduction to the company – visual and interactive.
- A tour of one production area – meeting appropriate people, who use visual aids to demonstrate what is taking place in closed vessels.
- A visit to a laboratory – to talk to scientists and see demonstrations of scientific testing (such as fading tests for dyed fabric, drying tests for paints, mixing, filtration, cooling, etc.).
- A visit to the control room – to see the computer control of production.
- A chance to meet professional engineers.
- A visit to the warehouse (fork-lift truck drivers prove to be popular, next to scientists).
- A question and answer session with key personnel (e.g. from a scientific/technical background).

Site visits can be wide in scope or remain simple, depending on what resources a company wants to commit to the visit. One particular series of teaching units, *Site-Seeing* (Parvin, 1995) was developed in conjunction with ExxonMobil in Fife and provides an interesting example of what can be achieved by a company that actively wants to promote educational links with its primary schools. The hazards associated with the production area are such that pupils cannot walk freely around the site. However, this did not deter ExxonMobil management, or the CIEC team. The activities were devised so that pupils tour the perimeter of the main production area on a coach. They have a variety of pre-determined stopping points, at which the tour guide helps pupils locate specific areas of interest, and mark them on drawings or maps of the site on their clipboards. For example, in the safety topic, pupils look for people wearing different types of safety clothing and discuss why they are being worn. They also study safety signs, emergency showers, lifebelts near the pond, etc. The pupils get off the coach at designated safe points, e.g. control room, warehouse, workshop (depending on the focus of their visit). In addition, they carry out activities in the Training Centre, such as dressing in safety clothing required for specific jobs, such as 'working at height'. They sort a range of safety gloves according to the use and properties of the materials from which the gloves are made.

Research into the project outcomes

Large quantities of data have been, and continue to be, collected from teachers and pupils, regarding changes to their perceptions of science–industry links as a result of participating in the CCI project. The foci of the research have remained the same and are to ascertain whether the project aims have been, and continue to be met; whether the CCI project has any long-lasting impact on teachers and pupils, and what pupils' and teachers' current views of science and industry are. Data have been collected in the ways and for the purposes stated in Table 9.2.

During the 3-year pilot of CCI, data were collected from 44 teachers and over 1,300 pupils in a northern region of the UK. The longitudinal study involved eight teachers and 89 pupils from this region, 4–6 years after their initial involvement. Data are gathered in all current CCI regions, using questionnaires

Table 9.2 CCI research purposes and methods

Period of data collection	Method	Purpose
1996–98	Pre- and post-project interviews and questionnaires	To ascertain whether teachers' and pupils' views of science and its relationship with the chemical industry changed as a result of project involvement
2002	Interviews and questionnaires	To determine any long-lasting impact, and current views held by teachers and pupils of science and its relationship with the chemical industry
2000–to date	Pre- and post-project questionnaires	To ensure project aims continue to be met, and to inform programme developments and improvements

shortened from the pilot versions. This provides data from about 100 teachers and 400 pupils each year.

At the time of writing, data from both the longitudinal study and the current regions to date are still undergoing analysis. It is, however, possible to refer to some of the early findings from these studies, but unless otherwise stated, the discussion below relates to the findings from the pilot study.

Data collected in both the pilot phase and current regions (2000–2003) suggest that the majority of 9–11 year olds perceive manufacturing as taking place in large mills or warehouses with lots of chimneys (see Figure 9.3). Inside it is hot, dark, noisy, and has production lines, ovens, furnaces, and lots of people and machines. The people who work there do predominantly manual jobs, such as operating machinery, and pouring, heating and mixing raw materials. Science and scientists play no part in the process.

Pupils often get their ideas from television, family, and passing industrial sites, and school was rarely mentioned as a source of information about industry. This was supported by the teachers' descriptions of their industrial links. Only 12 per cent linked industry to their science teaching, and 41 per cent linked

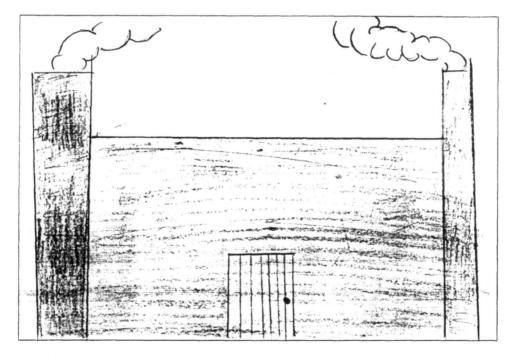

Figure 9.3 A typical 10 year old's impression of the chemical industry.

industry with history (mostly when teaching about the Victorian era, and the Industrial Revolution) and 'pollution' via the geography curriculum. However, this is not surprising when one takes into account the fact that 85 per cent of teachers in the pilot study (84 per cent in current regions) had no experience of working in industry, and half the teachers were not confident enough to describe the chemical industry in detail, other than to say 'it makes things'.

Therefore, pupils describing modern industry had little up-to-date information from school on which to base their analyses.

The emerging picture is somewhat better in the current CCI regions. The pupils' initial description of industry is still quite depressing, but they do not perceive it as being a dark and dirty environment, as the pupils in the pilot study did. This may be helped by the increased numbers of teachers who now describe science–industry links prior to involvement in CCI (38 per cent in one current CCI region, compared with 9 per cent in the pilot study), and by the lower number of teachers linking industry with 'pollution' (10 per cent in the same current region, compared with 23 per cent in the pilot study). However, a high percentage of teachers continue to teach about industry through history topics, and particularly the Victorian era (55 per cent and 40 per cent, respectively). Although it is clearly important to teach pupils about the history of our manufacturing industry, it is also important to teach them about how industry has changed, becoming less polluting, and a safer place to work. This has clearly not been happening in the past.

So, how do pupils' perceptions of industry change, as a result of participating in CCI? First it should be recognised that all pupils expressed new ideas about industry (see Figure 9.4). These new ideas ranged from a completely different image of industry to the one originally held, to specific details, such as the size and scale of an industrial site. Measurement of the change of individual views was possible with 65 pupils. Most of these pupils (90 per cent) had altered their views and were better informed.

Overall, a more accurate awareness of industry was seen in the following areas:

- raw materials used;
- processes involved, and the number of processes per site;
- equipment used to carry out processes;
- general appearance of a chemical site;
- working environment;
- range of jobs carried out and their desirability, especially those requiring scientific and technical knowledge;

■ industry's involvement in scientific research ('testing').

Gains were found in these areas whether or not a pupil had been on a site visit. Greater changes were measured when pupils had visited a company which had modified their site visit to meet the needs of the pupils and their science curriculum. Cases where pupils were given a 'standard' site tour (in which pupils were given a simplified version of the tour offered to other visitors), resulted in little change of views and, indeed in some cases, reinforced the negative stereotype of industry. This provides evidence for the need to train companies to offer effective visits for pupils.

Did the project result in any changes to teachers' practice or perceptions of industry? Three-quarters of the teachers cited new knowledge about the chemical industry and, as with the pupils, this new knowledge ranged from providing a totally new image of industry to specific pieces of information about industrial jobs or processes. The outcomes that were most significant for teachers were those that related to their teaching. Sixty-four per cent of the teachers felt they had learned how to teach about industry, 40 per cent had learned about how to teach science more effectively, and 31 per cent had learned about using industrial contexts to teach science.

All of the teachers felt the pupils had responded positively to the classroom activities. Seventy per cent of the teachers described the motivation and enthusiasm with which the pupils responded. They could see that the real

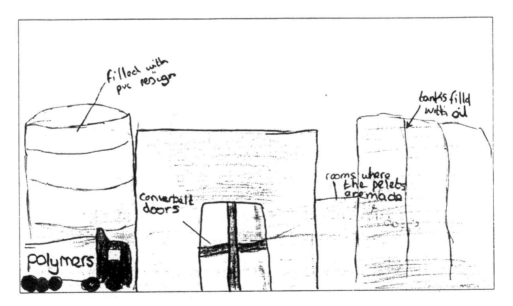

Figure 9.4 A typical 10 year old's post-project impression of the chemical industry.

industrial context and contact with industry provided pupils with a reason for doing science.

Teachers rated the industrial visit highly, with all those visiting industry feeling the experience had been valuable. The majority of those who were unable to visit industry, would have liked the opportunity to do so.

The emerging findings of the longitudinal study show that over half of the pupils involved in the pilot phase remembered doing the CCI project 5 years after its completion. Of these pupils, the dominant memory of the classroom activities was that they were *actively engaged* in science. Of them, 91 per cent remembered that the lessons had been either 'quite' or 'very' interesting and 61 per cent remembered the site visit in some way. The language used to describe the visit was very similar to that used 5 years previously. This suggests that the pupils' knowledge of the companies they had visited, and the scientific processes within, had not been further developed since the primary school input.

Almost all pupils saw links between science and industry, with 53 per cent stating that industry is based on scientific knowledge, investigation and/or technologies. Only one pupil responded negatively, commenting about science and industry producing pollution. Half of the pupils felt positive about the impact of industry on their lives, in relation to (in descending order): the products, the improved quality of life that industry offers, and the jobs that are available within the industry.

Pupils had participated in industry-link activities in their secondary school curriculum to varying degrees. The analysis has yet to determine any links between the pupils' current attitudes to industry and the number/type of secondary school links made. Similarly, comparisons are yet to be made with national MORI poll data (MORI, 2003), on teenagers' perceptions of industry.

The impact on teachers had also been positive, with seven out of eight teachers remembering the project impact, its value and the materials. The investigative approach to science was strengthened in several schools, despite the national imperatives of SATs. The context-led approach to science had been adopted throughout one school, and six out of eight schools continued to use the project materials with some of the classes.

The programme continues to be refined and developed as a result of the data collected and analysed, and it is heartening to see that the impact of the project is long-lasting for both teachers and pupils taking part. The data provide clear evidence for continuing to provide such valuable experiences to our pupils. It is to be hoped that the approach will expand geographically and become more commonplace for pupils throughout their secondary schooling. The next section will provide examples of how this can be achieved.

The case for secondary school visits to industry

Why take secondary students to industry? The benefits of a site visit include:

- providing a context for learning in the classroom;
- contributing to an improved scientific and technological literacy in society;
- helping to inform young people of the career opportunities in industry;
- demonstrating how companies are responding to issues such as sustainable development.

The Chemical Industry Education Centre encourages industry to take parties from secondary schools on carefully tailored visits to their sites. Publications such as *On Site* (Mapletoft, 1996) and *Educational Site Visits for Schools* (Ratcliff and Westin, 2000) (see Resources box) give detailed guidance on how to initiate and organise a visit to local industries.

In addition to these publications, courses such as *Salters-Nuffield Advanced Biology*, *Salters Advanced Chemistry* and *Salters Horners Advanced Physics* also provide thorough support in their course materials (see Resources box for details). The main reason for these visits is to emphasise to students how science is applied in industry. The Biology and Physics courses both require visits to industry as an assessed component of the course, whereas in the chemistry course teachers are encouraged to take the visit to enhance the not inconsiderable industrial component of the assessed course. Chapter 11 gives more details about the Salters Horners physics course.

Research at the University of Durham (Feasey, 1998) has shown that the negative perceptions children acquire of industry, referred to in the sections on primary school initiatives, are also present in trainee teachers. The research also found, however, that a minority is positive towards industry and science links and that a majority showed indifference or hostility. The perceptions of many trainee teachers were improved following well-designed visits to chemical companies. This is echoed in further research by Key (1998), who found that young people who have had a positive experience on one or more visit view manufacturing industry more favourably.

In the words of some Salters Advanced chemistry teachers, students gained from the experience of visiting a chemical site through:

'motivation'

'more confidence'

'improved problem-solving skills'

'meeting with industrial chemists improves the relevance of school chemistry'

'better understanding of large-scale production'

'insight into career opportunities (some students are reported to now work for the company they visited)'

'the visit provided an opportunity to do "real" investigations'.

Research has shown that a visit that has a proper purpose and is planned has a very positive influence on the opinions of students (Key, 1998). As a successful visit requires effort at the planning and execution stages, to justify this effort, both the company and school need to aim to generate as many positive outcomes as possible through the visit. A visit that does not have a clear purpose, or one that is poorly planned, is likely to reinforce the many negative images students have of industry.

One of the most effective site visits reported to CIEC was one in which a teacher spent some time on an industrial placement, courtesy of the local Business–Education Partnership. During his time at the company the teacher made a study of one of the chemical plants, in which a pharmaceutical, Ibuprofen, was being made. The chemistry was simple enough for his post-16 chemistry students to tackle. The teacher devised a series of mini-research exercises for the students to do prior to visiting the site. These included: yield calculations, a study of materials being used in the plant and process, processes such as crystallisation and purification, quality control and disposal of waste. During the visit the answers to the research questions emerged at various stages of the tour. The students were able to discuss their own work and compare this with the real solutions adopted by the company and thus both valued and enjoyed the visit greatly.

This short example illustrates the key features of an effective visit:

- The purpose was clear to all parties – the teacher, students and company personnel.
- The visit was carefully researched and planned.
- The students were actively engaged in gathering information and interacting with personnel they met.
- The knowledge the students acquired supported and enriched the knowledge they needed for their course.

It is not always possible for teachers to be released from school to experience an industrial placement. A preliminary visit to the company willing to host your party of school students is, however, very desirable. The preliminary visit should involve a tour of the plant for the teacher followed by a meeting with the person in the company responsible for organising the visit. The site map and some company literature are always useful for briefing the students, so should be requested at this meeting. Items for the meeting could include:

- Objectives of the visit.
- How the visit links with the curriculum, classroom work, and experience before and after the visit.
- Students' knowledge and level of understanding in science.
- Appropriate language to use with the students.
- The structure of the visit, site route and timings.
- Description of the site in terms of what it manufactures, emphasising links with consumer products if these are not obvious.
- Practicalities (health and safety, risk assessment and insurance), date and duration, transport, size and age of group, needs of any students with learning difficulties of physical disability, meeting venue, attire, refreshments, and, if appropriate, display materials.
- Publicity.

Once everything has been agreed, the students will need to be briefed about the company and the purpose of the visit. It is a good idea to prepare questions with the students prior to the visit to encourage them to talk to company personnel. Unlike primary-aged pupils, secondary school students are often awkward in these situations, but once the ice is broken they will happily engage in discussion with their tour guides.

The questions that the students might ask could be about: the company, the scientific process they are going to see or the products that are made, for example:

- What does the company make and where in the chain of manufacture does this product come in relation to consumer products (is it an intermediate or end-product)?
- Who does the company employ? (The students often want to know about job satisfaction, career routes, salaries!)
- Why the company is located where it is.
- Why the site is laid out the way it is (especially if they have gone to a chemical site, which can look fairly randomly organised).
- What are the raw materials being used, including issues to do with sustainability?
- What are the issues to do with marketing and packaging?

- What are the issues to do with health and safety on the site?
- What are the issues to do with the environment, again with reference to the company's sustainable development policy?
- What are the chemical reactors and pipelines made from?
- How is energy conserved on the site?
- How is science harnessed to the job in question?

Following the visit, the students may make use of their experience in a variety of ways including: discussions with other students, pooling their data into a common report, making presentations to the school governors or older students, and producing an information booklet about the company and processes they have seen.

Following the visit, companies appreciate feedback. This can be tackled in a variety of ways, for example: by the students holding discussions with company staff (chemists, managers, public relations personnel), making presentations, submitting reports from investigations or simply by sending letters stating what they have learnt and the aspects of the visit they enjoyed most. More creative feedback has included students writing articles for the company journal or for a local newspaper. A photograph of the event may enhance these.

Finally, it is important for the teacher and company representative in charge of the visit to debrief to ensure both parties felt their objectives were met, and to consider how the visit could be improved. More formal evaluation could involve either following a quality assurance process or using a student questionnaire. Once a relationship with a company is established it is important to nurture it in order to make the most of the effort they and you have put into the visit.

Summary

Whether a visit is to support primary-aged pupils or secondary students, if it is carefully prepared to support the curriculum in consultation with the company, the visit is likely to enrich and enhance young people's appreciation of science and its applications. The stages of setting up a visit include:

- Identifying a suitable company.
- Negotiation with personnel at the company to achieve a visit to meet the curriculum need.
- Working with the company, if necessary, to assist their staff tailor the visit to the interests and ability of the pupils or students.
- Proper levels of communication before and during the visit.

■ Good feedback, which both acknowledges the efforts made by the company and opens the way to future collaboration.

References

Burton, G. *et al.*, 2000, *Activities and Assessment Pack*, Salters Advanced Chemistry, London: Heinemann.

Department for Education and Skills, 2002, *Changes to Assessment 2003: Sample Materials for Key Stages 1 and 2*, London: Qualifications and Curriculum Authority.

Feasey, R., 1998, 'Science and industry links in initial teacher training', *Education in Science*, November, pp. 12–13.

Hubbard, E. M. J. S. and Stephenson, M., 2000, *The Contribution of the Pharmaceutical Industry to Science Education in Schools*, unpublished.

Key, M. B., 1998, *Student Perceptions of the Chemical Industry: Influences of Course Syllabi, Teachers, Firsthand Experience*, York: University of York.

Parvin, J., 1995, *Site-Seeing: Safety*, York: University of York.

Parvin, J., 1999, *Children Challenging Industry: The Research Report*, York: University of York.

Mapletoft, M., 1996, *On Site*, York: Chemical Industry Education Centre, University of York.

MORI, 2003, *Public Image of the Chemical Industry*, London: Chemical Industries Association.

Ratcliff, B. and Westin, U., 2000, *Educational Site Visits for Schools*, Brussels: European Chemical industry Council, CEFIC.

Roberts, G., 2002, *SET for Success: Final Report of Sir Gareth Roberts' Review*, treasury.gov.uk/documents/enterprise and productivity/research and enterprise/entres roberts.cfm

Stephenson, M. and Wingfield, W., 1998a, *The Contribution of the Chemical Industry to Science Education in Schools*, London: Chemical Industries Association.

Stephenson, M. and Wingfield, W., 1998b, *Polymer Education Provision for Post-16 Year Olds in Schools, Further Education, Higher Education and the Polymer Industry*, Telford: Polymer National Training Organisation.

Resources

Responsible Care is the chemical industry's commitment to continual improvement in health, safety and environmental performance and to openness in communication about its activities. Websites such as www.cia.org.uk and www.cefic.be provide further details about this programme.

Websites to help make links with industry:
www.SETNET.org.uk
www.STEMpartners.org
www.industrialtrust.org.uk
www.ciec.org.uk
www.psep.org

How to contact the Chemical Industry Education Centre: Chemical Industry Education Centre, Department of Chemistry, University of York, Heslington, York YO10 5DD. Tel.: 01904 4325232. Fax: 01904 434460. Email: ciec@york.ac.uk

About the Salters Advanced courses:

Reiss, M. *et al. Salters Nuffield Advanced Biology*, London: Heinemann.

'The exam specification and assessment', *Salters Horners Advanced Physics*, London: Heinemann.

Burton, G. *et al.*, 2000, 'Activities and assessment pack', *Salters Advanced Chemistry*, London: Heinemann.

Chapter 10

Chemistry trails

Peter Borrows

Overview

Pupils don't see chemistry as related to their 'real' world. A chemistry trail attempts to correct this impression by identifying a few examples of chemistry actually happening in the immediate environment of the school, preferably fairly simple chemistry that is accessible to pupils in Key Stages 3 and 4 – and some even to Key Stage 2. The development, use, presentation and format of chemistry trails is discussed and exemplified. Examples are given relating to various types of building materials, to metals and to air pollution, and further ideas suggested.

Origin and development

To most students and their teachers, chemistry is something which happens in test tubes in laboratories or in tangled masses of pipes in factories. They need to be shown that chemistry is not something remote but that it is going on all around us, all the time. Biologists and geologists are very familiar with this idea and field trips are an essential part of these subjects. More informally, many families happily spend Sunday afternoons, leaflet in hand, following a nature trail – a way-marked route through the countryside, with numbered stops where the leaflet points out matters of biological or geological interest. Geologists have also developed town trails, drawing attention to the wide variety of rocks used as building stones. Historians, too have their town trails where the leaflet identifies buildings of historical interest.

It seems people are willing to take an interest in their surroundings and learn about and from it. So why not the chemistry of their surroundings? The revised Nuffield GCE O-level Chemistry option, *Change and Decay* (Dilloway and Sykes, 1976), has long since disappeared, but it required students to look at the corrosion of stonework and metals and the causes – pollution and so on. Teaching this course in the early 1980s, I realised that, either within the school building itself, or in the immediate vicinity of the school, there were real examples of the corrosion required by the syllabus and direct evidence of some of its causes. Thus the first chemistry trail was born – *The Pimlico Chemistry Trail* (Borrows, 1984). Once accustomed to looking at the environment through chemical eyes, it was almost impossible to avoid spotting further manifestations of chemistry in the surroundings. The *Pimlico Chemistry Trail* got longer and longer! The idea took off. The BBC filmed Professor Ian Fells on a trail around Ealing in 1986 for its popular science series, *Take Nobody's Word For It*. Other schools developed their own trails. The Royal Society of Chemistry put up some money for printing leaflets. Chemistry trails were developed around: Norwich Cathedral, the *Techniquest* Hands-on Centre in Cardiff, the Science Museum in London, the town centres of Bedford, Cambridge, Walthamstow, Harlow, West Ham and, to add an international dimension, the University of Witwatersrand in South Africa – and doubtless many other locations. Leaflets were made available, usually free as a result of sponsorship, in libraries, tourist offices and museum shops. Some of these trails stemmed from a poster presentation and, of course, a chemistry trail, at the 11th International Conference on Chemical Education held at the University of York in 1991. Examples and extracts from some trails can be found in Borrows (1993).

If chemistry trails, why not physics trails? The late Stephen Foster took up the challenge (Foster, 1989). However, he developed the concept further by taking various measuring instruments and tools with him. His physics trail around the streets of Barking in East London required a Geiger counter, a stop watch, a ruler, a thermometer, a calculator, a plotting compass – and a hammer! (the latter was used to strike a long, steel fence; pupils standing 60 m away heard two sounds, showing the different speeds of sound in steel and air). Oliver Sacks, in his chemical autobiography *Uncle Tungsten*, tells us that he walks around Times Square with a pocket spectroscope, seeing the city lights of New York as atomic emissions. Most chemists, however, don't manage much more than a piece of pH paper.

With physics added to chemistry, it was inevitable that science trails would develop. Locations included the town centres of Croydon, Oxford, Colchester (partially sponsored by the local Education Business Partnership) and Sheffield (with support from the Committee for the Public Understanding of Science). The last two were targeted at Key Stage 2 pupils. Some schools including primary schools, developed their own trails (Sherring, 1990). Instead of producing a leaflet, one primary school produced a tape to be used with a 'Walkman'. Although the Sheffield trail (Peacock, 1994) had some ideas about materials, it would be fair to say that, so far, the concept of chemistry trails has not been much developed in primary schools. Some suggestions for physics trails (Smith, 1996) and for teaching about forces in the environment have, however, appeared (Hann, 2002).

Presenting and using the trail

At Key Stage 2, a chemistry trail allows children to see changing materials in different contexts, including non-reversible (but not very useful) changes and also to look at the appearance of some rocks. At Key Stage 3, however, a trail can be used to develop understanding of the reactions of metals and a good deal of acid/base chemistry. Rates of reaction and patterns of chemical reactions can be illustrated at Key Stage 4, as well as some aspects of transition metal chemistry. Teachers would teach these concepts anyway but by doing so using the surroundings of the school, children's understanding is enhanced whilst making a significant contribution to the breadth of study requirement of the National Curriculum in England. Even the gifted and talented can be challenged, for example, to understand the electrochemical nature of rusting.

One of the developments initiated by Foster was to make the trails more interactive. The *Pimlico Chemistry Trail*, like most nature trail leaflets, simply presented the information, although of course the teacher working with the class could question the pupils about what they were looking at, how it might have happened, and so on. However, the Year 10 class accompanying Foster had clipboards with worksheets. There were measurements and observations to be recorded, calculations to be carried out, questions to be answered.

The style of the trail, whether a paper leaflet or a tape-recorded guide, obviously depends on the intended audience. A leaflet may inspire the teacher to take pupils around the trail. Perhaps the pupils themselves do not need the leaflet – that serves simply as the teacher's notes, a bank of local resources to be brought into the lessons as necessary. Nor do the pupils have to go around the whole trail in one session. Visiting just one or two stops, to illustrate one specific piece of chemistry, may be sufficient. Such a short visit can then be fitted into the last 10 minutes or so of the lesson, without too much disruption to the normal routines or disturbance to adjacent classes. Does the class as a whole need to visit the site of interest, accompanied by the teacher? Perhaps pupils could be asked to visit one or two stops as part of their homework, with questions to be answered.

Of course, pupils learn much more by creating their own trail, with their own questions to be answered. The *Salters' Chemistry Club Handbook, Volume 1* (Holman, 1997) gives guidance to pupils trying to create their own chemistry trails. There is a copiable double-page worksheet of ideas to think about, questions to consider and suggestions for recording the trail. If paper copies of that handbook cannot be tracked down, it can be downloaded from the club's website (see Resources box). I have even come across an establishment that put its trail on the school web site. This is an excellent collaborative project for a science club and a better advertisement for the school than much that appears on such web sites.

If pupils learn from constructing their own chemistry trails, so, too, do teachers. Two trails in Cambridge were constructed by PGCE students. The Open University, in its *Chemistry for Science Teachers Pack* (Taylor, 1992) has a booklet on *The Environment* (Theme 5), one section of which is devoted to chemistry trails. There is an accompanying video, showing the development of a trail around Bedford. The main point of chemistry trails is to open the eyes of teachers to the chemistry going on in the world around them, so that they can then introduce this into their day-to-day teaching. Most teachers, when first meeting the concept, welcome the idea of chemistry trails but then go on to regret that unfortunately, purely by chance, they happen to live or work in a very chemically impoverished environment. They are wrong; they just don't know what to look for. Hence, the next sections of this chapter go into some detailed examples of chemistry that can be found in almost all environments, with suggestions for questions that teachers might want to ask pupils, although of course these will need to be tailored to the capabilities of the audience.

Building materials

Many modern buildings are made of concrete – not only office blocks and shopping centres, but also car parks, flyovers and underpasses. Whatever you may think of the aesthetics of concrete, it does have some surprisingly interesting acid/base chemistry, well within the comprehension of pupils at Key Stage 3 or 4. The full story is very complicated but an easily accessible account is available (MacLauren and White, 2003). Concrete is made by mixing cement, sand, water and small stones. Cement, in turn, is made by roasting ('calcining') a mixture of crushed chalk and clay at about 1400°C in huge rotating kilns. The chemistry of the reaction is complex but can be approximated to:

$$3CaCO_3(s) + Al_4Si_4O_{10}(OH)_8(s) \rightarrow Ca_3SiO_5(s) + Al_4Si_3O_{12}(s)$$
$$+ 4H_2O(g) + 3CO_2(g) \tag{1}$$

Some talented and gifted pupils will enjoy the challenge of balancing an equation such as this. However, this is not really the point. In addition to the reaction shown by Equation (1) a further reaction takes place – the thermal decomposition of calcium carbonate.

$$CaCO_3(s) \rightarrow CaO(s) + CO_2(g) \hspace{4cm} (2)$$

This reaction should be quite familiar at Key Stage 4 but one result is that cement is strongly basic because of the presence of calcium oxide and so too, therefore, is concrete. The calcium oxide will gradually pick up acidic gases from the air, mainly carbon dioxide, in a reverse of reaction (2).

$$CaO(s) + CO_2(g) \rightarrow CaCO_3(s) \hspace{4cm} (3)$$

Reaction (3) takes place first where there is a plentiful supply of carbon dioxide – on the surface of the concrete. Carbon dioxide gradually diffuses through the concrete, reacting as above. This can be demonstrated quite dramatically using phenolphthalein solution (highly flammable!). In principle any indicator solution will work, but phenolphthalein has the advantage that it is colourless in neutral or acid conditions but pink in alkali. Take a lump of concrete – it is surprisingly easy to find lumps lying around. Pour some phenolphthalein solution on to it. No change is observed, the phenolphthalein stays colourless – the lump is carbonated on the surface. Now, wearing eye protection to prevent possible injury from flying fragments, smash open the concrete with a hammer and quickly pour phenolphthalein solution on to the newly exposed surface. It turns bright pink. If you are careful, you may be able to spot a crust near the old exposed surface which remains colourless. Although the rate of carbonation, typically about 1 mm per year, depends on factors such as the porosity, it is possible to date concrete by measuring the depth of carbonation.

The presence of calcium oxide in concrete has another effect. Rain water, gradually leaching through the concrete, slowly dissolves the calcium oxide, forming calcium hydroxide solution, hopefully familiar to pupils as lime water.

$$CaO(s) + H2O(l) \rightarrow Ca(OH)_2(aq) \hspace{4cm} (4)$$

The calcium hydroxide solution will slowly work its way to the edge of the concrete, perhaps dripping down from a beam or archway. As soon as it meets the air, it reacts with the carbon dioxide, precipitating calcium carbonate.

$$Ca(OH)_2(aq) + CO_2(g) \rightarrow CaCO_3(s) + H_2O(l) \hspace{3cm} (5)$$

The water dripping down gradually forms a stalactite (see Figure 10.1). Such stalactites, a few centimetres long, and perhaps 0.5 cm diameter, are very common on modern concrete buildings – just look up! However, when looking up, don't stand directly underneath the dripping stalactite. The drops, a nearly

Figure 10.1 A drip of lime water is just about visible at the bottom of this concrete stalactite, photographed in central London.

saturated solution of calcium hydroxide (about 0.05 mol dm^{-3}), have a pH about 9–10, as a quick check with universal indicator paper will show.

To avoid possible confusion, it is important to stress that stalactites (and stalagmites) in show caves in limestone areas form as a result of different chemistry. There, the calcium carbonate rock dissolves in water with carbon dioxide dissolved in it.

$$CaCO_3(s) + H_2O(l) + CO_2(aq) \rightarrow Ca(HCO_3)_2(aq) \tag{6}$$

The calcium hydrogencarbonate solution flows through the rock until reaching a cave roof, where it drips down, reversing reaction (6).

$$Ca(HCO_3)_2(aq) \rightarrow CaCO_3(s) + H_2O(l) + CO_2(aq) \tag{7}$$

Another consequence arises from the basic nature of concrete. The ability of concrete to neutralise acid gases in the air means that concrete walls provide a good surface on which algae and lichens may grow. Lichens are usually taken as good indicators of air quality. You can often find them growing on concrete but not on other nearby building materials.

In comparison with concrete, bricks display relatively little chemical behaviour, although they display an interesting range of colours. Bricks are made by baking clay, in tunnel kilns, at a temperature of 1000–1200°C. Clays are sedimentary rocks composed mainly of silicates such as kaolinite $Al_4Si_4O_{10}(OH)_8$, formed by the decomposition of granite. The presence of iron(III) oxide gives the characteristic red colour of many bricks, a good opportunity to remind pupils of the colours of many transition metal compounds. However, clays themselves tend to be a grey colour, implying the presence of iron(II), so the red bricks indicate some oxidation has occurred. In fact, blue bricks do exist, presumably forming under more reducing conditions than the red ones. The presence of 1 per cent manganese(IV) oxide gives black bricks and smaller amounts give a muddy grey colour. In the London area, yellow bricks are common. This colour arises when the clay contains calcium (carbonate) and London is certainly ringed by chalk-rich hills – the Downs, the Chilterns, etc. The reason why calcium carbonate results in the yellow colour does not seem to be known. It does no harm at all for pupils to learn that science does not have all the answers.

Powdery white crystals can sometimes be spotted on brick walls, especially on newer ones. In the building trade, this is known as efflorescence, although it is not what chemists mean by the term. Bricks are very porous and 'efflorescence' tends to appear when a wet autumn is followed by a dry winter. A further wet spell may cause it to be reabsorbed. The crystals are the result of soluble salts in the original clay, mainly magnesium, potassium and calcium sulphates, plus traces of sodium from the cement. Rainwater leaches the sulphates through the pores, with the water evaporating when it reaches the surface. If the salts actually crystallise in the pores, they can cause the brick to disintegrate. Magnesium sulphate is the most destructive because of its much greater solubility. Calcium sulphate, although unsightly, is less so. Such damage can be very evident on old brick walls, although frost will also contribute. Frost damage is the result of water freezing in the pores. When water turns to ice, there is an increase of about 9 per cent in volume, and this can exert very considerable pressure in the pores.

Both concrete and bricks are, of course, artificial building materials, but many natural ones can also be found, often on old churches, town halls, banks and other prestigious buildings. The fact that the buildings are old is quite useful from the chemists' point of view, as there has been time for some rather slow reactions to take place.

Limestone, chalk and marble are all forms of calcium carbonate. What may be less obvious is that sandstone also contains calcium carbonate – it comprises grains of sand (silicon dioxide) cemented together by calcium (or occasionally magnesium) carbonate. Although silicon dioxide is chemically unreactive, carbonates are likely to dissolve in rain water which is acidic.

$$CaCO_3(s) + 2H^+(aq) \rightarrow Ca^{2+}(aq) + H_2O(l) + CO_2(g) \qquad (8)$$

Thus buildings of any age constructed from carbonate-containing stone are likely to show the same effects of acids that pupils find in their test tubes.

One building stone which does not contain carbonates is granite. This very hard stone may be found as kerbstones and granite setts (cobbles). Many of these may be undamaged after 150 years' use. Granite may also be found as decorative stone on banks and building societies. Granite comprises coloured plates of mica, e.g. $KAl_2Si_3O_{10}(OH)_2$, small clear crystals of quartz, SiO_2, and quite large crystals of feldspars, e.g. $KAlSi_3O_8$. Granite was formed as a result of the cooling of molten magma; the slower the cooling the larger the crystals. Can the pupils find different samples of granite, formed by cooling at different rates? Because granite does not have a neutralising effect on acid rain, only rarely can you find algae and lichens growing on its surface.

One of the best places to compare a range of building stones is in a cemetery or graveyard, providing the pupils can be encouraged to show due respect (Williams, 1990). As gravestones carry a date on which they were erected, they can be regarded as a long-term experiment in rates of (slow) reactions. The incised lettering on granite is usually as clear after 100 years as it was at the

---

Questions you might ask the pupils about building materials
- On which types of building materials can we find stalactites? Why don't they grow elsewhere?
- What is the difference between these stalactites and those found in show caves?
- How big were the stalactites? How fast do you think they are growing?
- How could we measure how quickly the stalactites were growing? What will affect the rate at which they form?
- Were there any signs of stalagmites forming?
- How could you show that the liquid dripping down from the stalactite is lime water?
- Was there any staining of the concrete? If so, what colour and what does that tell you?
- If we crack open a piece of concrete and test it with an indicator, what will happen to the indicator after a few minutes? Why?
- Which types of building materials seem to be most corroded?
- In which types of building materials can you see crystals? What types of rock are these?

start, in contrast to sandstone, for example, which may be almost illegible. On the other hand, sandstone may be host to a rich variety of lichens (see below), whereas the granite remains smoothly polished. A useful source of information on building stones is a series of three articles by Byrne (1981a, 1981b, 1982).

Metals

A surprising variety of metals can be found in most environments, demonstrating many interesting examples of corrosion and other chemical phenomena. A fuller discussion will be found in the *Nuffield Advanced Chemistry Materials Science Special Study* (Vokins and Hitchen, 1995).

The most obvious metal is iron, or its alloy steel, and its corrosion product, rust, is equally obvious. Syllabuses at all levels usually just expect pupils to know that rusting requires water and oxygen but the truth is rather more complicated. Rusting, and corrosion of metals generally, is in fact an electrochemical process. The iron behaves as an anode, atoms losing electrons and turning into iron(II) and then iron(III) ions.

$$Fe(s) + aq \rightarrow Fe^{2+}(aq) + 2e^- \tag{9}$$

$$Fe^{2+}(aq) \rightarrow Fe^{3+}(aq) + e^- \tag{10}$$

The lost electrons travel through the iron (as a metal, it is a good conductor of electricity) to a part of the iron where there is a good supply of oxygen. At this point, the iron acts as a cathode. The electrons are transferred to water molecules, which, in the presence of oxygen, become hydroxide ions.

$$2H_2O(l) + O_2(aq) + 4e^- \rightarrow 4OH^-(aq) \tag{11}$$

The ions then diffuse towards each other, producing rust where they meet.

$$2Fe^{3+}(aq) + 6OH^-(aq) \rightarrow Fe_2O_3.H_2O(s) + 2H_2O(l) \tag{12}$$

The important point is that this is action at a distance. If you have a large piece of iron, some of which is exposed to a plentiful oxygen (or air) supply and some of which is not, it is the latter, the oxygen-poor area, which corrodes. The iron in contact with plenty of oxygen merely acts as a conductor to pass electrons on to the water molecules. Thus, if a piece of iron is partially covered with paint, it is the painted bit which actually corrodes, unseen beneath the paint. It is usually not too difficult to find painted iron, where the paint has been scratched. The iron under the scratch may not appear rusty but when iron turns to rust, the volume doubles so look out for blisters of rust which may well be forming under the remaining paint. Thus protecting iron from corrosion by painting it could actually make the situation worse, if it becomes scratched. These days, iron railings are often set into concrete. The protruding iron may well be free from rust as most of the corrosion will be hidden in the concrete, although eventually the iron nearest the concrete will also start thinning, and this is often obvious. The increasing volume as the iron rusts may well crack concrete or stone work into which the iron is embedded. Examples are usually not difficult to spot.

The type of rusting just described relies on differential aeration – parts of the iron being in a more oxygen-rich environment than other parts. Another cause of corrosion is the contact between iron and a less reactive metal. Reaction (11) takes place on the surface of the less reactive metal. I have seen examples where steel screws were used to hold aluminium window frames in place, the more reactive steel having almost completely corroded away. In the past, molten lead was used to hold iron railings firmly in place in holes drilled into stonework. However, good examples may be difficult to find, at least if the architects or builders have understood any chemistry!

As a way of protecting iron from corrosion, putting it in electrical contact with a more reactive metal, such as zinc, is far more effective than painting it. This is the principle behind galvanised iron. The iron is coated by dipping it into molten zinc. Even if the zinc coating becomes scratched, the more reactive zinc dissolves in preference to the iron, i.e. reaction (13) occurs, rather than reaction (9).

$$Zn(s) + aq \rightarrow Zn^{2+}(aq) + 2e^- \tag{13}$$

Reaction (11) occurs on the surface of the exposed iron. The zinc is sacrificed to protect the iron – a sacrificial anode. Even more reactive metals, e.g. magnesium may also be used. I once spotted a sign saying 'gas anode' – a gas pipeline protected by sacrificing another metal.

It is usually easy to spot examples of galvanised iron – fences, rubbish containers, roof sheeting material. Look at the zinc coating and you are likely to spot feathery patterns (grains) – crystals of zinc, formed as the molten zinc cooled and solidified. The more rapid the cooling, the smaller the crystals, because crystallisation takes place at many centres at the same time. It may well be possible for pupils to find samples of zinc with different crystal sizes, i.e. implying different rates of cooling. The opportunity may be taken to remind pupils that the crystal form gives evidence of the underlying regularity of the arrangement of atoms. Etching of the metal surface may render the crystal grains more obvious. Acids are usually responsible, for example acid rain, or generations of sweaty hands on a door knob.

Copper is easy to spot with its characteristic browny-pink colour. It may often be seen snaking up church towers as a lightning conductor, relying on good electrical conductivity and relative chemical inertness of copper. Its alloys are also common. Bronze (about 90 per cent copper, the rest tin) is often used for statues and brass (about 70 per cent copper, the rest zinc) may, for example, be found as the fittings in public lavatories. Both copper and its alloys are characterised by the attractive green patina which they develop over time as a result of corrosion. The coating is usually said to be basic copper carbonate $CuCO_3.Cu(OH)_2$, but is likely to include the basic sulphate, $CuSO_4.3Cu(OH)_2$, or, in salt-rich environments, the basic chloride, $CuCl_2. 3Cu(OH)_2$.

Given the toxic nature of its compounds, lead metal is surprisingly common, especially around churches, where it may be found forming down-pipes for rainwater, or holding pieces of coloured glass in stained glass windows. As usually seen it is a rather dull grey, but if a small amount of the surface coating is scratched away, a soft shiny metal is revealed. Lead is even used for the lettering on some gravestones. If you see black lettering set into carved letters on a white marble stone, the lettering is likely to be lead, blackened over the years by the formation of a surface layer of lead sulphide. Another use for lead in the past was as a filler. Iron railings were fitted into holes in stone, molten lead being poured into the hole, to fill the gap and hold the railings firmly in place. Of course, over a period of time, iron, as the more reactive metal, would corrode (see Equation (9)), and so the railings are often now in poor condition (see Figure 10.2).

Other metals can be found in most environments. For example: chromium, protecting steel from corrosion; tin, on the inside of food cans; aluminium, for window frames; nickel, made into cheap jewellery; gold and silver, made into not-so-cheap jewellery and tungsten in light bulb filaments. One author of chemical trails even discovered rhodium plating on candlesticks in Norwich Cathedral. But the characteristic of all of these metals is that they are fairly, or extremely, resistant to corrosion. Therefore, there is usually not much sign of any chemical changes happening. The Chinese for chemistry translates literally as 'change-study'. If there are no changes, is it chemistry? But perhaps you could play a sort of periodic table bingo!

Figure 10.2 This iron railing was photographed in Bath. The iron has corroded, the lead in which it was embedded having acted as a cathode. The pressure exerted by the resultant expansion of the iron as it turned to rust has split the Bath stone in which the railing was set. The surface of the lead has also oxidised and then reacted with carbon dioxide to give a white crust of lead carbonate.

Questions you might ask pupils about metals in the environment
- How can we usually recognise the presence of iron (or steel) in the environment?
- What factors tend to increase the rate of corrosion?
- Where does the rust form? Where does the iron corrode?
- What methods are used to protect iron from rusting?
- To what extent do these methods seem to be successful?
- What evidence can you find that iron expands when it rusts?
- For which other metals can you find evidence of corrosion?
- Can you find examples of crystals of metals other than zinc?
- Does the corrosion of these other metals matter as much as the corrosion of iron?
- Why do you think lead has been widely used in the past?
- Why are gold and silver popular for jewellery?

Figure 10.3 This picture of a soot-blackened church in central London, partially washed clean by an over-flowing drain pipe, shows very dramatically the effects of a century or more of urban pollution by carbon particulates.

Air pollution

Pollution, especially of the air, features increasingly in chemistry and science syllabuses at all levels, but it often tends to be treated in an abstract way. However, there may be direct evidence of pollution in the immediate environment of many schools (see, for example, Figure 10.3). The soot is formed by the incomplete combustion of hydrocarbons.

$$C_xH_y + y/4\ O_2 \rightarrow xC(s) + y/2\ H_2O(g) \tag{14}$$

In the past, the main cause of air pollution generally was coal, although in fact the overall level of soot is much lower than it was 50 years ago. Diesel engines are now the main source.

Other atmospheric pollutants include sulphur dioxide and nitrogen oxides. Coal and most fuel gases contain small amounts of sulphur compounds. When the fuel is burnt, sulphur dioxide forms. Nitrogen oxides are formed when a spark is passed through air. This may happen when there is a lightening flash but also from the spark plugs in an internal combustion engine.

$$N_2(g) + O_2(g) \rightarrow 2NO(g) \tag{15}$$

$$2NO(g) + O_2(g) \rightarrow 2NO_2(g) \tag{16}$$

The mixture of NO and NO_2, of variable composition, is often referred to as NO_x. Sulphur dioxide and nitrogen dioxide both dissolve in water, giving an acidic solution – 'acid rain'. Due to air oxidation, sulphuric and nitric acids will eventually form.

$$2SO_2(aq) + 2H_2O(l) + O_2(g) \rightarrow 4H^+(aq) + 2SO_4^{2-}(aq) \tag{17}$$

$$4NO_2(aq) + 2H_2O + O_2(g) \rightarrow 4H^+(aq) + 4NO_3^-(aq) \tag{18}$$

Many environments will show signs of acid rain. Carbonates react with acids and hence limestone, marble and sandstones are all likely to be attacked.

$$MCO_3(s) + 2H^+(aq) \rightarrow M^{2+}(aq) + H_2O(l) + CO_2(g) \tag{19}$$

Although Equation (19) gives the general reaction, it is actually slightly misleading because what happens is not completely independent of the metal ion. For example, virtually all nitrates are very soluble but this is not true of all sulphates. Calcium sulphate has only limited solubility, a saturated solution contains about 2.1 g dm^{-3}, whereas for magnesium sulphate it is about 330 g dm^{-3}. Where a carbonate-based building stone is attacked by nitric acid, the carbonate dissolves completely and is washed away with the rain. This would be equally true for an attack on magnesium carbonate by sulphuric acid. However, if building stones containing calcium carbonate form an overhang where the solution of calcium sulphate drips down, its much lower solubility results in the formation of a deposit of solid calcium sulphate. The deposits are often blackish, as a result of soot being incorporated as crystallisation occurs. Sometimes, old sandstone building blocks look as if they have lost their shape, almost as if they had melted (but don't mention the word 'melt' to children at this point – they are already far too confused between melting and dissolving for this to be helpful).

$$Ca^{2+} (aq) + SO_4^{2-}(aq) \rightarrow CaSO_4(s) \hspace{4em} (20)$$

Lichens tend not to grow well under acid conditions. In the past, some urban areas were a lichen desert. However, because of the ability of carbonate-containing rocks to neutralise acid rain, it is often possible to find lichens growing on limestone or sandstone (or indeed on concrete) but not growing on granite. A graveyard is a good place to look. You can often spot orange patches of *Xanthoria parietina* or the grey crusts of *Lecanora conizaeoides*.

Because of its importance, government agencies regularly monitor air pollution. Air pollution is continuously monitored at many sites throughout the country (see Resources box). Data are fed directly to a web site. Any surfer can see and download figures for the concentration of each pollutant, updated hourly, every hour of the day, every day of the week, every week of the year, with an archive of 3 years of figures. Whilst it is easy to get swamped by the mass of data, the figures lend themselves to all sorts of hypothesising by children: is there less pollution at weekends? Is the afternoon rush hour spread over a longer period than the morning rush hour? Is there a correlation between the weather and

---

Questions you might ask pupils about air pollution
- What evidence can we find of pollution by particulates?
- What evidence can we find for the erosion of building stones by acid rain?
- If the stones contain fossils, have the fossils eroded at the same rate as the matrix in which they are set? Why?
- Is there any evidence of the formation of calcium sulphate deposits?
- Which types of gravestone have the most growth of lichens?
- Is this because of the age of stones or the material from which they are made?
- Why is air quality monitored at a particular local site?
- How do you think the air pollution figures would differ if the monitoring site were just outside the school?

pollution levels? Are the peaks in the same place for all the pollutants? Hypotheses could be tested by predicting what the pollution levels will be for today – and then going to the website to check. In order that children realise that these are not disembodied figures, but relate to their environment, it is best to identify a site in the vicinity of the school.

Further ideas for chemistry trails

This chapter has focused mainly on three key aspects, which are likely to be found in almost any environment – building stones, metals and air pollution. However, there are many other possibilities.

Sometimes, place names give a clue to a chemical past. There may be a statue of a famous chemist, or a plaque on the wall to record that they lived there once, although sadly such commemorations are far rarer than those for royalty, soldiers and politicians. Many towns have their Tanners Lane or their Dyers Row, indicating a former chemical industry. Salt (sodium chloride) was very important for food preservation and in tanning hides, hence the proliferation of salt-related names, for example, Salter Row (Pontefract) and Salter's Hill (the Norwood area of London), reminders of the time when trains of pack-horses carried this valuable commodity across the country. Less obvious are those places which take their names from the Celtic word *heli* (brine) or *halen* (salt), for example Pwllheli in Wales or Hayle in Cornwall. In Hampshire, you can find Saltern Lane and Kings Saltern where water was evaporated, from brine partly by the action of the sun but usually finished by boiling in metal pans. You can also find place names based on bittern, which was the solution (mainly magnesium sulphate) remaining after most of the sodium chloride had been crystallised out. Many environments give evidence of the importance of salt even today – look out for roadside salt bins.

For about 10 years the journal *Education in Chemistry* (a copy of which is supplied by the Royal Society of Chemistry free of charge to every secondary school) has carried a regular column (in alternate issues), usually about 600 words, exploring one particular aspect of environmental chemistry which could be incorporated into a trail. Table 10.1 lists the main focus of each of the articles.

Conclusion

Chemistry trails are a way of making the subject more relevant to pupils by getting them to realise that chemistry is happening all around them. It is often quite easy to spot one or two places of chemical interest but the challenge of

Table 10.1 The *Education in Chemistry* series

Year	Volume	Month	Issue no.	Page	Main focus
1994	31	January	1	7	Concrete
		May	3	63	Granite and sandstone
		September	5	118	Bricks
1995	32	January	1	6	Limestone
		May	3	62	Iron
		September	5	120	Other metals
1996	33	January	1	7	Glass
		May	3	63	Salt
		September	5	119	Plant pigments
1997	34	January	1	8	Famous chemists
		May	3	63	Place names
		September	5	120	Swimming pools
1998	35	January	1	8	Hydrocarbons
		May	3	63	On the beach
		September	5	118	Plastics
1999	36	January	1	6	Air pollution
		May	3	63	Water
		September	5	118	At the supermarket
2000	37	January	1	10	Fireworks
		May	3	66	Transporting chemicals
		September	5	118	Light sources
2001	38	January	1	23	Tea, coffee and fizzy drinks
		May	3	63	Food: E-numbers
		September	5	121	Bread, butter and jam
2002	39	January	1	14	Air
		May	3	64	Lead metal
		September	5	119	Lead compounds
2003	40	January	1	9	Gases
		May	3	62	Smelly gases
		September	5	119	Jewellery metals
2004	41	March	2	33	Gemstones

trying to produce a complete trail will enhance teachers' awareness of the potential of the school's environment, even if pupils are not expected to follow the trail in one go. Pupils will learn even more if they are challenged to produce a trail themselves – as a leaflet, tape-recording or website. The idea can be widened to include physics or science trails. Although most obviously relevant to secondary schools, there have been some successful developments in primary schools.

References

Borrows, P., 1984, 'The Pimlico chemistry trail', *School Science Review*, 66 (235), 221–33.

Borrows, P., 1993, 'On the chemistry trail', *Education in Chemistry*, 30, 18–19.

Byrne, M., 1981a, 'Building materials and buildings. Part I', *School Science Review*, 62 (220), 452–64.

Byrne, M., 1981b, 'Building materials and buildings. Part II', *School Science Review*, 62 (221), 675–86.

Byrne, M., 1982, 'Building materials and buildings, Part 3', *School Science Review*, 64 (226), 63–75.

Dilloway, P. and Sykes, A., 1976, *Revised Nuffield Chemistry Options. Option 6 Change and Decay*, York: Longman Group Ltd.

Foster, S., 1989, 'Streetwise physics', *School Science Review*, 71 (254), 15–22.

Hann, K., 2002, 'Forces in the world around us', *Primary Science Review*, 71, 11–12.

Holman, J. (ed.), 1997, 'Create your own chemistry trail', *The Salters' Chemistry Club Handbook, Vol. 1*, London: Salters' Chemistry Club, pp. 50–1.

MacLauren, D. C. and White, M. A., 2003, 'Cement: its chemistry and properties', *Journal of Chemical Education*, 80, 623–35.

Peacock, G., 1994, 'City science trail', *Primary Science Review*, 34, 19–22.

Sherring, P., 1990, 'Science trails', *Primary Science Review*, 12, 14–16.

Smith, R., 1996, 'Physical science trails', *Primary Science Review*, 43, 15–17.

Taylor, P., 1992 (Chair of PS547 Course Team), *Chemistry for Science Teachers*, Milton Keynes: The Open University.

Vokins, M. and Hitchen, B. (eds), 1995, 'Environmental effects on materials', *Nuffield Advanced Chemistry. Materials Science: A Special Study. Teachers' Guide and Students' Book*, 3rd edn, Harlow: Longman Group Ltd for the Nuffield-Chelsea Curriculum Trust.

Williams, J., 1990, 'Ecclesiastical geology', *Teaching Science (Journal of the School Natural Science Society)*, 8, 7–9.

Resources

The Salters' Chemistry Club Handbook, Volume 1, to be found on the Salters' Chemistry Club website: http://www. salters.co.uk/.

Chemistry for Science Teachers (PS547), Video Cassette 2 (VCO643).

Air pollution data for London from the South East Institute of Public Health. Website: http://www.weiph.umds.ac.uk/envhealth/table/htm

Air quality data from www.airquality.co.uk

Drinking water quality data from http://dwi.detr.gov.uk/water/drinking/

Education in Chemistry, published every two months, a copy is supplied by the Royal Society of Chemistry free of charge to every secondary school.

Chapter 11

Learning physics and astronomy outside the classroom

Elizabeth Swinbank and Martin Lunn

Overview

This chapter begins with activities that are school-based but take place outside the classroom. Here the focus is on astronomy, where star-domes and star parties bring to life a somewhat remote area of the curriculum. Next, we see how visits to telescopes, the National Space Centre and research organisations can help students learn about so-called 'Big Science'. In the two final sections, we outline how visits can help students learn physics in context and become aware of areas of future study and careers while also enhancing their enjoyment of the subject.

Planetaria and star-domes

The 'Earth and beyond' is one of the most abstract parts of the National Curriculum for science at Key Stages 1 and 2. At the other end of the school age range, astronomy is a popular option in A-level physics courses but brings challenges, as there is little scope for conventional practical work. It is possible to construct some simple models to demonstrate concepts such as day and night and phases of the moon, but in order to study astronomy in a more realistic way, it is useful to visit a planetarium or bring the night sky to the classroom in the form of a star-dome. In these places pupils see the stars in the same way that the ancient astronomers saw them. It is so dark inside that pupils can see so many stars and this might make them believe that they are seeing more than there really are. The reason is that today light pollution (light from street lamps and so on, scattered upwards to the sky) has made stars far more difficult to see.

A planetarium allows pupils to see the stars we normally see at night during the day. It takes pupils on a magical journey across the galaxy looking at the stars and is the closest many will get to looking at the stars without actually being outside.

Most planetaria offer a choice of programmes, so you should be able to find one suitable for your pupils. Some programmes are general tours of the sky, while others may be linked to particular curriculum areas. The Federation of Astronomical Societies (FAS) produces a handbook listing planetaria and other related places to visit. The handbook can be ordered from the society, at a cost of about £2, via their website (see Resources box).

A star-dome is a portable planetarium that can come to your school. It looks something like a giant igloo, 4 metres tall and 8 metres across. Due to its size, a star-dome is normally accommodated in the school hall. Inside the dome the pupils can sit around the edge surrounded on all sides and above by stars.

The unit is inflated by air and comes in three separate sections: the dome itself, the fan unit and the projector system. All three containers will fit into the back of a medium-sized car. Most star-domes are hired through commercial companies or from private individuals. To find out what is available, consult the website of the British Association of Planetaria and/or the handbook of FAS (see Resources). Some local authorities own their own star-domes and allow suitably trained teachers to pick up and return the domes after use. As with a fixed planetarium, pupils of any age can benefit from a session in a star-dome, but the programme will clearly need to be pitched at the right level, so you should discuss this with the presenter in advance.

A star-dome takes about 20 minutes to inflate and can typically accommodate 35 primary-school pupils, their teacher and the star-dome presenter. It is sensible to screen off the fan unit using benches or chairs, to prevent people getting too close to it. The dome is not sound-proof, so it is important that people are aware that presentations are being made and are quiet when they are in the vicinity of the star-dome, otherwise the presenter not only has to speak over the noise of the fan unit but also has to compete against whatever background noise is being made outside.

The star-dome itself appears much larger from the inside. However, be aware that there might be problems of claustrophobia, because once inside people will be surrounded on all sides. In addition, because it has to be dark to see the stars, there is the additional problem of young pupils being frightened while in a dark environment. This can become a very serious problem if the teacher is also unwilling to go into the dome! A dome can accommodate wheelchair users. The entrance tunnel is very flexible and there is sufficient room for wheelchair access, although the number of people who can use the dome at any one time is reduced.

Inside a star-dome or planetarium, one point to notice is that not all stars are the same colour. Stars are red, blue and orange as well as white. The colours of stars indicate their temperatures. A blue star is much hotter than a red star. The light pollution, which makes it difficult to see the stars, also makes it difficult to see their true colours.

With pupils of any age, a planetarium or star-dome provides a good way of showing constellations. The ancient astronomers divided the stars into patterns which tell the stories of heroes and villains from ancient mythology. Many of the stories tell about characters such as Hercules, Perseus and Orion, names that even young pupils may recognise from characters who appear in various television programmes and from their studies of Ancient Greece. In the dome pupils will, however, quickly realise that these constellations bear little resemblance to the images they are supposed to represent.

Astronomers were probably telling the stories of constellations over 2,000 years ago and it is reasonable to assume that these same stories will still be told in 2,000 years time. Today we use the stories from Ancient Greece but, although most of the stories and constellations names we use in Europe were originally Greek, some of the individual star names we use (e.g. Aldebaran, Altair) are actually Arabic. Many other cultures have their own stories concerning the same patterns. For example, the constellation pattern we call the Plough is known as the 'Great Bear' in Ancient Greece, a 'Horse and Cart' in China, a 'Crocodile' in Egypt and a 'Hippopotamus' in Mesopotamia. Pupils will have to use their imagination, just as the ancient astronomers did, to see these pictures in the sky.

There is some practical follow-up work that pupils could undertake. On the next clear evening following their star-dome or planetarium experience, they could be asked to look at the stars from their garden at home or another safe location. Young pupils could try to design their own constellations, by using the stars in a dot-to-dot fashion. These pictures could be anything from an object to a person or animal. After they have drawn the picture a short story could be added. The pupils would be simply making their own mythology just as the ancient astronomers did all those thousands of years ago.

With older pupils, a planetarium or star-dome programme can be used to show how stars move during the course of a night, and from one night to the next. This motion can be explained in terms of the earth's rotation and its motion around the sun. Afterwards, pupils could be asked to identify particular stars or planets in the night sky, and might be asked to observe for themselves how the stars' positions alter during one night, or from one night to the next.

Observing the night sky

The atmosphere under the night sky is quite unlike anything that can be achieved in the classroom. Almost everybody has looked at the stars at some time. It is incredibly satisfying to be able to identify real stars and constellations. A planetarium or star-dome goes part of the way but there is nothing to beat being under the stars and identifying the Plough or Orion. The 'wow' factor is beyond description.

If you want pupils to see real stars and be able to identify them, you could organise a star party with the help of a local astronomer. While the idea has been developed mainly for primary-school pupils, a star party can be enjoyed by students of any age provided the activities are tailored to them. A good way to find a 'tame' astronomer is to contact your local reference library which should be able to give you the address of your local astronomical society. Another good source is the FAS website which lists contact addresses for all UK astronomical societies.

A star party enables pupils to do things which they cannot do in the classroom; a unique opportunity to look at the stars. The star party occurs after school hours, typically lasting for about an hour and a half. It provides an informative but relaxed environment in which to meet parents and friends. Even parents who don't like more formal school events might be tempted to come. It allows parents to be genuinely involved in their children's learning.

It is sensible to organise a star party during the winter months, when sunset is early in the evening, so that the event can start at 6pm. The period from November to February is the best time. As the clearest winter nights are also likely to be frosty, it is important that people dress warmly. The length of time spent outside will vary, but it is unlikely to be more than 20 minutes, as people will get too cold. The party can continue indoors with suitable activities and refreshments. If possible, arrange a viewing area that is shielded from the glare of street lights, and ask for any external security lights to be turned off so that there is a clear view of the sky.

Some people might want to bring binoculars or even a small telescope if they have one. However, the most important aspect of the star party is to try to identify some bright stars and constellations using just the naked eye. The only torches that should be brought are ones that have a red cover, as red light does not damage night vision as much as white light does.

As well as stars, sometimes there might be one or more planets on view. Many parents and pupils find it amazing that it is possible to see planets such as

Jupiter and Saturn with the naked eye. Once identified, these planets can be watched over a period of several weeks and observers will see, just as the ancient astronomers did, that these star-like objects do in fact move against the starry background. The Greeks called these objects 'wandering stars' and when translated into English the term becomes 'planet'. If you are incredibly lucky you might even see an artificial satellite moving across the sky or a meteor (shooting star) burning up as it enters the earth's atmosphere.

If the sky is cloudy it will be impossible to see the stars. It is therefore important to have other plans in hand. A slide show or Powerpoint presentation could take people on a journey through the solar system. A space quiz or wordsearch is always fun. Participants could be asked to devise these themselves, and could also be asked to bring or suggest appropriate music (e.g. the 'Planets Suite', or tracks from 'Starlight Express').

What would Earthlings eat at a star party? Depending on the age of the pupils, there could be an opportunity to develop ideas in food technology, and parents may want to help their children at home to produce some food for the party. Whatever food is produced it is important that it links to the theme of astronomy and space. Table 11.1 shows some tips for having fun with space food. For example, you could provide a bowl of cashew nuts labelled 'astronuts', while a drink called 'Jupiter juice' with a 'red spot' is really fruit juice with a glacé cherry.

If the party involves young pupils, you might consider organising games with cosmic or planetary themes.

Table 11.1 Some examples of food for a star party

Space food	Earth equivalent
Astronuts	Cashew nuts
Comet crush	Ice cream balls with biscuit bits
Phase cakes	Crescent shaped cakes
Meteors	Hundreds and thousands
Mercury munchies	Munchie sweets
Venus sweets	Love hearts
Venusian curry	The hottest curry in the solar system
Martian soup	Tomato soup
Jupiter juice	Fruit juice with a glacé cherry
Saturn slush	Fizzy lemon with ice cream
Saturn rings	Hoola hoops
Neptune nibbles	Crisps, popcorn
Hot total eclipse	Hot chocolate

After a star party, pupils might become keen to get a clearer view of the sky so consider arranging some follow-up activities. Binoculars are easier for beginners to use than telescopes and, if you want to arrange an evening's viewing with small telescopes, your local astronomical society will probably be able to help. Some astronomical societies own, or have access to, larger telescopes – for example, in university observatories. The listings in the FAS handbook indicate telescopes that you can visit.

Big Science

Big Science is a term often applied to astronomy, space research and subatomic particle physics. It refers not only to the size of equipment needed (huge telescopes, space rockets or particle accelerators) but also to the cost of the endeavour and the numbers of people involved. Big Science experiments generally involve large teams of people based in several institutions, often in different countries, and the cost to governments is such that few countries, with the exception of the USA, can undertake Big Science on their own.

People can find Big Science both inspirational and controversial. On the one hand, there is the excitement of international collaboration and research into big questions such as 'what are we made of?' and 'what will be the ultimate fate of the universe?'. On the other hand, there are questions about whether the cost can be justified.

A visit to a research telescope, particle physics laboratory or space science centre is an excellent way to give pupils a real appreciation of Big Science. Seeing the vast radio telescopes at Jodrell Bank in Cheshire, or the space rockets at the National Space Centre in Leicester, is much more impressive than any picture or video can ever be. Students can benefit from seeing the connections between frontier research and their own studies and may be inspired to consider a career in science. As well-informed future citizens, older students, in particular, should also be encouraged to discuss arguments for and against governments (i.e. tax-payers) supporting costly fundamental research. Older students (at GCSE level or above) will be in the best position to appreciate both the details of the research programmes and the wider socio-economic implications of Big Science. If you are planning a visit with younger pupils, check to see what will be available for them to see and do, as some Big Science centres do have visitor centres with exhibits designed for young pupils.

Within the UK, there are several centres devoted to astronomy, space and particle physics research that welcome school visits. These include:

The *Jodrell Bank* radio telescopes and *Science Centre*, Cheshire
The *National Space Centre* and *Challenger Learning Centre*, Leicester
The *Rutherford Appleton Laboratory*, Oxfordshire
The *Goonhilly Satellite Station*, Cornwall
The *Royal Observatory Edinburgh*
The *Armagh Observatory*.

The format of a visit will depend on the venue and on the age of the visitors. Some centres have a permanent exhibition that includes hands-on activities. Some can arrange guided tours. Some hold open days. Some offer the opportunity to talk to researchers about their work. The Challenger Learning Centre (part of the National Space Centre) enables pupils to experience working in a space-science research team, which not only helps them to learn aspects of science but also develops team-working skills.

Whatever the ages and interests of your pupils, you should contact the venue well in advance to find out what is available and to arrange a suitable programme. As with all visits, the value will be enhanced by preparatory and follow-up work. Beforehand, alert students to some of the things they will encounter. Ask them what they will expect to see, and encourage them to think of questions that might be answered during the visit. Afterwards, ask them to recall particular highlights and to say what they have learnt.

If you want a really ambitious and memorable visit for older students, you could go to the European Particle Physics Laboratory (CERN) in Geneva. This is Big Science on the grandest scale. The accelerators occupy a tunnel 27 km in circumference, passing beneath the French–Swiss border, and the underground experimental areas are the size of cathedrals. Over 20 different nationalities work at CERN and, while the official working languages are English and French, you will hear many other languages being spoken around the site and in the canteens. A tour of the laboratory and a visit to the on-site 'Microcosm' exhibition centre would be particularly relevant for students of A-level physics.

A visit to CERN can be combined with a visit to the city of Geneva, or perhaps with a skiing trip in the nearby Alps. Many UK schools have taken groups of students, and some return year after year. CERN is keen to encourage visits from schools and their visits service can provide comprehensive advice on all aspects including travel and accommodation. A very useful *Guide to Visiting CERN from the UK* can be downloaded from the web.

Physics at work

Young people are sometimes reluctant to choose physics for post-16 study or as a degree subject because they and perhaps their parents think, erroneously, that 'there are no jobs in physics'. A visit to observe physics in the workplace can do a great deal to counter this misconception. Such a visit can also help students learn physics. If students can recognise 'school physics' being used in 'real life' this can help them to make sense of what they are studying and can also increase their motivation to tackle demanding concepts.

A workplace visit, where the focus is on identifying the physics being used, will be most beneficial for students who already have some experience of the subject, although this will depend on the venue. Most of the examples given in this section would be suitable for students in the 14–19 age range, although in some cases a well-planned visit could also work well with younger pupils.

The *Salters Horners Advanced Physics* course (SHAP) requires students to make a visit during their AS year and to report in depth on some of the physics they have observed in action. Teachers have noted that such visits are very successful in opening students' eyes to possible careers and also in helping them to learn and apply physics concepts. The visit report is assessed and contributes to students' overall AS and A-level grades. This assessment tool values distinct abilities not otherwise assessed (e.g. the ability to recognise and describe physics principles). Teachers also comment that, compared with their experience of unassessed visits, the assessment makes students take the visit more seriously and focus more clearly on its outcomes (Parker, Swinbank and Taylor, 2000; Lubben, Campbell and Hogarth, 2001).

Some teachers initially express doubts about the feasibility of organising a visit to see physics in the workplace, particularly if they are based in an area where there is little or no obvious physics-related industry. While an industrial visit can indeed be very worthwhile, there are many other possibilities. Once you start to look, you might be surprised how easy it is to identify physics at work. It is impossible to list all suitable venues, but here are just a few examples of some that have hosted successful visits:

- Power station
- Hospital
- Optician
- 'Big Science' centre (see previous section)
- Engineering research lab (university or industry)
- Engineering structure (e.g. a suspension bridge)
- RAF airbase

- Hi-fi manufacturer
- Cement works
- Car factory
- Chocolate factory
- Cinema
- Swimming pool
- Superstore
- Tyre-fitting workshop.

Those near the bottom of the list may be less 'obvious' than some of those higher up. A visit to a cement works, for example, while promising some obvious links to physics, might sound less glamorous and appealing than going to a particle physics laboratory. However, teachers often find that some of their most successful visits have been to venues 'just down the road', where physics might be used in surprisingly interesting and unexpected ways. For example, on a visit to a cement works, students and their teacher were intrigued to find that raw materials from a quarry 50 miles away were transported not by road or rail but were blown along a huge underground pipeline – a process that uses physics to sense and control the motion of large masses of material. The physics involved in the fire-protection system of a superstore is likely be more accessible than that in a particle physics experiment.

What makes a successful workplace visit? Regardless of the age of the visitors, or whether the visit will contribute to assessment, there are some guidelines to bear in mind. These have been set out and discussed by some SHAP teachers (Astin, Fisher and Taylor, 2002), and in summary they are as follows.

- Try to find a venue that will appeal to students' interests (e.g. those students with a medical interest would be keen to visit a hospital). Look for somewhere relatively close at hand, to avoid long expensive journeys.
- Time the visit so as to minimise disruption to students' other commitments, and to avoid upsetting colleagues by taking students out of their classes at crucial times.
- Contact the venue well in advance – ideally, visit it yourself – and check that the physics will be accessible to the students, i.e. not too advanced and not obscured by complex technology.
- Try to ensure that someone with appropriate physics knowledge, briefed to pitch the information at a suitable level, will be on hand to guide the visit and answer questions, and if this is not possible be prepared to do so yourself. The careers aspect of the visit is enhanced if people who work there can talk about their own physics background and the route that took them to their present job.

- Make sure that you, the students and the host are fully aware of any health and safety issues.
- Prepare students thoroughly beforehand so that they know what to do during the visit. Even if the visit is not to be assessed, consider getting students to produce a record so as to focus their attention. Afterwards, hold a debriefing to identify key points, deal with outstanding questions and reinforce what students have learnt.

As well as the intended outcomes of helping students to learn physics and raise their awareness of careers, workplace visits can bring other benefits. A well-organised visit can help build good relationships between the students and local employers. Students who are well-behaved and interested, and a thank-you letter following the visit, will go a long way towards this. An article in the local paper and in the school magazine, preferably accompanied by a photograph, can be good publicity for all involved. Students might get ideas for project work. Contacts made initially for visits can lead to work-experience placements. Occasionally, industries may offer to donate materials and equipment to a school or college whose work they wish to support.

Physics for fun

A physics-related visit will not only help students learn physics and open their eyes to career opportunities; it can also have social benefits. A visit can help students get to know one another and their teacher, to enjoy one another's company and to work productively together. Any visit will provide a shared experience that can help students to enjoy their study of physics, but sometimes the 'fun' element can be made even more prominent by visiting a venue associated primarily with leisure activities. Make sure the visit also has a clear physics purpose. A good way to do this is to collect data for later analysis. Sometimes data collection will involve estimation – which is itself a valuable physics-related skill.

An amusement park provides great opportunities for learning physics. The rides often illustrate physics principles on a large scale. For example, a roller-coaster ride demonstrates energy conservation as the cars slow down while climbing and accelerate on the downhill runs. While at the amusement park, you could use a camcorder to film rides such as a roller-coaster in action, then after the visit freeze-frame the motion to deduce speed and acceleration and relate changes in kinetic energy to changes in height. Some large amusement parks produce materials designed to support school visits. The Alton Towers theme park, for example, provides a range of educational materials that can be downloaded from their website. They contain information and activities for pupils of various ages.

Amusement park rides can also be used as a laboratory for carrying out experiments in rotating and accelerated reference frames. Bagge and Pendrill (2002) describe how rides in the Swedish Liseberg park have helped students perform classic experiments such as the Foucault pendulum (by observing the swinging of a small cuddly toy suspended on string held by someone on a slowly rotating roundabout). They advise that such experiments are performed only after pupils have become familiar with the rides, otherwise the novelty of the ride will occupy much more of their attention than the experiment. It is also important to consider safety. Visitors to rides will not be allowed to carry loose objects that could cause injury so you need to plan experiments so that they use only small, light, soft objects – and consult those in charge of the park in advance of your visit.

Another example of a physics-related leisure activity would be a ride on the London Eye. During the visit you could ask students to time the wheel's revolutions and estimate the dimensions of the structure (for example by comparing the wheel's diameter to the height of a person). After the visit, estimates can be compared with the actual dimensions provided by the engineers. See, for example, Tear (2000), which also provides information on the forces acting within the structure and the materials used in constructing the wheel.

A boat trip on a canal provides many opportunities for students to collect data by measurement and by estimation, and to discuss physics principles. Health and safety are paramount here, and students need to be well supervised near any water. The activities you plan will depend on the age of the pupils. For example, pupils at Key Stage 2 and above could estimate the volume of water that flows into, or out of, a lock when the sluices are opened (see Figure 11.1). Knowing that each cubic metre of water has a mass of 1 tonne (1000 kg) they could also estimate the mass of that water.

GCSE and A-level students could go on to estimate the pressure acting against the lock gates when there is a difference in water level, and hence estimate the force needed to open the gates at various stages during the filling–emptying cycle. The pressure at the lower water level is equal to the density of water ($\rho = 1000$ kg m^{-3}) multiplied by gravitational acceleration (g, roughly 10 m s^{-2}) multiplied by the difference in water level, h, either side of the gate, and the average excess pressure, p, is half of this (1).

$$p = \rho g h \tag{1}$$

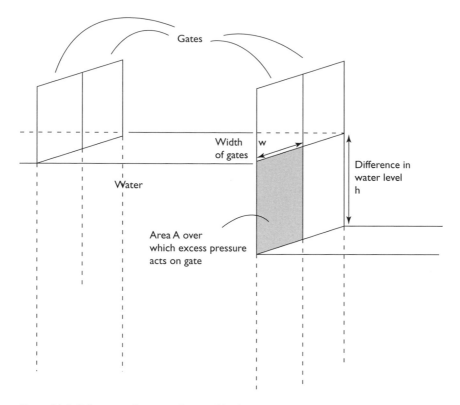

Figure 11.1 Schematic diagram of a canal lock.

With the level difference, h, in metres, this gives the excess pressure in pascals (N m^{-2}). Pupils can now estimate the force F (in newtons) needed to open the gate by multiplying the average excess pressure by the area, A, of gate that has water only on one side, that is, by width, w, of the gate (in metres) and by the difference in water level, h (2).

$$F = pA = pwh = \rho gh^2w \qquad (2)$$

Even for a water level difference of a small fraction of a metre, the force required is large. Students can compare this to their own body-weight (a student of mass 60 kg has a weight of about 600 N). In a manually operated lock, this force can be experienced directly by leaning on the lever to open the gate. Suppose the force F_1 due to the water to be acting at the mid-point of the gate, then estimate the length, l, of the lever that operates the gate and hence calculate the force F_2 you need to apply at the end of the lever (Figure 11.2).

$$F_1w/2 = F_2l \qquad (3)$$

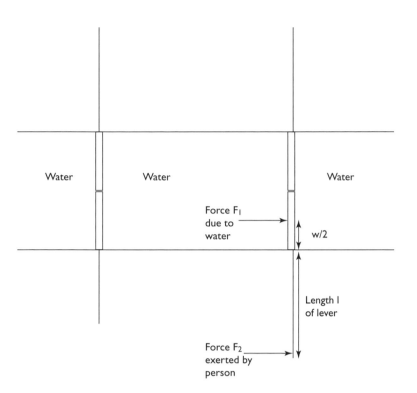

Figure 11.2 Aerial view of Figure 11.1 showing forces acting on a lock gate.

Only when the water levels are almost equal does it become possible to produce any movement, even if several people lean hard against the lever. Once the water pressure either side is equalised, then it is relatively easy to move the gate.

Extreme natural phenomena can also provide an opportunity for data-gathering and learning physics. Unfortunately most such phenomena are both infrequent and unpredictable. An exception is the Severn Bore, a step-shaped wave of water that is forced inland along the river Severn by high tides in the Severn estuary. The Severn Bore website indicates when 'good' bores can be expected by giving them star-ratings; it also lists times when the bore is predicted to pass various viewing locations (see Resources box). A 'good' bore can be spectacular and attracts surfers as well as riverside observers.

A-level students are most likely to be able to understand the physics behind the bore (Figure 11.3). Simple models predict that a bore of height h, travelling along a straight, parallel-sided river of much greater depth than the step height, will have a speed v given by

$$v = \sqrt{(gh)} \qquad\qquad (4)$$

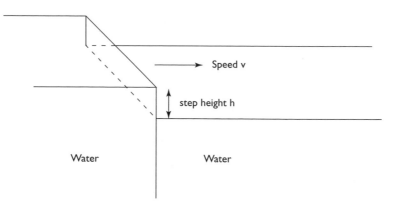

Figure 11.3 Schematic diagram of a bore.

where *g* is the acceleration due to gravity (about 10 m s^{-2}) and *h* the step height in metres. Observers could estimate the step height and the speed and discuss the extent to which the speed matches the prediction.

High tides ('spring tides') occur approximately every 2 weeks, when the sun, earth and moon are aligned – which brings us back to the astronomy discussed at the start of this chapter. The height of the bore depends on the distances between the earth, sun and moon. A-level students will know that the earth and moon have elliptical orbits, and can appreciate that these distances change with time and the bore height therefore varies in a way that, though complex, is predictable. However, the bore height is also affected by rainfall and by atmospheric conditions, which are less easy to predict, so if you are planning an expedition it would be wise to include some additional activities such as a workplace visit as discussed earlier.

Summary

We have described a variety of opportunities for learning physics and astronomy outside the classroom. Planetaria and star-domes simulate ideal conditions for viewing the night sky, and star parties provide an experience of geniune astronomical observation coupled with a social occasion. A visit to an observatory or the National Space Centre helps make connections between school work, personal observation and current astronomy research, while a visit to CERN provides a memorable experience of another area of Big Science – particle physics. Nearer home, visits to explore physics in the workplace can also help bring 'school physics' to life and open eyes to possible careers. Finally, leisure activities can provide opportunities for learning physics while having fun. The activities and venues we have described range from the ambitious to the apparently mundane, but all have the scope to provide an enriching experience to enhance the learning of physics or astronomy.

References

Astin, C., Fisher, N. and Taylor, B., 2002, 'Finding physics in the real world: how to teach physics effectively with visits', *Physics Education*, 37(1), 18–24.

Bagge, S. and Pendrill, A.-M., 2002, 'Classical physics experiments in the amusement park', *Physics Education*, 37(6), 507–11.

Lubben, F., Campbell, B. and Hogarth, S., 2001, 'Assessment through reports of "physics-in-action" visits', *School Science Review*, 82(301), 47–53.

Parker, K., Swinbank, E. and Taylor, B., 2000, 'Piloting Salters Horners Advanced Physics', *Physics Education*, 35(3), 209–12.

Tear, C., 2000, 'The London Eye', *Physics Review* 10(1), 22–6.

Resources

Federation of Astronomical Societies. Website: www.fedastro.org.uk

British Association of Planetaria. Website: www.planetarium.org.uk

National Space Centre, Exploration Drive, Leicester LE4 5NS. Website: www.nssc.co.uk

Jodrell Bank, Macclesfield, Cheshire SK11 9DL. Website: www.jb.man.ac.uk

Rutherford Appleton Laboratory. Website: www.rl.ac.uk

Goonhilly Satellite Station. Website: www.goonhilly.bt.com/visitors_frame.htm

Royal Observatory Edinburgh, Blackford Hill, Edinburgh EH9 3HJ. Website: www.roe.ac.uk

Armagh Observatory. Website: star.arm.ac.uk

European Particle Physics Laboratory (CERN). Website: public.web.cern.ch

Guide to visiting CERN from the UK. Website: www.pparc.ac.uk/Pbl/Cern.asp

Salters Horners Advanced Physics Website: www.york.ac.uk/org/seg/salters/physics

Alton Towers. Website: www.altontowers.com/education.htm

Severn bore. Website: www.severnbore.ndirect.co.uk/boretable.htm

Chapter 12

Learning with newspapers

Ruth Jarman and Billy McClune

Overview

This chapter explores the use of newspapers as a resource for teaching and learning about science. It begins by suggesting why they have a place in both the primary and secondary classroom and how they may be employed. The use of newspapers as a context for reading activities is then considered in more detail, focusing on news stories, feature articles and graphics. The use of newspapers as a context for writing activities is discussed and illustrated by a 'front page' prepared by primary school children and a published article written by secondary school students. Finally some characteristics of news reporting are outlined.

Introduction

When children and young people think of 'Learning Science Outside the Classroom', they think of television, the Internet and science centres. They do not, as a rule, think of newspapers. In a study we undertook as a starting point for this chapter, 200 12 year olds and 200 15 year olds in Northern Ireland were invited to name as many ways as they could for learning about science outside-of-school. Only 12 per cent of the former and 13 per cent of the latter included newspapers in their list! This compares rather unfavourably with television, mentioned by 77 per cent of 12 year olds and 84 per cent of 15 year olds, the Internet mentioned by 51 per cent of 12 year olds and 70 per cent of 15 year olds and science centres mentioned by 61 per cent of 12 year olds and 43 per cent of 15 year olds. Despite this, indeed perhaps because of this, we believe there is a strong case for using newspapers as a resource for teaching and learning about science.

Why use newspapers for teaching and learning about science?

On the face of it, newspapers do not appear a particularly attractive resource. Typically, they are black and white. They have large blocks of text and small sizes of print. The most appropriate 'science interest' stories are surrounded by the most inappropriate 'human interest' stories. Sooner or later, they turn yellow and disintegrate.

On the other hand, there are some obvious advantages associated with newspapers as a resource for teaching and learning about science. Almost by definition, they are up-to-date, dealing with current developments in the subject and contemporary issues in society. Indeed, this intrinsic topicality has prompted some to describe newspapers as 'living textbooks', although, as we shall see, there are important differences between the two. By the same token, regional and neighbourhood papers have a strong 'local' perspective which can lend them a particular relevance for their reader. These characteristics ensure that although, unlike other approaches advocated in this book, the child may not actually move into the community, nevertheless, through the use of newspapers, the community – indeed the world – moves into the classroom.

Science-related stories in newspapers are written for lay audiences. The articles have to attract and hold their readers. As a consequence, they are often written and illustrated in an arresting and accessible style which can make them a useful resource for teaching and learning in a school setting. Although scientists (Allan, 2002; Gregory and Miller, 1998) and science teachers (Jarman and McClune, 2002) tend to be rather sceptical of science in the media there is, in fact, great merit in much that is written. Significantly, the House of Lords' Select Committee on Science and Technology concluded, in its report *Science and Society* (2000), 'science journalism is currently flourishing in the United Kingdom'. That said, there are also examples of dubious science reporting. It could be argued that this is further justification for studying newspapers in the science classroom.

Finally, many teachers have found that children and young people often relish the opportunity to relate to, as they see it, 'adult material' (in the other sense of that phrase!) and are captivated by the 'real world' quality of newspapers.

These could be considered, perhaps, as surface reasons for exploiting newspapers in the science classroom. Digging deeper, though, we can begin to build a foundation for identifying possible teaching objectives and learning outcomes associated with their use. First, newspapers can be a valuable resource for illustrating important ideas about science, for example, those linked with: the content of science, particularly as it applies to and is applied in everyday life; and the 'processes' of science, particularly in relation to 'scientific enquiry' including so-called 'science-in-the-making'. Second, newspapers can be a valuable context for developing important skills associated with science, for example those linked with: 'general literacy', particularly in relation to reading, writing, research and discussion; and 'scientific literacy', particularly in relation to critical engagement with science in the media, 'science for citizenship' and 'science as lifelong learning'.

Such a framework can facilitate the all-important task of specifying objectives for using print media in a particular way in a particular lesson. Research shows that most teachers use newspapers simply to show the 'relevance' of school science 'content' in everyday life (McClune and Jarman, 2001; Jarman and McClune, 2002). Important as this intention is, if the resource is employed solely to enliven science lessons with examples from everyday life, we believe valuable opportunities are being lost. Newspapers have, as shown above, the potential to contribute much more to education in and through science.

This framework also highlights a 'present' and 'future' dimension to newspaper use. In school, they represent a lively and timely resource capable of catching the interest of pupils and developing their knowledge and skill. As young people move on from formal education, however, the media becomes their major source of information about science and, significantly, about science-related issues which are impacting society. One important way we can help prepare children for their future, then, is to encourage and equip them to engage critically with science in newspapers.

How to use newspapers for teaching and learning about science

Clearly, newspapers are not written with the school science curriculum in mind. However, it is often the science content behind a newspaper article which catches our attention. It is the case that a wide range of school science topics do make it into the quality and popular press (Wellington, 1991). Figure 12.1, for example, shows an article on air pollution which could readily be used in the classroom.

Simply reading good science journalism to children and young people can be rewarding. The sheer quality of some of the writing, particularly the feature writing, can fire their interest and imagination; it can inform and it can inspire. Furthermore, through the act of turning to a newspaper (or looking up a

Belfast gets ultimatum to come clean on pollution

Seven years to clear the air

BELFAST City Council has been given seven years to improve the quality of its air, currently the worst than any other region in the UK.

The rigorous clean-up operation to improve air quality, is part of new legislation for all councils across Britain.

Belfast is at the bottom of the UK air quality league table because of its high levels of sulphur dioxide and PM 10 particles, from coal and fuel emissions.

Other factors include the city's location in the Lagan basin, poor weather conditions and lack of cleaner fuel options.

Details of a survey into Belfast's air quality problems will be made public for the first time at an energy conference at the Balmoral Conference Centre on Thursday, January 29.

The presentation will be given by Heather Armstrong, a senior environmental health officer at Belfast City Council.

According to Heather, a number of health problems can arise from bad air. 'Sulphur dioxide and PM 10 can cause eye irritation, aggravate asthma and other respiratory problems.

'Air pollution is worse on cold, calm winter days, because the pollution gets trapped under a lid of cold air.'

'People should make sure that they burn only authorised fuels and walk instead of using the car all the time.'

'We can all help reduce the current high levels of air pollution by avoiding making unnecessary short car journeys wherever possible. By walking or making use of public transport instead, we can all do our bit to improve air quality.'

To help promote cleaner air, Belfast City Council have launched a smoke hot line.

'People should ring the number if they want to report a smokey chimney or car exhaust. They should note the car registration number and the address of the house.

'We will educate and advise people, but if they are persistent offenders, fines may be imposed,' said Heather.

Belfast Telegraph
19 January 1998

Figure 12.1 Newspaper article on pollution from the *Belfast Telegraph*, reproduced with kind permission.

clipping) we can serve as a role model for our pupils, highlighting the medium as a source of science communication.

A fun way to illustrate the same point is to have a science 'scavenger hunt'. Pupils work in groups, each of which is given a copy of the same edition of a newspaper. They are then challenged to find 'a story about energy', 'a letter about biodiversity', 'the phase of the moon today', etc. If you are concerned that the complete paper may be too unwieldy (or that some articles may be inappropriate!), pages can easily be removed.

There are, of course, other means for conveying that all-important message that newspapers are a source of science-related information:

- a bulletin board of 'science in the news' can be maintained;
- a time-line charting developments in science news stories can be constructed;
- articles on science-related themes can be archived and accessed by pupils;
- news diaries can be kept;
- a 'newspaper learning area' can be set up for use, for example, by 'fast-finishers';
- the school library can host displays.

Moving on, many teachers find it useful to prepare comprehension exercises, where a series of questions are devised to accompany a particular newspaper article or illustration (see Wellington and Osborne, 2001). Along with science-related questions, there is merit in including some that are more media-related, for example, 'Why do you think the headline writer used the phrase "Frankenstein Food"?'; 'What impact do you think this might have on the readers?' Crucially, children and young people should be invited to suggest what they would wish to ask the journalist and the scientists featured in the story if they had the opportunity. This promotes the questioning attitude which is so important when responding to science reports in the media. Comprehension exercises can be completed by children working individually. They can also serve as a basis for small group discussion. The text, graphic or photograph is cut out, laminated (but watch what is on the back!) and distributed, along with the questions, to each group. Ideas can subsequently be shared in a plenary session.

With younger children, newspapers can be used to extend vocabulary, both general and scientific. They can play 'stumped'. Children can search for words in an article that they think no one else in the class will understand. If they find a 'stumper' they get a point. The 'stumpers' are written on the board and, as a follow-up, the children find out what they mean and use each in a sentence.

Taking it further, children and young people can research the science behind a news story. They can conduct a 'Views on the News' survey, first devising a questionnaire or interview schedule and then questioning their friends or family. Subsequently, they can produce a graphic, collage, poster or PowerPoint display relating to the topic they have investigated.

Finally, newspaper articles and illustrations can be used as a resource or context for tackling teaching objectives which are more ambitious, particularly those that relate to 'science and society' and 'science and citizenship'. Thus, for example, they can contribute to learning outcomes such as understanding 'the strengths and limitations of science in the solution of everyday problems' and 'the interplay of rights and responsibilities, values and interests'. They can stimulate children and young people to 'consider other people's experiences' and to 'think about, express and explain views that are not their own'.

Such goals, however, generally call for teaching approaches which are more participatory than those outlined above. For example, for a particular article in the newspaper, pupils can, through discussion, try to distinguish between 'fact' and 'opinion'. For 'opinion' statements, they can conduct card-sorts (table-top activity) or post-it responses (walk-about activity) using I agree/I disagree/I am not sure or We support/We do not support, etc. Their views can be discussed in a plenary session. For a particular issue in the news, pupils can draw up a chart showing arguments for and against a particular position and then, in small groups, present the case from that perspective. They can carry out a structured discussion, debate, role play or drama exploring the goals, rights and responsibilities, values and interests of those involved. They can engage in 'imagine!' activities, picturing 'what might be' or 'what it might be like to be'.

As an example, consider Figure 12.1 again. The newspaper article was used to introduce the theme of pollution to a class of 12 year olds. The children then studied the topic as outlined in their textbook. At the end, the pupils returned to the article and discussed the council's smoke 'hot line'. They were then challenged, in small groups, to write a 2-minute script for a drama about a family debating whether they should report their neighbours. As you can imagine, a very lively discussion ensued! The planned learning outcomes for the lesson were also achieved. The young people began to understand that rights and responsibilities can conflict and that many factors, of which science is only one, contribute to our decision-making.

We have written a paper, Jarman and McClune (2003), which gives further ideas for science and citizenship education through the use of newspapers. Roger

Lock and Mary Ratcliffe's work (1998) also gives valuable advice on dealing with controversial social and ethical issues in science.

To end this section, some practical advice. Enlist help from others in looking for appropriate articles and remember some newspapers have an online presence and archive service. Consult both the broadsheets and the tabloids. Select articles to which pupils will relate, which are short and, preferably, accompanied by photographs or graphics. Consider abridging the text. With younger children, it may be necessary to read the articles with the class first. Structure the learning experiences carefully, explaining the purpose of the exercise and making explicit your desired learning outcomes.

Learning with newspapers: a context for reading

Turn the pages of any newspaper and you will quickly appreciate the great variety of elements which it combines – not only local and world news, but also sections devoted to lifestyle, business, travel and of course sport! Within these sections you will find news items, feature articles, editorial comment and letters, etc as well as carefully chosen images to help give the paper its visual interest. During the course of our research, we have seen science teachers use nearly every conceivable component of a newspaper from obituaries to stock market prices. In this section, however, we will focus on news stories, feature articles and images. We will illustrate with specific exemplars the potential which each has to support aspects of teaching and learning in science.

News stories to illustrate ideas about science

While it is often the underlying science 'content' which attracts teachers to a news story, in some articles the investigative process rather than the subject matter can be the focus for learning. News reports which include sufficiently detailed information about the scientists' approach to their research allow us to concentrate on the 'scientific enquiry' component of the National Curriculum (Sc1) irrespective of the specific science theme. This links well with pupils' own work on investigations.

An example, based on research linking chewing gum to enhanced memory illustrates this point. The findings caught the attention of the media and they were subsequently published in several national daily newspapers. This is not uncommon, and, when it occurs it presents a further learning opportunity in relation to science in the media, namely the merit of comparing information from a number of different sources. This is a valuable component of critical reading skills.

The news reports shown in Figure 12.2 have been used with a class of 14 year olds. A series of activities based on the articles required pupils to use their developing knowledge of 'scientific enquiry', encouraged them to approach newspapers with a questioning mind and illustrated the value of consulting a variety of sources of information. These formed the desired learning outcomes for the lesson. The *first activity* involved identifying what information we would hope to find out from reading a report about a scientific investigation. This provided an opportunity for the pupils to apply their knowledge of scientific enquiry as they compiled a list of information that would be important from the readers' perspective if they are to be able to evaluate the article.

After an introductory discussion about who chews gum and why, the headlines were used as a starting point:

> I've got an improved memory, by gum.
> Chewing gum can boost your brainpower.

Pupils were asked to look at the headlines and suggest:

- What question the scientists were trying to answer;
- The sort of experiment they might have carried out;
- Important information which should be included in a report of the scientists' work.

With appropriate guidance pupils should be able to generate a list of 'things I would want to know'. This list could include:

- Who did the investigation?
- Who paid for the investigation?
- Where was the investigation carried out?
- Where did the scientists report the results of their research?
- How was the investigation carried out?
- What were the observations or findings of the investigation?
- What conclusions were made?
- Is a possible explanation or a hypothesis included in the report?
- What do other scientists say about the research?

In the *second activity*, armed with their list of 'key questions', pupils examined Article A to see how many were actually answered in the news report.

As pupils used their 'key questions' to interact with the newspaper article they had further opportunity to work towards a deeper understanding of 'scientific

(Article A)

I've got an improved memory, by gum

CHEWING gum can improve your memory, scientists have found. The discovery will come as bad news for pavement-cleaners as well as parents, who are irritated by the perpetual motion of their children's jaws. But taking a packet of gum into exams might actually boost a student's performance. Neuroscientists at the University of Northumbria assessed the effects on memory of various substances – including rosemary, ginseng and aromatherapy oils.

They found that volunteers' ability to remember lists of words improved by more than a third if they were given a stick of gum. Dr Andrew Scholey told the British Psychological Society's annual conference in Blackpool: 'It was really quite a dramatic effect. It held up over and over again, so we are confident it is really helping.'

He is not certain why chewing gum quickens the mind, but said it may raise the heart rate, pumping more blood to the brain. The team also found that the smell of rosemary jogs the memory. It can help people recall faces and events from years earlier.

The scientists hope to use the information to produce drugs to combat dementia or Alzheimer's.

© *Daily Mail*
(14 March 2002)

(Article B)

Chewing gum can boost your brainpower

CHEWING GUM can greatly improve the performance of the brain, research issued yesterday suggests. People who chewed gum scored 40 per cent more in memory tests than those who didn't in a study presented to the British Psychological Society's annual conference in Blackpool. Dr Andrew Scholey, of the human cognitive neuroscience unit at the University of Northumbria, described the improvement in memory as 'quite dramatic'.

Although chewing gum was first marketed in America more than 150 years ago, Dr Scholey's work is the first to look at its impact on mental performance. Three groups of 25 people took part in the experiment. The first chewed gum throughout, the second had nothing and the third went through the chewing motion with nothing in their mouth. They then completed computerised tests to measure attention span, response times and long and short-term memory.

During tests to recall 15 words, the gum-chewers remembered two to three more than the non-chewers. There was no effect on concentration but the heartbeat of the gum-chewers increased by an average of three to four beats a minute compared with only a very slight increase improve memory because the heartbeat increased and delivered more oxygen and glucose to the brain. Alternatively, chewing could stimulate insulin production, which affected the part of the brain involved in memory.

Dr Scholey said: 'We found a very clear pattern of improved memory when gum among the fake chewers. Dr Scholey said chewing gum might was chewed. We think it is the effect of chewing that causes this rather than anything in the gum itself. There are lots of ways to improve mental function. This may be one of a series of interventions that people may want to try.'

Well known gum-chewers include Sir Alex Ferguson, Robbie Williams and Martine McCutcheon. Previous work by Dr Scholey has shown that ginseng can enhance the memory and gingko can improve memory and concentration.

By Lorna Duckworth
© *The Independent* (14 March 2002)

Figure 12.2 Using science-based news reports to support pupils' learning in science.

enquiry'. By scrutinising the report they were again applying their knowledge but also making judgements on the basis of that knowledge. How many questions were they able to answer? Which questions were they not able to answer from the article? How significant is the missing information? To be able to identify significant omissions is an important element in critical reading. It is necessary, however, to remind the pupils that when reading a newspaper report we are not reading the scientists' own account of their work – but the journalist's report. Missing experimental detail may not mean poor experimental design!

In the *third activity*, pupils read Article B which is an account of the investigation in another newspaper. Again they were challenged to answer their 'key questions'. How many questions were they able to answer using this article? Are there still questions they cannot answer? Do any important details in the accounts differ? If the experiment was carried out as described in the papers, how would you evaluate the investigation? How could you find out more information about this study?

Through this type of task, young people can learn a number of important lessons; for example, that newspaper reports may leave important questions unanswered and that different sources may provide different information. Furthermore, they can begin to internalise a framework for interrogating media texts of this sort.

As a *final activity* there is the opportunity to make personal sense of the news report and to explore implications for lifestyle. The following question makes an interesting starting point for a class debate or small group discussion: 'After reading these articles, do you think chewing gum should be permitted in class?'

Feature articles to enrich teaching and learning about science

In this section we will consider the use of science-based feature articles. Features differ from news stories in a number of ways. Although they cover topics that are timely, they are generally not breaking news and so are found toward the centre of the newspaper. Since they are not so time-sensitive, feature stories are often written further in advance of their publication than news stories. They also tend to be longer. As a consequence, they can contain more background information, explanation, analysis and speculation. The writing may be more interesting in style; the comments drawn from a wider range of sources. These characteristics ensure that many of these articles are especially appropriate for extending or enriching science teaching and learning, particularly with older students.

There are perhaps two related principles to bear in mind when considering using a feature article in the science classroom. The first is to aim to capitalise on its inherent interest value, on the reason it warranted coverage in the first place. The second is to exploit the specific characteristics of feature writing, for example, the broader contextualisation of an issue. Although the specific scientific content will undoubtedly figure in your judgement about the appropriateness of a particular article, too narrow a focus at an early stage may lead you to bypass useful material.

The extension and enrichment of teaching and learning about science through the use of feature articles may take many forms. In the example below, we consider activities which place science in social and historical contexts.

The potential of features to provide social and historical contexts is well illustrated by an article from the *Irish Times* (10 April 2003). It celebrates the life of Nobel Prize winning physicist Ernest Walton, one of the first to 'split the atom'. 'Making his name with a bang' was published in the week prior to the 71st anniversary of his landmark experiment and in the year which marks the centenary of Walton's birth. It describes events surrounding his pioneering work and gives an outline of the experiment which he and fellow researcher John Cockcroft carried out in April 1932. In highlighting Walton's involvement in later life as a campaigner against nuclear weapons, the article alludes to some of the ethical issues surrounding scientific research.

While pupils could simply be asked to read the article and draw up a concept map representing the science ideas described in the text, this section will indicate some activities which could be used to further support, extend and enrich pupils' learning in this area. Although most do not depend on detailed subject knowledge, one possible use of the article is as a starting point for further study for students following an advanced physics course.

A time line would make a useful starting point for this study. The article provides sufficient background information for pupils to construct a profile of Ernest Walton in this form. An extension, which would emphasise the social and historical context of his work, would be the construction of a parallel time line, drawing on pupils' own knowledge and research, charting events which they consider significant in the same period. The *first activity*, then, would centre around the following challenge:

Ernest Walton became famous for his work in nuclear physics; he was one of the first scientists to 'split the atom'. Use the information in the article to construct a profile of Ernest Walton in the form of a time line from 1903 to 1995. Can you find any additional information about him?

Construct a parallel time line for the same period placing on it events which you consider are important. Compare your time line with others in your group.

The article provides further opportunity to consider the experimental work in its social and historical setting. It highlights the role of other key figures such as Ernest Rutherford and the collaborative nature of the research. The article is supported by a picture of Cockcroft and Walton's apparatus including the 'packing-case dark room' in which observations were made. The bulky figure of Rutherford apparently had some difficulty squeezing into this confined space to confirm their findings. Detail like this is more than anecdotal embellishment; it gives pupils a real feel for science as human endeavour.

Pupils could engage with these issues through a second activity of the sort shown below. These aim to highlight aspects of the nature of scientific enquiry – the collegiality, the perseverance, the uncertainty, the frustration, as well as the pleasure and excitement associated with science in the making.

Read the article and try to imagine what it would have been like to work as a scientist engaged in this research. Describe your work and your feelings.

Or

This experiment attracted much media attention at the time. In not more than 150 words, write a news report that could have appeared in April 1932. Provide a headline for your story. Remember the model of atomic structure which you have today would not have been known in 1932!

A *final activity* develops the idea of ethical issues surrounding scientific research. Reference in the article to Walton's stance against the development of nuclear weapons provides a useful starting point for discussion of the beneficial and harmful outcomes of scientific research.

Developments in science can have beneficial and harmful applications that are not always obvious at the time. What evidence is there that Walton became concerned about some of the applications of nuclear physics research? What is Pugwash? Find out more about this organisation.

Do you think scientists bear some responsibility for the uses to which their discoveries are put?

Images to stimulate thinking about science

When considering newspapers as contexts for reading it may seem somewhat contradictory to include a section on images. It is sometimes said, however, that 'a picture is worth a thousand words'. The essential idea behind this statement is that images can play a powerful role in communication and newspapers concentrate a great deal of effort on their pictorial content, both to attract attention and to add to readers' understanding of the accompanying articles.

The graphic elements of a newspaper comprise photographs, montages, diagrams, maps, charts (of air quality, moon phases, etc.), editorial cartoons, strip cartoons, puzzles, logos and so on. We will highlight the use of three different types of images: photographs, editorial cartoons and explanatory graphics.

Photographs

In some cases the photograph is the story, but more often photographs, like headlines, are intended to catch the attention of the readers and to draw them into the article. The characteristics which make a photograph newsworthy can be exploited to support learning in science. The more famous the person, the more noteworthy the activity, or the more unusual the object, the more engaging the image. Pupils can describe the circumstances, discuss the underlying science, relate their prior knowledge to the situation, and use the image as a hook for memory or a springboard for further learning.

One image from the sports pages of *The Independent* (4 February 2003) had no associated story. It featured Australian fast bowler Bret Lee using the drag of a small parachute to increase his strength and stamina during training for the cricket World Cup 2003. This is a photograph with clear links to units on 'force' at various levels within the curriculum. The picture can encourage pupils to use their science knowledge to describe, explain and interpret. Equally important it is an opportunity to link science learning to newsworthy people and events.

An example of the unusual is 'the naked chicken' (*Daily Express*, 21 May 2002). Under the headline 'Fowl Play!' the picture shows a featherless chicken bred by Israeli scientists for use in hot climates. The image along with the associated story can be used to raise questions about genetic manipulation, inherited characteristics, selective breeding and animal welfare.

Some potentially useful images come from unexpected sources. A business section article featuring a well-known home-delivery Pizza company (*Daily Express*, 10 January 2002) was accompanied by a photograph of the familiar pizza delivery bag. Images like this can be used to prompt discussion and indeed investigation in relation to the insulating qualities of materials.

Editorial cartoons and explanatory graphics

The skill of the editorial cartoonist lies in the ability to get to the point of the story and to represent it with a simple and often amusing line drawing. Cartoons use few if any words, yet they often have a memorable impact.

The cartoon does not need to deal directly with a science story. One such example (Figure 12.3A) from Matt in the *Daily Telegraph* (15 November 2002) relates to the fire fighters' industrial dispute. However, those who take time to look will see that it links well to familiar science associated with mirrors and images. In contrast, some cartoons do relate to science in its social setting and the messages can be very compelling (Figure 12.3B; Matt, *Daily Telegraph*, 2002). Young people can be invited to identify the issue which prompted the cartoon, to try to tease out the position taken by the artist and to consider if there are alternative points of view on the subject. This can form the basis for a structured discussion or debate.

A well-designed explanatory graphic will also provide a useful resource for teaching. The rendering of complex scientific ideas into visual images, when done skilfully, can spark the interest of young people and scaffold their learning. In many cases the graphic can be used as pre-reading, providing information which will support the reader through the article.

In the example shown in Figure 12.3C (*Daily Express*, 1 February 2003), the graphic illustrates just a few sentences in a human-interest story which was reported in the news under the heading 'Doomed twins separated by laser surgery'. In the article we read that: 'their lives were saved after they were separated by pioneering laser surgery while still in their mother's womb . . . the laser was used to seal off blood vessels joining the twins together'. The accompanying graphic is similar to the images found in many secondary science texts. Use of the graphic may help students to value school science in understanding important subjects in people's lives. In addition to the obvious links to courses in human biology this image provides a link to the physical sciences, highlighting, for example, the use of ultrasound scanning and the endoscope.

(A)

(B)

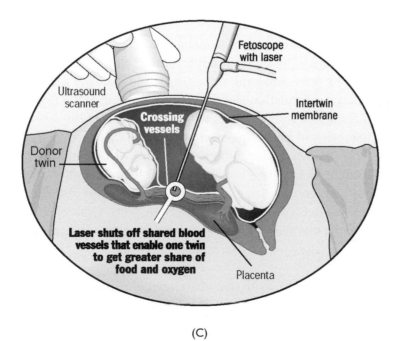

(C)

Figure 12.3 Using images to explore science ideas.

Pupils can also be challenged to become creators of newspaper-style graphics. They can caption photographs, prepare montages, design explanatory graphics, illustrate charts and draw editorial cartoons. For example, having examined instances from a number of papers, pupils could be invited to compose a cartoon about an environmental or health issue that they study in science. It should be humorous, but carry an important message. Stick drawings are welcome!

Learning with newspapers: a context for writing

Newspapers are written to be read. However, in the classroom, they can also be used as a springboard for developing pupils' competence in writing their own non-fiction texts. By their very nature, they offer a context (simulated or real) for encouraging young people to write for a particular purpose and for a particular audience. Not only can this contribute to their literacy skills, but, crucially, it can also contribute to their understanding of how media texts are constructed.

Writing with style

We tend to browse newspapers, scanning the pages until an article or image catches and holds our attention. Journalists, for their part, aim to make us stop and read. As a consequence of this, and other factors such as constraints of space, there are certain conventions associated with the writing of news stories. The headline is designed to attract attention and to convey what the article is about. The 'intro' or lead paragraph draws the reader into the account. In a news story, the important information is right at the beginning of the report, with the background information following in the body and close of the article. This is sometimes characterised as the 'inverted pyramid' style of writing, where the 'famous five W's' (the who, what, where, when and why of the story) appear early in the account and the less important detail later. In reality, however, this rather oversimplifies news writing, and is even less evident in feature writing. In the body of the article, ideas are expressed concisely. Quotations are often used. Generally, the sections of the story follow in order of importance. Small paragraphs break up the text, making it easier to read.

Pupils can be challenged to write science-related headlines, news stories, features, editorials, letters to the editor, problem page answers, etc. They can write about events, issues, scientists past and present and about their own science investigations. Figure 12.4, for example, shows a 'front page' prepared by a child from Kilkeel Primary School in Northern Ireland. This relates to experiments on static electricity, a topic introduced by their teacher with reference to his magic comb!

KILKEEL P.S. NEWS

FIRST WITH THE GOSSIP

1st APRIL 2003   50p

HARRY POTTER'S MAGIC COMB FOUND!

SPARKS FLY IN HAIR RAISING BATTLE

A pupil at a Northern Ireland primary school was at the centre of controversy today amid claims that he had found Harry Potter's magical comb.Matthew Quinn (11) claimed to have picked up the comb after it fell from Harry's pocket as he flew over Avenue On, near his home,on April the first.To back up his claims Matthew asked one of his classmates to pour water from a jug into a basin slowly.To everyone's amazement as he drew the comb near the water it" bent" soaking the pupils sitting alongside.He then set a 10p coin on its edge and balanced a matchstick carefully covering the lot with a clear,plastic tumbler.He challenged anyone to move the match without touching the tumbler!!After several failed attempts from pupils Matthew waved the comb over the glass and the matchstick fell.

Harry Potter is said to be livid at Matthew's claims and has commenced legal proceedings for the return of the comb.He claims Matthew is a fraud and that his "tricks" are all down to static electricity.Matthew was unavailable for comment today.

Figure 12.4 A 'newspaper report' of science experiments.

'Writing for real'

This final activity describes a project in which young people were given the opportunity to write up a science-based news story for publication in their local community newspaper. They were, as one girl observed, 'writing for real'.

The first step required the selection of a 'storyline'. The issue, clearly, needs to be newsworthy. It should also interest the young people involved – in this case a class of 14 year olds. Finally, it should be one with which the school is content to be associated. Many socio-scientific issues are controversial and this needs to be considered at the outset. In this example, the pupils focused on a public consultation exercise relating to regional plans for waste management. The local council was contacted and officers agreed to visit and discuss with class members the survey results for their town. That the findings were released first in the school made the story something of a scoop!

In parallel with this process, the co-operation of the local newspaper was secured. The editor of the *Community Telegraph* was very positive about and supportive of the project. A journalist from the paper agreed to visit the school and speak to the class giving guidance, in simple terms, about how to proceed.

The project proper then began. Prior to the visits, members of the class were given individual resource packs comprising a 'press pass', 'reporter's notebook' and background information in the form of a 'press release' from the local council. The first visitors were representatives from the council. They presented information from two perspectives: first, dealing with general matters relating to waste management and second, providing specific information about the public's response to their proposed waste management plan. The pupils then had the opportunity to question the experts, as in a press conference. The second visit was from the journalist. She skilfully focused on the four key elements of the story production: researching the information, writing for an audience, composing a headline and selecting the images.

Following this, there is value in a whole class discussion, brainstorming possible ideas for inclusion in the newspaper articles. This provides the focus for future small group work and contributes to 'whole class ownership' of the final product. The young people subsequently divided into four 'specialist groups' to take on each of research, writing, headlines and graphics. Each group was given a 'training pack' to help them with their particular assignment; the graphics group, for example, completed an exercise based on illustrated charts from *USA Today*. As they tackled their tasks, early ideas were circulated to aid inter-group consultation. Special arrangements were made to give the writing group time to draft and redraft their copy.

The final article, together with the suggestions for headlines and graphics, was submitted to the newspaper editor. Showing wonderful sensitivity to the spirit of the project, he proposed publishing not only the text of the story along with his preferred headline and graphics, but also the other suggestions for headlines and graphics. The young people of Priory College in Northern Ireland were rewarded for their work by no less than a centre-page spread in their *Community Telegraph*!

Conclusion

Newspapers can help bridge the gap between the classroom and the 'real world'. They are a lively complement to the school textbook and, still more, to the ubiquitous revision guide. In the introduction, however, we stressed that newspapers are not textbooks. To read them with discernment, children and young people need to understand something about science, certainly, but they also need to understand something about the media.

There are certain characteristics of news reporting of which young people, ideally, should be aware. Journalists write within constraints of *time, space* and, sometimes, *expertise*. They write for an *audience*; they write to an *agenda*. Together, these interact to influence the presentation of scientific and socio-scientific issues in the press. Thus, for example, news reporting is a hectic business and exhaustive research is not always possible. Space is at a premium. This favours an economy of words which may mean that important details, including reservations and restrictions, are omitted. The absence of such conditionals may make information appear more certain than it is. This also favours reference to only a limited number of sources, which may influence the way opposing views are represented and weighted. Many science-related stories are written by generalists rather than specialist science correspondents.

Furthermore, news is not inherent in an event. An event *becomes* news when it is judged to be so by journalists or others. Thus, news production is a process of selection and also of construction. In its creation, writers are acutely aware of audience; the article must attract, as well as inform, its readers. This privileges, in all papers, stories with a human-interest angle. It also, in some instances, leads to a tendency to sensationalise, for example, to cast a development as a 'breakthrough' or to inflate expectations of what the new science can accomplish. Much science-in-the-media is science-in-the-making, where knowledge, by its nature, is tentative and is contested. This may be misrepresented as conflict or confusion. Finally, newspapers are free-market enterprises, dependent for income on advertising and on readership. They have agendas: commercial, proprietorial, political, ideological. Inevitably, media messages have embedded values and points of view. The *Impartial Observer* is not. Nor could it be!

Children and young people may meet many of these ideas in their English (or media studies) curriculum. Primary teachers of science will want to exploit these links. Secondary teachers of science can often benefit from working co-operatively with teachers from these subject areas. Additionally, the 'Newspapers in Science Education' group based at Queen's University in Belfast is developing approaches and resources to support the exploration of some of these complex issues in the science classroom.

In conclusion, we believe newspapers can bring science to life in exciting and unexpected ways. This is not to say, of course, that this resource should displace all others or that media-related aims should dominate all that we do. Any approach will become tedious if over-used. However, bringing newspapers into our classrooms can enrich the science curriculum and enliven science teaching. It can also encourage lifelong learning and empower our children and young people as citizens in a news-rich society.

References

Allan, S., 2002, *Media, Risk and Science*, Buckingham: Open University Press.

Gregory, J. and Miller, S., 1998, *Science in Public*, Cambridge, MA: Perseus Publishing.

House of Lords' Select Committee on Science and Technology, 2000, *Science and Society*, London: HMSO.

Jarman, R. and McClune, B., 2002, 'A survey of the use of newspapers in science instruction by secondary teachers in Northern Ireland', *International Journal of Science Education*, 24(10), 997–1020.

Jarman, R. and McClune, B., 2003, 'Bringing newspaper reports into the classroom: Citizenship and science education', *School Science Review*, 84(309), 121–9.

Lock, R. and Ratcliffe, M., 1998, 'Learning about social and ethical applications of science' in Ratcliffe, M. (ed.), *ASE Guide to Secondary Science Education*, Cheltenham: Stanley Thornes.

McClune, B. and Jarman, R., 2001, 'Making a place for newspapers in secondary science education, in de Jong, O., Savelsbergh, E. R. and Alblas, A. (eds) *Teaching for Scientific Literacy: Context, Competency and Curriculum*, Utrecht: CD-B Press.

Wellington, J., 1991, 'Newspaper science: school science: friends or enemies?', *International Journal of Science Education*, 13(4), 363–72.

Wellington, J. and Osborne, J., 2001, *Language and Literacy in Science Education*, Buckingham: Open University Press.

Resources

Organisations

The Newspapers in Science Education (NISE) Group can be contacted at Graduate School of Education, Queens University, Belfast.

Many newspapers have a 'Newspapers in Education' (NiE) service which provides general information and resources.

Websites

Many newspapers have an online presence and some an electronic archive service.

Some NiE groups, particularly those in the USA, have websites. For science, the New York Times Learning Network is particularly interesting. Website: www.nytimes.com/learning

The Why? Files is a US site which looks at the science behind the news. Website: http://whyfiles.org

CD-Roms

Ideas and Evidence published by the Pupil Researcher Initiative and Collins Education has a unit 'Getting into the Media'.

Only Connect? published for Science Year by the Association for Science Education has a unit 'Science EXTRA! Using Newspapers in the Science Classroom'.

Other resources

SATIS 8–14, Box 2 Unit 8 deals with 'Reporting Science'.

Chapter 13

Learning science through ICT at home

Jerry Wellington and Joey Britto

Overview

The use of ICT (information and communication technology) in homes is growing faster than its use in schools and colleges – and there are already more systems in homes than in educational settings. This chapter argues that science teachers and educators should take serious note of how, what, when and why children learn science via ICTs at home. What are the implications of ICT use at home for science teachers in schools? Do home systems interfere with school education or can they be used to enhance it? How should teachers respond to, and assess, work done using home ICT? Is the home situation widening the gap between one set of pupils (the 'haves' of ICT) and another? Suggestions for practice, school policies and action research for the future are put forward.

Why consider home learning of science with ICT?

One of the recurring findings in educational research over the last three decades is that the influence of the home and family background on a child's ability and achievement is at least as great as that of the school. For example, Schibeci writes, in reporting a review of a number of studies of relative influence that: 'Factors outside of schools have a strong influence on students' educational outcomes, perhaps strong enough to 'swamp' the effects of variations in educational practices' (Schibeci, 1989, p. 13). In addition, research by Heyneman (1997), using data from 29 countries, indicated that school science achievement is far more greatly affected by the home environment in so-called developed countries than in 'developing countries'. His research concludes that in India, 90 per cent of science achievement depends on school learning, with only 10 per cent due to home factors. The position is reversed in countries such as Holland, Australia, Scotland and England, where only 25 to 35 per cent of school science achievement is attributable to the school environment. Home factors are far more influential.

We therefore start from the premise that, although there is no substitute for properly structured science teaching in schools, the home has a major influence on student learning, attitude and attainment in science.

The extent of ICT resources in homes

Facts and figures on how many computer systems there are in homes are unreliable to say the least. An additional problem, discussed later, is that the presence of a home computer is no guarantee of easy, educational or productive access for a child in that home. In one of the few books reporting in-depth research in this field, Sanger *et al.* (1997, p. 5) cite a range of surveys, one of which indicated in 1995 that 39 per cent of British households had home computers. The survey also suggested that 'most middle-class parents see home computers as an educational tool', while 'fewer than a quarter of working-class parents agree, seeing computers as mainly for games playing'. Sanger also cited an Inteco forecast which predicted in 1995 that by 1998, 47 per cent of UK households would have personal computers with 66 per cent of those having CD-ROM drives and 9 per cent of them connected online. That forecast suggested that although '86 per cent of high income families will possess a PC, 53 per cent of homes are currently without access to computers' – an issue we return to later.

In 1999, Livingstone and Bovill found that 53 per cent of 6–17 year olds had a computer in the home. The growing trend of home computer ownership is clearly evident in more recent surveys such as *Young People and ICT* (DfES, 2002) where it was found that 81 per cent of households in the UK already had access to a personal or laptop computer in the home, compared with 78 per cent in 2001. Moreover, the survey found that 68 per cent of households had access to the Internet at home, compared with 64 per cent in 2001.

A few crude calculations show the magnitude of ICT at home when compared with schools. There are about 23,000 primary and 4,500 secondary schools in the UK. Based on DfES statistics we can put a rough figure of 100 computers per secondary school and 12 per primary (although DfES figures suggest that nearly a quarter of these may be used for administrative purposes). Crudely then, considering advances since the late 1990s, the UK probably has over one million computer systems in its schools. Compare this with the very conservative estimate of 5 to 7 million in homes – that represents a ratio of almost seven to one. The rapid rollout of broadband Internet services in most parts of the country means that purchases of home computers will continue to increase. The ImpaCT2 Report to the DfES (2002/2003) suggests that already, for most pupils, the amount of time spent on ICT at home greatly exceeds the time spent on ICT at school. The report also shows that many pupils enjoy greater autonomy to explore the exciting possibilities of ICT at home and the opportunity to use it for longer periods of time than that allowed at school. It is also true that many pupils have sustained, ready access to cutting edge ICT equipment and resources at home to support a wide variety of pursuits.

What are home computers used for?

One of the most widely cited studies of home computer use (Downes, 1999) indicated that children's use of ICT at home involved 'playful interaction with the computer, often leading to exploratory approaches to learning about both the computer and the task itself'. As we shall see, this has important implications for the learning of science.

The two main uses of home ICT in this study were for 'business and education' and for 'games playing'. Most surveys have produced similar findings: home computers are predominantly used for game playing (see Livingstone and Bovill, 1999). The latter found very little use of computers by 5–17 year olds for educational purposes in the USA. They put this down to: lack of parental encouragement and knowledge; poor communication between home and school; and poor communication between software producers and the domestic consumer. Parents surveyed mentioned the problem of cost and a lack of advice on what to buy. We return to these points later. The research certainly points to a gap or a 'discontinuity' between the home and school as learning environments. Finally, Livingstone and Bovill (1999) confirmed that most home computer activity (in their study, with 6–17 year olds) centres on game playing, despite the fact that parents had bought the computers with educational purposes in mind.

It could be argued, of course, that game playing is a vehicle for developing a wide range of skills, tactics and strategies. Hypothesising, speculating (what if . . .?) predicting, inferring, deducing, trial and error, learning from mistakes, problem solving: all these skills are seen as desirable in a science context. They formed the backbone of the Process movement in Science curricula in the 1980s and 1990s; they have been incorporated into the science programmes of study in the National Curriculum and would seem to form part of the new Key Stage 3 Science Strategy (DfES, 2002). However, the jury is still out on whether these skills are generic and transferable.

One other issue concerns the fact that access to computers at home is equally as complex and problematic in the home as it is in school. One cannot assume that 'home computer' equals 'free access for a child'. There are often parents and siblings with as strong, or stronger claims, on its use as the school learner. Location, security and control are as present in the ecology of the home as in the school setting. Constraints operate in both institutions.

The 'ecology of learning': comparing the school science environment with home learning using ICT

We find it useful to employ an ecological analogy in comparing informal, home learning with the more formal and statutory learning that occurs in schools. We define ecology as the investigation of the total relations of an animal to both its organic and inorganic environment (based on the Greek words 'oikos' meaning household or homestead, and 'logos' meaning study).

Kerawalla and Crook (2002) give an excellent discussion of 'domestic ecology' in contrast with that in school. They talk of the 'social envelope' (including social expectations and arrangements) and the systems of activity within which children learn in the two habitats. There is a huge contrast in the nature of the learning environment in the home compared with school: learning is linked to an adult at school (the teacher) compared with home learning which has little or no adult interference or engagement; social, paired, collaborative learning with school ICT is often an isolated, individual activity at home; the informal atmosphere of the home contrasts with the formal, more pressured environment at school.

The fact is, there are fundamental differences between learning in an institution which we know as a 'school' or 'college', and learning which does not take place under institutional constraints. Some of these contrasts are summarised in Table 13.1 which shows the differences in the ecologies of domestic and school learning, with some of the key features of learning with ICT in the middle column. The table illustrates that home learning and the domestic ecology are far more conducive to learning with ICT than are school or classroom learning, as we now discuss.

Although resource levels for ICT in schools are generally increasing, schools where levels are low find that this is a major factor in inhibiting its use. But, by considering the ecology of school learning, we can identify other factors in addition to resource levels which act against the use of ICT in teaching and learning in a school setting:

1   Control: secondary teachers, especially subject specialists, are reluctant to relinquish control over children's learning – quite rightly too, given the external pressures on them to increase attainment in tests and examinations.

Table 13.1 Comparing the ecologies of school learning and home learning with learning through ICT

Classroom learning	Learning through ICT	Home learning
Conformity and order is central; learning is compulsory and collective	Personal empowerment is central; learning is individualised (usually)	Voluntary; personal; individual (often)
Keeping people 'together', 'on track', on course; directed, staged, sequenced, paced learning	Exploring, having a free rein, going their own way; free access to information	Free range, undirected, haphazard, unstructured, unsequenced
Measurable learning outcomes; assessment driven; extrinsically motivated	Free-ranging learning outcomes	Many unintended outcomes (outcomes more difficult to measure); not always assessment driven or extrinsically motivated
Timetabled, 'forced' access; teacher control	Flexible access, when it suits them; learner or teacher control	Free access; learner (or parent) control
Clear boundaries and targets, e.g. times, deadlines, subject divisions	Unclear boundaries and targets	Few boundaries and limits; open-ended
Teacher-led, teacher-centred	Learner-led, learner-centred	Learner-centred
Teacher filtered, distilled, vetted	Unfiltered, not always vetted or censored	Often unfiltered or unvetted
Legislated for, e.g. by National Curriculum or other statutes	Not always governed by documents	Not legislated for

2   Supervision/intervention: past studies of ICT use show that teachers are sometimes prepared to allow unsupervised use of technology, but still want to intervene by imposing some structure on it, e.g. time limits, guided activity (worksheets). The instance one of us observed of a handwritten worksheet being used to structure and guide pupils' use of a CD-ROM may be ironic but not uncommon.

3   Curriculum dominance: the power of the centralised, subject-based curriculum and the need for ICT to have a clear curriculum 'fit' still dominate as much as ever.

4   Classroom and school organisation: fitting IT into the typical secondary school classroom is still a problem.

5   The 'logistics' of the school: split sites, stairs, subject blocks, separate buildings, subject boundaries and divisions – all these act as a constraint on school use of ICT.

6   Teacher practices and teacher attitudes: this is the most complex issue of all. There is an inherent tension between the ecology of the classroom and the culture of learning with ICT. Multimedia can provide access to vast quantities of information, give learners the power to explore and

manipulate information, and enable individuals to construct their own 'knowledge base'. In contrast, the ecology and culture of the classroom is governed by the need for teachers to control learning outcomes, to maintain authority, to meet the demands of content-laden syllabuses, and at the same time moderate the behaviour of a large group of young people. The strategies which teachers have necessarily developed for achieving the latter set of aims clash with their role in allowing or even nurturing the former. As Tyack and Cuban (1995) put it, 'computer meets classroom – classroom wins'.

Yet few people doubt the value of ICT and multimedia systems in teaching and learning. If one observes students of any age working with them, their potential for active learning, exploration and motivation is apparent. But when this marvellous platform for learning meets the institution, strange things happen. Innovations seem to die on contact with the inertia and 'institutional reality' of the school. Computers, video discs, IT and now ICT have generally (with a few important and fascinating exceptions) had little impact on life in the secondary classroom. Computers have not radically altered classroom activity; they are typically used to add to existing practices rather than replace them. For many teachers, ICT is seen as just 'another thing they have to do'. Rather than schools and teaching patterns adapting to *accommodate* the change, the innovation becomes *assimilated* to existing, unchanging patterns of schooling.

We need to recognise these trends, which are observable over the last century in the use of technology in education. Teachers will continue to use technologies that 'fit familiar routines and classroom procedures'; teachers will use technologies to 'enhance their regular instruction but rarely to transform their teaching' (Tyack and Cuban, 1995, p. 122). This is perfectly understandable given the management, curricular and societal constraints within which they work. The classroom itself has proved to be the hardest thing to change.

Home use and external pressures

The England and Wales National Curriculum (NC) for schools and initial teacher training (ITT)

Many of the NC programmes of study and attainment targets for IT can be fulfilled more effectively by home use than at school. For example, at Key Stage 3 pupils are expected to 'become critical and largely *autonomous* users of IT, aware of the ways in which IT tools and information sources can help them in their work'. As Sanger *et al.* point out (1997, p. 37) from the evidence of their research into schools, 'this is a forlorn requirement' – in the school context. At an earlier stage (KS1) pupils should be given opportunities to 'examine and discuss their experiences of IT' – again, home use could be brought in here, but as discussed later this would need sensitive handling to be equitable. Pupils are expected to use IT to 'communicate their ideas' (KS1) and to 'create good quality presentations' (KS3 onwards). To achieve level 7 of the attainment targets, they must 'identify the advantages and limitations of different data-handling applications, and select and use suitable information systems'. All these, and indeed most of the other statutory requirements of the NC, can be fulfilled by home use. Probably the most important is that pupils should become 'critical and autonomous users of IT'. However, to achieve these objectives at home requires good teaching at school – an important example of the need for home–school liaison.

Another very good reason for diverting our attention more towards the home in future planning for ICT in education can be found in elements that were introduced in the national curriculum for initial teacher training (ITT) in England and Wales (DfEE, 1998). Several statements in the standards document refer to ICT in the home. For example, 'trainees must be taught to identify in their planning . . . the fact that some pupils may already be very competent e.g. because of home access'. The same document talks of trainees 'structuring pupils' work to . . . maximise use of time and resource rather than, for example, allowing pupils to search freely on the Internet or CD-ROM'. Later statements are equally important to home use of ICT. For example, trainees are 'to ensure that assessment of ICT based work is based on the quality of their work within the subject and is not just based on the quality of the presentation or the complexity of the technology used'. In addition, trainees must be taught to 'ensure that all pupils have opportunities to use ICT, and that their experience takes account of any home use or other previous experience of ICT'.

Vocational rhetoric

Finally, it is clear that there will be increasing external pressures acting to increase the presence of ICT in homes and to increase the use of that ICT in education for young people and adults. All the political rhetoric of the last 20 years has referred to the vocational significance of IT in schools from Kenneth Baker's launch of the 'Micros. in Schools scheme' onwards. This alleged vocational importance of IT has been fuelled by advertising and parental pressure. The kind of rhetoric we frequently hear and read refers to the importance of preparing our children for the information age or 'the information society', or of giving them 'the skills for the jobs of tomorrow'. This rhetoric may be optimistic and overstated, but it is certainly influential.

What do we know about home use of ICT in learning science?

A search of the literature over recent years, including websites, shows that researchers have largely ignored the home. The Sanger study of young children (aged 4 to 9), videos and computer games (Sanger *et al.*, 1997) is one notable exception. Sanger *et al.* themselves admit the difficulty of researching this area. It is 'messy'; interviews with parents and children may not always be reliable, so first-hand observation is needed; access is difficult, e.g. into homes, private rooms, even bedrooms; data are difficult to categorise; it is impossible to construct a statistical sample. Despite these complications, Sanger and his team produced some fascinating data and reported them in a fair and honest way. Perhaps this is what future research on this field should aspire to. Their work is too extensive and wide ranging to summarise here, but they report on several issues pertinent to this chapter, some of them quite worrying, which are mentioned later.

Clearly, there are difficulties in probing home use of ICT and the home–school link (what Sanger has described as the 'air lock' between home and school). But, despite the difficulties and the 'messiness', in our view it is essential to concentrate on this area, for the benefit of the future of ICT in learning science. Teachers in training and practising teachers could valuably conduct their own qualitative studies on:

- pupils' views on ICT at home and school;
- teachers' reactions to ICT work at home and its implications for their role at school;
- examples of 'good practice' in developing home–school links;
- case studies of individual children and their use of ICT at home;
- difficulties and issues presented by home use of ICT, such as equity, the role of the parent or siblings, gender differences.

There is a lot of work to be done – it is too important to be neglected just because it is messy and time-consuming. One of the saving graces, however, is that teachers can become involved in it, as active agents for researching and developing their own practice.

Case studies carried out in the past (Wellington, 2001) raise interesting points about such issues as: family 'status'; the role of parents; the attitudes and reactions of teachers; the potential of home computers to fulfil many of the requirements of the National Science Curriculum; the lack of knowledge by teachers of the excellent resources which pupils have at their fingertips at home.

Difficulties, issues and ways forward

Key issues and outline strategies

In this section the key issues are raised and practical strategies for addressing them are briefly presented.

Access and inequality

As with so many issues in education, the problems of equity and access with ICT are perennial and recurrent. The problem of equity occurs in three areas, all of which feature prominently in home use of ICT: the areas of gender, social class and economic status. Even in the very early days of micros. in schools (and homes) Hannon and Wooler in Wellington (1985, p. 93) warned that 'the gulf between children of different classes will widen'. Huge differences continue in home access, and use. There are large differences between even pupils in the same class, let alone between different schools. It can be argued that this inequity has always existed – with books, pencils, a quiet room and a desk on which to work but undoubtedly, the use of ICT can exaggerate these differences. The issue of equal opportunity needs to be addressed both at school level (e.g. by the IT co-ordinator) and by individual classroom teachers. Are homeworks set which rely on IT use? For those without home access, should the school policy on access favour them – or will this create stigma? How should access to IT outside of timetabled hours be shared out and managed?

Control and guidance

A second issue for teachers in considering ICT use at home, referring back to Table 13.1, concerns the degree of control and guidance which they can and should exert over pupils' learning. The very nature of home learning, i.e. free rein, uncontrolled, unstructured, can be both a virtue and a vice. One of Sanger *et al.*'s (1997) most barbed findings was that 'significant adults' (and this included parents *and* teachers) were unable to discern what elements of ICT would be beneficial for children's learning. He reports a *laissez-faire* attitude among parents when it comes to new technology. Given the uncontrolled, unfiltered and unchecked nature of much of the material on the Internet, this can be a dangerous stance to take – much of the material that young people encounter may be educationally inaccurate and inappropriate as well as being morally dubious.

Schools need to audit, in a sensitive way, the extent and nature of home use of ICT. Without this information they cannot begin to improve or exploit it, or develop a school policy towards it. It needs to be recognised that home and family life is as complex and varied as school and school life. For example, we cannot always assume that parents are willing participants in introducing and using ICT in the home. Nor can we assume that school pupils have unlimited, uncontrolled access to the home ICT system: other family members may be in direct competition; access and use may also be controlled and constrained for other reasons, such as the phone bill!

Given these qualifications and cautions, parents do need, and will probably welcome, guidance on improving and developing the educational use of ICT at home. One suggestion is that a small leaflet could be produced, perhaps by an IT co-ordinator, giving ideas, guidance and encouragement to parents, with concrete examples of the kind of work which can be expected and accepted.

Bypassing the brain and plagiarism: whose work is it?

A third issue is concerned with the obvious fact that material on a computer, a CD-ROM, DVD or the Internet can find its way straight from the machine (or cyberspace) on to a piece of paper with no cerebral intervention by the student whatsoever. We have all heard the cliché about the marvel of the information age when, at the press of a button, we have a 'world of information' at our fingertips. Well, at the press of another button or a click on the mouse, the same information can go straight from the CD-ROM or the Internet on to a piece of paper, into a plastic wallet and be handed to the teacher. The brain has been bypassed. Teachers will be familiar with the huge, unfiltered chunks of text and illustrations printed straight from the web or a CD/DVD (but, as some teachers have asked in discussion, is this any different from copying from a book? Yes, we would answer, in some ways). More seriously, some students are handing in such work and claiming it as their own.

The first stage is for teachers to foster and develop a critical outlook in pupils (a sort of 'healthy scepticism') towards IT. When is it appropriate to use IT and when not? What are the problems, dangers even, of using IT at home? For example, is the Internet material they are using accurate? Where did it come from? Is it biased? The same healthy scepticism needs to be applied to use of multimedia on (say) CD-ROM, although such material has usually been filtered, checked and vetted before being 'packaged' on to a disc. The aim of educating pupils to become critical users of ICT should be at the centre of the school's role.

The more contentious issue concerns teachers' reactions to pupils' work on computer. It has been suggested that some teachers are more favourably disposed to work which has been (say) desktop published or simply word-processed – while others react negatively and with (sometimes justifiable) suspicion towards coursework or homework presented via ICT. Above all, a school policy needs to be developed (perhaps by the IT co-ordinator) relating to home use of IT. For example: is word-processed or desktop-published homework acceptable: always, sometimes or never? How should it be judged and marked, e.g. in comparison with hand written work? Should teamwork at home around one pupil's system be encouraged and how should it be assessed? Where is the line to be drawn on plagiarism, e.g. with GCSE science coursework?

A threat to the teacher?

Finally, and more fundamentally, the teacher's role is brought into question as a result of home use of ICT. Some teachers do feel vulnerable in the presence of the 'pupil classroom expert' on ICT, when the teacher is using IT as a teaching tool in his or her lesson. Home use of ICT can also create students who genuinely know far more about a topic than a teacher, as a result (perhaps) of long hours on the Internet or other focused (even obsessive) study of a subject at home – whether it be the dinosaurs, the spread of AIDS, the geology of Europe, the solar system, the human body, UFOs or water divining. The potential for young people to become genuine 'experts' on specific topics has always been there, but has been greatly enhanced by the spread of ICT. These issues may not be a problem for some teachers, but our discussions with groups suggest that they are a real concern for many. In short, the presence of ICT in homes may threaten the teacher's authority both as a 'subject expert' and as someone in authority or control over the learning situation.

This points to the need to research and implement a programme of staff development in the area of 'the changing role of the teacher'. This could happen at school level, for example in departmental and whole staff meetings and discussion or as a theme for in-service training days.

Further practical advice and suggestions

Using ICT at home can play a vital role in the affective domain of science learning, by developing enthusiasm, curiosity, interest and fascination for science. School-based ICT provides children with a huge array of possibilities for the learning of science but this will normally entail the deployment of additional equipment and resources that will *usually* only be accessible in school (e.g. data-logging equipment, measurement and analysis software and so on). Home-based ICT is therefore primarily used for two purposes: to access, prepare and present information (e.g. for a school assignment) or to follow-up some science interest the student may have. In both cases, the finding of information is central to the endeavour.

Schools need to be in a position to provide advice for parents and older pupils when it comes to using ICT for learning science at home. One of the most obvious ways in which children can do this is through the use of the world-wide-web. There are some wonderfully crafted websites (see later), which provide extremely good resources both for the teacher and the student. The advent of broadband services to many parts of Britain (again, issues of equity are raised here – there are some areas which will be disadvantaged because of the technical limitations in older telephone exchanges and therefore no broadband internet access) means that children now have very fast access, and competition between technology providers becomes fiercer. Children can now visit a host of interactive UK-based science websites of which those listed in Table 13.2 are representative.

The last two entries in Table 13.2 are of particular interest to parents and teachers in that they provide useful and independent advice and reviews of web-based resources for learning. The Parents Information network (PIN) is especially impressive, in giving examples of good quality software for science at different key stages and listing useful criteria for judging quality.

Judging quality on the WWW

There is a great deal of excellent Internet science content created by educational bodies and organisations but, generally speaking, children should be advised that they cannot always assume information on the internet has been *carefully* evaluated and is *always* accurate and reliable. The website content of the sites

Table 13.2 Examples of useful science websites

---

www.bbc.co.uk/education/dynamo/lab/index.shtml
www.bbc.co.uk/science/humanbody/standard/index.shtml
www.4learning.co.uk/ict/ourbodies/health/index.shtml
www.channel4.com/science/index.html
www.hhmi.org/coolscience/
www.issen.org.uk/links_science.htm
www.schoolscience.co.uk/content/index.asp
http://www.sci-journal.org/
http://www.ngfl.gov.uk/search
http://www.learn.co.uk
http://www.nhm.ac.uk/science/index.html
http://www.ase.org.uk/
http://www.dfes.gov.uk/parents/learning/
http://www.pin.org.uk/
http://www.teem.org.uk

---

in Table 13.2 has already been tried and tested by teachers, especially the BBC and Channel 4 ones, but the reality is that anyone can post content on the Internet in an unvetted state.

Advice to children should include the fact that a great deal of content is North American and not really aimed at a UK audience. The problem with this is that the information will probably not be set out in such a way as to coincide with the National Curriculum's Key Stages. A means of getting around this is to ensure that the search facility in use is filtered for the UK. It is best to keep to a few of the better known search engines such as Google (www.google.co.uk), Lycos (www.lycos.co.uk) or Yahoo (www.yahoo.co.uk), always ensuring that the .uk suffix is used as this limits the search to websites that are hosted within the UK. Search terms should also always include a reference to the Key Stage as this, in effect, limits the returns to English and Welsh educational sites.

In recent trial searches specifically for the purposes of this chapter, it was found that there was no problem accessing valuable, quality resources on the internet for use by teachers and children. Using a well-known search engine, the search term *the states of matter + KS3* returned a total of 610 hits. The first page of results is shown in the screen-grab in Figure 13.1.

GCSE CHEMISTRY REVISION NOTES ... The Three **States** of **Matter**. ...
www.wpbschoolhouse.btinternet.co.uk/ page03/3_52states.htm - 39k - 30 Mar 2004 - Cached - Similar pages

btmpiwpb **KS3**-KS4-GCSE CHEMISTRY matching pair QUIZ Q's at Doc ...
KS3-KS4-GCSE nifty and short matching pair CHEMISTRY Exercises. ... pictures); (2. particle
pictures); (3. state changes) on the **STATES** OF **MATTER** (gas, liquid ...
www.wpbschoolhouse.btinternet.co.uk/page17/page17.htm - 12k - Cached - Similar pages
[More results from www.wpbschoolhouse.btinternet.co.uk]

[PDF] **States** of **Matter** Activities
File Format: PDF/Adobe Acrobat - View as HTML
Page 1. http://www.collaborativelearning.org/statesofmatter.pdf **States** of **Matter**
Activities We ... 3. Another Connect Four activity for **KS3** up from Rose Elgar in ...
www.collaborativelearning.org/statesofmatter.pdf - Similar pages

BBC - Schools - **KS3** Bitesize - Science - Chemistry - Materials 1
Classifying Materials 1 The **states** of **matter**. There are three **states**
of **matter** - solid, liquid and gas. Each state has particular ...
www.bbc.co.uk/schools/ks3bitesize/science/ chemistry/materials1_1.shtml - 18k - Cached - Similar pages

BBC - Schools - **KS3** Bitesize - Science - Chemistry - Materials 2
... In this Revision Bite we cover: More on the three **states** of **matter**; Molecules,
atoms and sub-atomic particles; Naming metal and non-metal compounds; ...
www.bbc.co.uk/schools/ks3bitesize/science/ chemistry/materials2_intro.shtml - 16k - Cached - Similar pages
[More results from www.bbc.co.uk]

Teacher Resource Exchange
... Download | Similar]. Last Updated: 2 Aug 01. 2. **States** of matter **KS3**:7G.
Developing Idea, Liz Beatty, ovingdean hall (20 Sep 03). A pupil ...
tre.ngfl.gov.uk/ server.php?request=c2l0ZS5zZWFyY2g%3D&sf%5BsimilarResourceId%5D%5B%5D=5853 - 39k -
Cached - Similar pages

TEEM - Teachers Evaluating Educational Multimedia

Figure 13.1 Hits for search terms 'the states of matter + KS3'.

Judging the quality of what is available on the Internet is really not difficult, especially if a few simple rules are followed:

- Define your search terms – think carefully about this.
- If you want to search for a phrase, enclose it in quotation marks: 'the states of matter' or 'kinetic energy' searches for occurrences of the *exact* phrase within the quotation marks.
- Check the source of the information; government and related agencies will normally provide reliable information (e.g. www.xxxxx.gov.uk).
- Check the date when the website was last revised – this should ensure that the information is current.
- Try it out, spend some time using the website and evaluate it. Ask yourself if it provides something that no other resource provides; e.g. can the children find this information in their course or textbook anyway?
- Look at the *science* rather than eye-catching presentation, graphics and special effects alone. ICT-based educational materials can be embellished by the use of special effects, graphics, video, sound clips and so on but this should not be at the expense of appropriate science content.

Of course, public websites are but one type of resource for the learning of science. The possibility of more direct home–school electronic links are a very real possibility, making it possible for a school to set up a private website or similar resource bank that can be accessed from the home. This could include lessons, notes, homework and project outlines, and schemes of work so that children know where they should be and so on. The use of e-mail also provides a means of discussion.

There is also a wealth of software available (see below for examples), interactive CD-ROMS, SATs practice test-papers, science content on CD-ROM or DVD for all the Key Stages. A quick search within any of the booksellers with an internet presence (e.g. www.amazon.co.uk; www.foyles.co.uk) will reveal an extensive range of suitable software for the learning of science. The content of any software should, of course, conform to the National Curriculum programme of study and to the correct Key Stage to avoid home-based learning conflicting with what goes on in the school. This information will usually be supplied along with a brief description of the actual software.

Much of the guidance on judging quality for software is similar to that for web-based resources. Currency is vital so users have to check the date of publication. The software should be aimed at a British audience because only then will it follow an appropriate structure. All British software should at least mention the Key Stage audience it is designed for. Science software for Key Stage 1, for

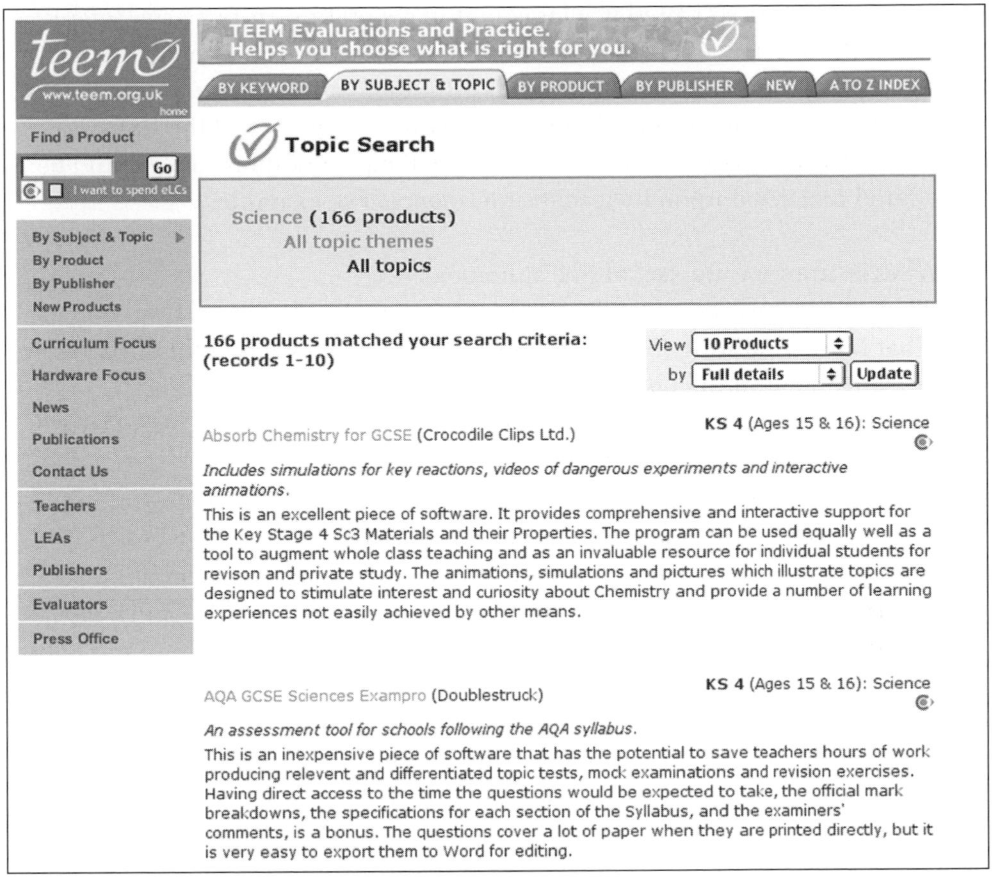

Figure 13.2 The *Teachers Evaluating Educational Multimedia* website.

example, will contain a great deal of graphics, moving images and special effects and less use of text. Remember that even for modern computers, this tends to be a drain on resources and will slow the machine down to some extent.

Luckily, much of the work involving the evaluation of educational software and websites has been done as part of the government's *Curriculum On-line* initiative and comprehensive guidance can be found in the *Teachers Evaluating Educational Multimedia* website (www.teem.org.uk) which is both approved and funded by the DfES. It provides an extremely useful portal for teachers wishing to evaluate educational software and Internet-based resources (Figure 13.2).

In summary

The use of ICT at home is a vitally important part of science learning. Home ICT can provide the possibility of quality time for the individual learner, which not every classroom can. It can play a large part in generating enthusiasm, interest and curiosity in science. It can help to fulfil some of the requirements of the National Curriculum, in science and in IT. But there are numerous issues and difficulties to be resolved – not least those of access, equity and the links between home and school in the use of ICT. A long list of questions should be considered and acted upon by teachers of science. For example:

- What is 'appropriate use' of ICT at home?
- What relevant experiences do children bring to the classroom from home?
- What kind of training (both ITT and in-service) do teachers need in order to take advantage of the opportunities which ICT can offer at home?
- How should teachers design learning tasks for individuals at home? (If at all?)
- How should work done with ICT, perhaps involving small groups of pupils working together at someone's home, be assessed?
- More generally, how can teachers achieve greater congruence and concordance between home learning in science and school learning, so that the two domains complement and enhance each other rather than possibly being discordant or simply unrelated to each other?
- Finally, what might be the long-term effects of growing ICT use in the home on the school science curriculum, and on pupils' general orientation to learning science and to the world around them?

However we address these questions, one thing seems certain – we ignore home use of ICT at our peril. If we fail to take account of home learning in science we take the risk of having what Green and Bigum (1993) call 'aliens in the classroom'. The contrast between the learning ecologies at home and school may reach breaking point. Teachers will then be faced with pupils whose style, attitude to, and environment for learning at home are so different to the ecology of school and classroom that for certain children, as Downes (1999, p. 77) puts it, 'schooling no longer works'.

References

DfEE, 1998, *Teaching: High Status, High Standards – Requirements for Courses of Initial Training*, London: DfEE.

DfES, 2002, *Impact2: Final Report*, London: Department for Education and Skills/British Educational Communications and Technology Agency.

Downes, T., 1999, 'Playing with computing technologies in the home', *Education and Information Technologies*, 4, 65–79.

Green, B. and Bigum, C., 1993, 'Aliens in the classroom', *Australian Journal of Education*, 37(2), 119–41.

Heyneman, S., 1997, 'Economic growth and the international trade in educational reform', *Prospects*, 27(4), 501–30.

Kerawalla, L. and Crook, C., 2002, 'Children's computer use at home and at school: context and continuity', *British Educational Research Journal*, 28(6), 751–71.

Livingstone, S. and Bovill, M., 1999, *Young People, New Media: Report of the Research Project Children, Young People and the Changing Media Environment*, London: London School of Economics.

Sanger, J. with Wilson, J., Davis, B. and Whittaker, R., 1997, *Young Children, Videos, and Computer Games*, London: Falmer Press.

Schibeci, R., 1989, 'Home, school, and peer group influences on student attitudes and achievement in science', *Science Education*, 73(1), 13–24.

Tyack, R. and Cuban, L., 1995, *Tinkering toward Utopia: A Century of Public School Reform*, Cambridge, MA: Harvard University Press.

Wellington, J. (ed.) 1985, *Children, Computers and the Curriculum*, London: Harper and Row.

Wellington, J., 2001, 'Exploring the secret garden', *British Journal of Educational Technology*, 32(2), 233–44.

Chapter 14

Managing learning outside the classroom

Michael Reiss and Martin Braund

Overview

In this chapter we bring together some of the threads expressed throughout the rest of the book. We examine why there is renewed interest in learning science outside the classroom and go on to discuss the implications of this for learning. We explore how such teaching can be unsettling for some teachers but can bring rich dividends to many pupils, including those not always best served by conventional classroom teaching. We close by examining the implications of learning science outside the classroom for scientific literacy and lifelong learning.

Introduction

Most school teachers are trained – as the two of us were – to see the classroom as their main professional base. The classroom is 'home', so outside the classroom is 'other'. This is true for all subjects in primary schools; in secondary schools it may be especially true of science, as 'the science lab' is a special (and financially expensive) construction dedicated to the teaching of science. Most non-science teachers dislike teaching in science labs as much as secondary science teachers prefer it. We can contrast the usual 'science lab-as-home' feeling for teachers of science with what we suspect is the typical attitude of most PE teachers, namely that real PE takes place on football pitches, in swimming pools and in gymnasia, in other words *outside* the classroom.

In this book, the authors argue strongly for the potential of out-of-classroom science activities to enhance science learning. In this chapter we begin by examining the renewed interest in learning science outside the classroom and then go on to discuss the implications this has for a broader education in science. We close with some crystal-ball gazing in relation to educational policy, scientific literacy and lifelong learning and the contribution that the contexts considered in the book might make in these areas.

The renewed interest in learning science outside the classroom

There have long been enthusiasts for learning school science outside the classroom. In many schools the 'biology fieldtrip' has existed for decades (see Chapter 5 by Anne Bebbington). Although there are fears that fieldwork in biology may be declining (Lock and Tilling, 2002), the last decade or so has seen a renewed interest in learning science outside the classroom and this has manifested itself in a number of ways.

Not just biology

While ecology has long enjoyed a place outside the classroom (e.g. Collins, 1984; Oakes, 1996; The Living Churchyard and Cemetery Project, 1998), science learning outside the classroom is no longer confined to biology. This book provides a number of non-biological cases. For example, in Chapter 10, Peter Borrows looks at the ways in which chemistry trails, which include earth sciences too, can help students to connect what they learn in the classroom with what is going on in the everyday 'real' world. As he puts it:

> To most students and their teachers, chemistry is something which happens in test tubes in laboratories or in tangled masses of pipes in factories. They need to be shown that chemistry is not something remote but that it is going on all around us, all the time.
>
> (p. 151)

Elizabeth Swinbank and Martin Lunn, in Chapter 11, review how the learning of physics and astronomy is enriched by planetaria, star-domes, observing the night sky (we write this in late August 2003 as Mars is at its brightest in human history – and the brightest object in the night sky) and visits to centres devoted to astronomy, space and particle physics.

Growth in the educational role of museums, science centres, zoos and botanic gardens

The last decade has seen a massive growth, not just in the UK but in many other countries too, in the educational role of such out-of-school sites of learning as museums, science centres, zoos and botanic gardens, as discussed by Sue Johnson in Chapter 6 for botanic gardens, Sue Dale Tunnicliffe in Chapter 7 for zoos and farms, and Martin Braund in Chapter 8 for museums and hands-on centres.

To a primary or secondary teacher of science, such sites can cause one to feel rather envious. They frequently seem to be extremely well financed, the objects on display or with which pupils interact are typically far more interesting than the standard fare served up in the classroom, group sizes are smaller and the high motivation of pupils often results in fewer discipline problems. Of course, education officers and others running such establishments see things rather differently. These establishments lack the state funding enjoyed by most schools; they exist in a cut-throat competition not just with one another but with all the other members of the leisure and entertainment industries; and they don't have the luxury of uninterrupted, guaranteed, regular chunks of contact time with pupils.

As is often the case, the truth probably lies in between these two extreme views. In this book our intention is *not*, of course, to reduce the extent and importance of school science. Rather, what we would like to see is an increasing acknowledgement of the complementary roles that schools and out-of-school establishments have in supporting learning in science. One way in which these complementary roles can be realised is by a better integration of the learning experiences of pupils in the school and the out-of-school site. For all that 'a day out' can and should be an enjoyable and special experience, it should link with the on-going learning of pupils. The greatest benefits for pupils' learning in science often arise when the activity extends what has been or will be learned at school, making the best use of what the out-of-school situation has to offer. Sue Johnson in Chapter 6 stresses the links that should exist between inside and outside the classroom when learning about plants. For example:

> At primary level the bean's life cycle is commonly drawn as a diagram. Some teachers grow beans indoors in pots and, if children are fortunate, they themselves may plant the growing beans outside in the school garden. The latter only happens where the teacher has the knowledge, skill and land to do so. In a botanic garden there is the possibility of seeing at least one species of leguminous plant at some stage in its life cycle whatever the time of year. A number of botanic gardens still have order beds where plants of one family are grown in a single bed. All botanic gardens have many examples of the bean family in their vegetable gardens, flowerbeds and borders. A visit can certainly enhance the underlying biodiversity element relating to the bean-in-the-jar experiment.
>
> (pp. 85–6)

Recognition by government bodies

As long ago as the 1950s, the Department of Education and Science was exhorting schools to develop their school grounds for educational uses (Department of Education and Science, 1955). Things have moved on a pace since then. In July 2002 the House of Commons Select Committee on Science and Technology called for fieldwork to be strongly recommended in all 14–19 science courses (the House of Commons Select Committee on Science and Technology, 2002). The training of teachers has now begun to catch up with these developments. Since September 2002 one of the standards for the award of Qualified Teacher Status expected of all trainee teachers in England and Wales is:

> As relevant to the age range they are trained to teach, they are able to plan opportunities for pupils to learn in out-of-school contexts, such as school visits, museums, theatres, field-work and employment-based settings, with the help of other staff where appropriate,
> (Department for Education and Skills, 2002/3, p. 10. Standard 3.1.5.)

This clearly indicates an increasing recognition by the Department for Education and Skills and the Teacher Training Agency that out-of-school learning is a core part of school-age education. The handbook of guidance that accompanies the requirements talks about 'the added value' that such opportunities for learning bring (Teacher Training Agency, 2002, p. 41).

Implications for learning

Learning outside the classroom has the potential to transform learning in science. It can do this partly by enlarging the scope for work in science. School grounds can form an extension of or alternative to the school laboratory. Experiments done outside can include those that are unsafe or impractical inside or where the environment makes an obvious contribution, e.g. experiments involving flight, rocket propulsion, combustion, measurement of weather conditions, etc. Experiments exploring measurement of speed, e.g. of cyclists, sound, etc., can best take place 'outside'. Susan Rowe and Susan Humphries give plenty of examples in Chapter 3 of activities making full use of their grounds for a wide range of science and other curriculum-related activities.

Even small additions to the outside environment of a school can have high impact for pupils. For example, a school pond makes learning about freshwater life much more meaningful and every school can have one, even if space is limited to a concrete yard (see Chapter 4).

Handing control over to pupils

We rather like the way one long-established USA book on short field trips titles one of its chapters 'Of the value of saying "I don't know"' (Russell, 1998). Of course, there are many occasions in the classroom when a teacher should say 'I don't know'. This is particularly so if their view of scientific knowledge is one of 'science as validated uncertainty', rather than the transmission of unchallengeable and unarguable truths. But these occasions of uncertainty are likely to multiply themselves greatly in out-of-school contexts. For some of us that can be threatening; for others it can be liberating. The more general point is that learning outside the classroom not only entails a geographical shift in the site of learning, it also entails a shift in the culture of learning. There is now an increasing realisation of the importance of place in learning. All learning, indeed all experience (Malpas, 1999), is situated. Of course, the place alone cannot assure learning; pupils and adults and the interactions between them also play their part. We discuss the interplay between these different aspects of the out-of-classroom learning experience in Chapter 2.

In Chapter 13 Jerry Wellington and Joey Britto talk about how the ecology of learning in the school science environment compares with home learning using ICT. They see home learning, compared to classroom learning as:

- voluntary
- less structured
- more intrinsically motivated
- open access
- learner-centred
- less filtered and vetted
- less supervised
- not legislated for.

Similar generalisations can be made about other forms of science learning outside of school (Falk, 2001). Such learning entails greater pupil autonomy. Classrooms are 'governed by the need for teachers to control learning outcomes, to maintain authority, to meet the demands of content-laden syllabuses, and at the same time moderate the behaviour of a large group of young people' (Wellington and Britto, p. 212). Given this, what happens when a potentially transformative practice, such as ICT, arrives? Jerry Wellington and Joey Britto's answer is that:

> Computers have not radically altered classroom activity; they are typically used to add to existing practices rather than replace them. For many teachers, ICT is seen as just 'another thing they have to do', rather than

schools and teaching patterns adapting to *accommodate* the change, the innovation becomes *assimilated* to existing, unchanging patterns of schooling.

(p. 212)

Indeed, Jerry Wellington and Joey Britto go so far as to suggest that today's ICT can be seen as a threat by some teachers, as the teacher's role is brought into question because of the home use of ICT. Such use can result in students who know more about a topic than their teachers. For a teacher whose model of pedagogy, even if subconsciously, is of 'me as expert telling them as learners', this can be deeply undermining. The two of us have observed much the same phenomenon when outstandingly able biology graduates with specialisms in molecular biology or genetics attempt to shun biology fieldwork on the grounds that they can't identify all the organisms their pupils ask them about. This is a bit like never going on holiday abroad because you aren't completely fluent in the language. For some teachers the broadening of pupils' experience is thwarted by the fear of entering foreign territory.

Different styles of learning

Any good classroom should provide experiences to suit pupils with different learning styles but with out-of-the-classroom learning it is easier to avoid always favouring pupils who learn best through words. Pupils who learn best through words are auditory learners. Visual learners think in pictures and have pictorial imaginations; they have a tendency to recall concepts that are presented as diagrams, graphs, photographs or in concept and mind maps. Kinaesthetic learners express their feelings physically and these students learn most effectively through activity. It has been suggested that more than 30 per cent of students may have kinaesthetic learning preferences. According to Reiff (1997), many of the students who are underachieving at school are kinaesthetic learners, and consistent instruction that does not accommodate their requirements can mean that they lose confidence, fall behind and experience repeated failure.

The diversity of experiences and activities afforded by out-of-the-classroom learning means that visual learners and, in particular, kinaesthetic learners may do better than in conventional classrooms. So learning in contexts outside the classroom offers opportunities for greater inclusion of learners. In Chapter 6 Sue Johnson writes about how botanic gardens can provide for a range of styles of learning including a liking for sensory stimulation. Attempts to broaden the audience and appeal of museums, libraries and archives have resulted in some highly innovative schemes that have involved previously disaffected and disengaged young adults in improving their own learning. (Several examples of such projects are described in *GEM News*, published by the Group for Education in Museums.)

Relationships between teachers and pupils

Learning science outside the classroom can powerfully transform relationships between teachers and pupils. We are not so naïve to believe that one or two field trips or visits will permanently transform a difficult group of immature youngsters into a caring group of responsible young adults. Nevertheless, relationships outside of the classroom can be more authentic that in school. This is perhaps especially the case at secondary school where, in the absence of suspended timetables or the sorts of events suggested in this book, a science teacher may never work with a group of pupils for longer than a double period framed by bells.

Working outside the normal constraints of the classroom and school timetable offers some unique and memorable experiences for pupils. These might not always be seen by pupils as conventional learning – but therein lies some of their power. In Chapter 11 Elizabeth Swinbank and Martin Lunn write about after-school star parties, and one of us used annually to take biology students out for a cream tea on their residential biology field trip. Out-of-the-classroom experiences can bring out the best (and occasionally the worst!) in pupils. Most people who have taken young people on residential activities, whether science-related or not, have tales of kindness and sudden growths in maturity. As Anne Bebbington notes in her quotation of a teacher accompanying a group of 9–10 year olds:

> I have always noticed how the children bond and become a much closer-knit group as a result of their residential field trip. Jackie had never been away overnight and both she and her Mum were very worried about this. We approached it a day at a time and I gave her the option that if she was really unhappy she could go home. Even though I was woken up in the early hours of the morning a couple of times during the week and she had to be comforted and reassured, she made it to the end of the week. Jackie was so pleased that she had managed a whole week away and her Mum was delighted by this milestone. Interestingly, the rest of the class was really proud of Jackie and made a big fuss of her.
>
> (p. 70)

Out-of-the-classroom activities can also deepen relationships between teachers and pupils' parents/guardians or other adults. It can certainly be valuable to involve any adult helpers in the learning activities as well as the general running of out-of-the-classroom activities. In Chapter 7 Sue Dale Tunnicliffe discusses how such 'chaperones', if suitably briefed, can help considerably by asking pupils appropriate questions and encouraging them to talk among themselves about what they are observing.

Scientific literacy and lifelong learning

Out-of-the-classroom learning in science gives one a new perspective on scientific literacy and on lifelong learning. We argue here, first, that out-of-the-classroom learning in science broadens what the term 'scientific literacy' is often taken to mean, and second, that it provides a natural link between school learning and lifelong learning.

Scientific literacy

The term 'scientific literacy' has been used in a variety of ways but these centre on the notion that effective functioning in today's society requires a certain scientific knowledge (Ryder, 2001). A 'rich' scientific literacy would include knowledge about the scope of science, its nature, how it is undertaken and how scientific knowledge is built up as well as knowledge of particular scientific content. It seems clear that in most societies only a small proportion of the population leaves school scientifically literate (Shamos, 1995; Driver *et al.*, 1996). In Chapter 12 Ruth Jarman and Billy McClune argue that newspapers can be a valuable context for developing the skills associated with scientific literacy. In addition to researching the science behind a news story, pupils can come to understand the strengths and limitations of science in the solution of everyday problems.

Authentic learning is achieved when pupils learn what they are genuinely interested in. We maintain that a science education that confines itself to the classroom is less valid and provides for less authentic learning than one that also embraces the diversity of learning environments that exist outside of the classroom. It has long been a tenet of environmental education that it takes place 'about the environment, in the environment and for the environment'. More generally, understanding how science operates is almost certainly enhanced when pupils work in the community on meaningful science-related projects (see Roth and Désautels, 2002; Ratcliffe and Grace, 2003). Some examples of suitable projects and how these might be linked with examination syllabuses are provided by Elizabeth Swinbank and Martin Lunn in Chapter 11. The work of industry provides a wealth of opportunity for authentic learning of science and ways of making the most of this resource are discussed by Joy Parvin and Miranda Stephenson in Chapter 9.

Lifelong learning

One caricature of schools is that they are the only places where learning takes place. To some extent this view has been reinforced in recent decades as schools have increasingly been seen as the potential answer to every societal woe. Is there a perceived problem with teenage pregnancy? Require schools to deal with it in sex education. Is there a perceived problem with political apathy and growing selfishness in society? Introduce citizenship education. And so on. The opposite caricature is that 'real learning' only takes place outside schools. 'You wait till you get into the real world.'

The growth in the acknowledgement of the importance of lifelong learning recognises that while much important learning takes place during the years of full-time education, much of it takes place outside these years too. In terms of science education, people of all ages, including school children, learn about science by going to science museums and hands-on science centres (Chapter 8), by visiting zoos, farms and botanic gardens (Chapters 6 and 7), by working in science-related industries (Chapter 9), by watching the television, listening to the radio and reading newspapers (Chapter 12) and increasingly, through the Internet and other IT-mediated means (Chapter 13).

We suspect that lifelong learning is prompted by a good primary and secondary school education although, conversely, poor schooling might also result in people's desire to educate themselves later in life, to make up for perceived deficiencies. In Chapter 3 Susan Rowe and Susan Humphries describe how they have helped transform the grounds of Coombes School since it opened in 1971 into a wonderfully rich and aesthetically pleasing environment. (Have a look at http://www.thecoombes.com/grounds/txt_smp.html for a photographic record to complement the account in Chapter 3.) The advantages of the richly developed curriculum that they describe surely provides a sound start and promotes the desire in pupils to explore the world in more detail and ask questions about it.

The chapters of this book and the examples they contain offer us great hope and we believe that they lead us to a science education that can be rich, broad, inspiring, relevant and motivating. We hope that the experiences described act as a springboard for future and continued learning – a hunger in pupils to find out more and engage with the scientific issues of the day. As we discuss in Chapter 1, we can no longer tolerate a population increasingly disinterested in science and suspicious of it and so unable to engage with many of the pressing concerns of the twenty-first century. Scientific literacy is as much an educational goal and right as are basic literacy and numeracy. We hope that this book goes some way to providing the wherewithal and insights for teachers to make the most of the many and varied opportunities that there are for pupils to enrich and complement their in-school (more formal) learning of science. Ultimately the capacity that will provide for improved scientific literacy and the desire to want to know more about the world, that are the foundations of lifelong learning, must come from within learners themselves. However, this capacity for learning has much to do with how we, as teachers, provide, structure and make best use of the stimuli from all the places and situations that are described in this book and that we hope will ensure that this capacity is developed in meaningful ways.

References

Collins, M., 1984, *Urban Ecology: A Teacher's Resource Book*, Cambridge: Cambridge University Press.

Department of Education and Science, 1955, *Building Bulletin*, London: Department of Education and Science.

Department for Education and Skills, 2002/3, *Qualifying to Teach: Professional Standards for Qualified Teacher Status and Requirements for Initial Teacher Training*, London: Teacher Training Agency. Available at www.tta.gov.uk/qualifyingtoteach

Driver, R., Leach, J., Millar, R. and Scott, P., 1996, *Young People's Images of Science*, Buckingham: Open University Press.

Falk, J. H. (ed.), 2001, *Free-Choice Science Education: How We Learn Science Outside of School*, New York: Teachers College.

House of Commons Select Committee on Science and Technology, 2002, *Third Report: Science Education from 14 to 19*, London: Stationery Office.

Lock, R. and Tilling, S., 2002, 'Ecology fieldwork in 16 to 19 biology', *School Science Review*, 84(307), 79–87.

Malpas, J. E., 1999, *Place and Experience: A Philosophical Topography*, Cambridge: Cambridge University Press.

Oakes, M. (ed.), 1996, *Investigating the Environment at Key Stages 3 and 4*, Hatfield: Association for Science Education.

Ratcliffe, M. and Grace, M., 2003, *Science Education for Citizenship: Teaching Socio-Scientific Issues*, Maidenhead: Open University Press.

Reiff, J., 1997, *Learning Styles*, Washington, DC: National Education Association.

Roth, W.-M. and Désautels, J. (eds), 2002, *Science Education as/for Sociopolitical Action*, New York: Peter Lang.

Russell, H. R., 1998, *Ten-minute Field Trips: A Teacher's Guide to Using the School Grounds for Environmental Studies*, 3rd edn, Arlington, VA: National Science Teachers Association.

Ryder, J., 2001, 'Identifying science understanding for functional scientific literacy', *Studies in Science Education*, 36, 1–44.

Shamos, M. H., 1995, *The Myth of Scientific Literacy*, New Brunswick, NJ: Rutgers University Press.

Teacher Training Agency, 2002, *Qualifying to Teach: Handbook of Guidance*, London: Teacher Training Agency. Available at www.tta.gov.uk/qualifyingtoteach

The Living Churchyard and Cemetery Project, 1998, *Hunt the Daisy: Encouraging Children to Discover the World of Nature in Churchyards and Cemeteries. Linked to the National Curriculum Key Stage 2 (7–11 years)*, Stoneleigh Park, Warwickshire: The Arthur Rank Centre.

Index